CRITICAL ACCLAIM FOR
The Best Travel Writing Series

"Travelers' Tales has thrived by seizing on our perpetual
fascination for armchair traveling (there is a whole line of site-
specific anthologies) including this annual roundup of delight-
ful (and sometimes dreadful) wayfaring adventures from all
corners of the globe."   —*The Washington Post*

"*The Best Travel Writing 2006: True Stories from Around the
World*: Here are intimate revelations, mind-changing pilgrim-
ages, and body-challenging peregrinations. And there's
enough to keep one happily reading until the 2007 edition."
                    —*San Francisco Chronicle*

"There is no danger of tourist brochure writing in this collection. The story subjects themselves are refreshingly odd....
For any budding writer looking for good models to learn
by or any experienced writer looking for ideas on where the
form can go, *The Best Travel Writing 2005* is an inspiration.
And a fine read for anyone who is missing the open road."
                    —*Transitions Abroad*

"Travelers' Tales, a publisher which has taken the travel piece
back into the public mind as a serious category, has a volume
out titled *The Best Travel Writing 2005* which, to my mind,
wipes out its best-of competitors completely. During the deeps of
the winter, this one, taken a bit at a time, may just preserve your
sanity and calm down your itchy foot."   —*The Courier-Gazette*

"Travelers' Tales books are a sweet relief indeed. These titles
luxuriate in that complicated, beautiful, shadowy place where
the best stories begin, and the most compelling characters
roam free. *The Best Travelers' Tales 2004* is a collection of
memories from travelers who visit both the exotic and the
familiar, and come away with rich stories...a zesty mix."
                    —*ForeWord Magazine*

TRAVELERS' TALES

THE
BEST
TRAVEL
WRITING
2007

TRUE STORIES
FROM AROUND THE WORLD

TRAVELERS' TALES

THE BEST
TRAVEL WRITING
2007

TRUE STORIES
FROM AROUND THE WORLD

Edited by
JAMES O'REILLY, LARRY HABEGGER,
AND SEAN O'REILLY

Travelers' Tales
Palo Alto

Art Direction: Stefan Gutermuth
Interior design and page layout: Melanie Haage using the fonts
Nicolas Cochin, Ex Ponto and Granjon.

Distributed by: Publishers Group West, 1700 Fourth Street,
Berkeley, California 94710.

ISBN 1-932361-46-4
ISSN 1548-0224

First Edition
Printed in the United States
10 9 8 7 6 5 4 3 2 1

"Come to the edge," he said.
They said, "We are afraid."
"Come to the edge," he said.
They came.
He pushed them...
And they flew.

—GUILLAUME APOLLINAIRE

Table  of Contents

Publisher's Preface

TRAVEL TO NEW PLACES, ESPECIALLY THOSE FAR AWAY, is surely one of the most rewarding ways to spend time. But it is also better than just about any other activity for the purpose of grasping the paradox of human existence: your life, and everyone else's, is only a drop of water in the ocean, but is more valuable than all the stars in the galaxy. To paraphrase a line from the movie *Gladiator*—"Is all of Rome worth the life of one good man?" I think most of us know the answer to that question, but travel underlines the enduring truth of the answer.

Some years ago I was on a travel panel and was asked who were, in my estimation, the most amazing travelers. "Refugees," I answered, and an uneasy murmur passed through the crowd; I think I'd been expected to canonize Wilfred Thesiger or Isabella Bird, or sing the praises of backpackers and do-gooders roaming the globe.

But no! I said refugees and I mean it still. Millions of souls cross borders without food, documents, clothing, health, or hope, and are preyed upon by weather, wild animals, and human jackals—their own kind who hack at them, rob them, rape them, kill them. These are the travelers we should admire and study and care the most about, for our cardboard wall of law and borders is flimsy, and expensive weaponry is mostly an illusion, and while that wall keeps the demons from snapping at us in our well-washed and well-fed splendor, if it collapses we will all too quickly join our brothers and sisters who suffer unimaginably every day. We, the lucky ones who can cross borders with impunity, need to do so as often as we can to see how the rest of the world lives, to wake up and spread the honest news of our fellows to people at home who don't get out much, or who think that Bono and Bill and Melinda Gates have it handled out there beyond the bubble.

Recent research concluded that if you have assets of—get this—$2,200—you are in the richest half of humanity. So chances are if you are reading this, whether you are well off or struggling to make ends meet, you are, in the eyes of most of your fellow humans, unimaginably rich. And not just in fact, but in opportunity, in education, and most of all, freedom.

The traveler today continues to enjoy an unparalleled opportunity to bear witness, do good deeds, and have fun and fantastic life experiences at bargain basement prices. And while it is not new to say that the traveler is a nation's best ambassador, it is worth repeating, for the lives and ethics and views of individuals are often, as Tony Wheeler points out in the Introduction which follows, dramatically different from those of governments the world over. The U.S. Army recently had a recruiting slogan I like very much and think we should all apply to ourselves: "An Army of One." That's you, bringing warmth and hope and a fresh perspective to others wherever you go, even when you're just on holiday.

So I say look kindly on all those bereft of home for any reason, political, economic, or religious, and encourage your leaders and fellow citizens wherever you live and travel to craft shrewd and honest immigration policies so that those who wish to live in freedom and prosperity be allowed to at least try out for the privilege. Do not let them languish in the gray lands where they are prey to the wicked and the greedy and to the hideous inertia and cruelty of state bureaucracy.

I just got back from my first trip to Antarctica, an intoxicating and terrifying continent, but one that so far doesn't suffer from the confusion of fences and borders we have up north. Sure, many countries have made territorial claims, with more in the wings, but so far the Antarctic Treaty of 1959, and the awesome power of the continent's climate and remoteness have kept us, the would-be carpetbaggers, at bay.

Consider the penguin, that goofy bird that has forgotten how to fly (except underwater). The penguin, while it has a few natural predators, can go where the krill are without being machine-gunned by Janjaweed or brainwashed child-soldiers, blown up by fanatics strapped to explosives, or restrained at every turn by the kudzu of government regulation. The penguin can go home again, back to the same nest, unlike the world's homeless, from the Lost Boys of Sudan to the Dalai Lama, who has been in exile from his Tibetan homeland since that very same year the Antarctic Treaty was signed.

So enjoy your next trip with deep appreciation that you can do it at all! And I will accept your forgiveness in advance if I seem overly cranky. I must still be thawing out.

—James O'Reilly
Palo Alto, California

Introduction

Tony Wheeler

We TRAVEL TO TRY TO UNDERSTAND, A COUNTRY, A people, perhaps ourselves. We may fail to find what we're searching for, but we're many miles ahead of the stay-at-homes who've not embarked on that search, and way ahead of the stay-at-homes who believe they understand the world, even though they've not even ventured out the front door.

I've been regularly reminded of that important quest in my own recent wanderings, visits to a roll call of countries which, we're repeatedly informed, deserve to be described as "bad." I won't claim I've come anywhere near understanding them, but I've certainly had plenty of opportunities to contemplate that essential truth that every story has two sides. We may resolutely believe one side of the tale, but it's foolish to ignore the reality that other people may believe the flip side with equal conviction. It's by traveling that we meet people and come face to face with how they see the world or, even better, start to see how the world looks from their viewpoint and begin to understand why they think the way they do. We're much less likely to discover that alternative perspective by sitting at home and watching the news on TV.

So many of the tales in this collection are reminders of this other essential truth: that it's at ground level, in the streets, where we have the best hope of making that connection. Perhaps we'll only emerge dazed and confused, perhaps the person we come to understand best is simply somebody else from our own culture, like "The Girl Who Drank Petrol" in Tanya Shaffer's intriguing tale of a spell in Ghana. Or perhaps it's some long ago family relationship like Michel Moushabeck's seemingly (until we dig further) aloof and unfriendly grandfather in "The *Mukhtar* and I," a story that so positively brings home a completely different interpretation of a place, Jerusalem, where we so often only hear one story. Or its polar opposite.

Some of my favorites in this year's collection remind us that how you travel is just as important as where you travel. For instance, there's no better way of finding understanding in India than riding the rails, as Gregory Kennedy does on "The Howrah-Puri Express." Along the way he hears of hopes and aspirations and how simply going somewhere—to the sea when you're from the mountains—can define you. Watching the daughter of that man from the mountains, embarking on her first big trip, whisks Gregory back to contemplate his own initial travel inspiration.

Road trips can be equally enlightening, particularly if hitchhiking also comes into the equation. Following the waves in Costa Rica, J. Spencer Klein discovers that it's really not such a "Bad Country," although bad karma can certainly play its part. His tale is also a nice reminder of how much fine travel is inspired by some other pursuit, surfing being one of the best.

"The Adventure of La Refrita" starts as road trip, but soon changes gears to remind us that some of the best travel adventures are the unexpected ones. Nobody wants their road trip interrupted by a long breakdown, but would Steve King ever have discovered Chamberlain, South Dakota if the injector pump hadn't gone kaput? It's an illustration that some of the best travel doesn't involve travel at all, it can be just as important to become part of the scenery, as Richard Sterling (and his hat) do in "Mr. Hat's Neighborhood."

We've all lost umbrellas. They're probably the most losable of personal possessions and it's remarkable how a shower of rain in a city almost anywhere in the world will bring out umbrella salesman just as assuredly as it will turn the grass green. My last two new umbrellas started their short life with me—for undoubtedly their turn to be lost will come—in Munich and Seoul. "The Purple Umbrella," Karin Muller's fine little tale of international misunderstanding, inverts that umbrella basic: her umbrella proves unlosable and in the process underlines some basic rules of life in Japan. Railway travelers in Japan may observe that bicycles are equally unlosable, they pile up outside terminals all over Japan, unloved, divorced, but still waiting in vain hope for their fickle riders to return on the evening commuter service and reclaim them. Until finally they're rounded up and shipped off to North Korea.

Nicholas Seeley's Red Sea voyage in "Bread" is another reminder of those connections that travel brings and how people are people, even in the most foreign of environments. Bread is the other side of the equation here: food, of course, is a big part of travel and there's no better way of coming to grips with somewhere else, or someone else, than over a meal. Pickett Porterfield's "The Mexican Taco Stand" is a perfect song of praise for that most Mexican of dishes while Maciej Ceglowski analyses another country's culinary preoccupations with

"Argentina on Two Steaks a Day." "Never underestimate the importance of the first steak of the day," is clearly a piece of advice essential to Argentinian understanding.

But it was Bonnie Smetts's perfect small tale "Only Fish" that brought the biggest smile to my face. Racing from restaurant to restaurant trying to find that perfect "vibe" is just as consuming a preoccupation to a guidebook writer as to a traveling chef. Yes, I thought, I've been there. I'd also already traveled, although only on paper, with Rory Stewart. His foot-propelled wanderings in "Dervishes" take place in Pakistan, but only a few months ago I followed his wonderful book *The Places In Between* across Afghanistan. My Toyota Hilux may have been beat up, but it was clearly a far more comfortable means of travel than the boots that carried Stewart on a truly amazing journey. He, however, appears to have had the deeper experience. At the end of the day it's walking that really gets you there.

❧ ❧ ❧

A lengthy jaunt along Asia's "Hippy Trail" in 1972 led Tony Wheeler to create Lonely Planet Publications, a story he tells in Unlikely Destinations *(Periplus, 2007). The account of his recent wanderings around nine pariah states (including Afghanistan, Iran, Iraq and North Korea) also appeared in 2007 as* Bad Lands *(Lonely Planet). Tony's footloose ways can probably be traced back to his childhood: born in England, he grew up in Pakistan, the Bahamas, and then the USA where he went to high school near Detroit and Baltimore. Today he lives in Melbourne, Australia.*

NICHOLAS SEELEY

❧ ❧ ❧

Bread

Aboard a cargo boat, a traveler bridges
the gulf between cultures.

IT'S THE LAST NIGHT OF RAMADAN, AND I'M ON A FERRY crossing the Red Sea to the Sinai. Now, I seldom pay much attention to holidays, and as a non-Muslim in the Middle East, I do my best not to get involved with Ramadan. It's an interesting display of devotion to God, but it's not mine. For the first few days, it's a curiosity, an intriguing departure from the familiar. Later, it's an annoyance: the Jordanian government closes down all but the swankiest tourist restaurants during fasting hours, and many shops and grocery stores close out of solidarity. You can get ticketed or harassed by cops for eating, drinking, or smoking in public. It's not a big deal for most foreigners, who try to be respectful, but it's a lousy break if, say, you happen to be diabetic, or pregnant, or

1

on vacation with small children. By the end of the month of fasting, Ramadan is simply a fact of life, an event one tries to be respectful of, but need not comment on.

This particular year, I happen to be traveling with friends to the Egyptian beach-party town of Dahab for the Eid al-Fitr, the feast that follows the end of the holy month. The overland passage is closed, or as-good-as, since it would require crossing the Palestinian territories, so the alternative is a three-hour bus trip to the south of Jordan, followed by a boat ride across to Egypt. Two types of boats make the crossing. The "fast boat" is a slick and fairly expensive commuter service. The "slow boat" is a cargo freighter that happens to take passengers. Our bus had arrived too late for the fast boat, and so, with some trepidation, we bought tickets for the freighter.

Now that we're here, we don't quite know what to expect. I've ridden enough cargo-and-passenger ferries in other countries to know that they are seldom particularly comfortable or fun, but nothing prepares me for the boat to Egypt.

The boarding dock is crowded with Egyptian migrant workers waiting for jobs, or perhaps coming off them. Some squat on the hot pavement, while others shout at each other, or at the dock workers, or else sit in silence, squeezing themselves into the tiny corners of shade etched out by the noonday sun.

Stepping aboard the boat feels like stepping onto a plague ship. There are no seats or benches, and every inch of the oil-slicked black deck is covered with sprawled human figures. Barefoot old women sit slumped on blankets against the rails and crowd into the narrow walkways like so many bundles of rags, while men with

yellow nails and tired faces try to sleep, or brush away
the swarming flies with dirty fingers.

Crowds of eyes follow us as we pick our way over the
bodies; vacant, uninterested eyes, bleary with exhaustion
or sickness. I think of *Heart of Darkness*, or *The Fever,* or
the nightly news images of African famines. I think I am
going to vomit.

So we find ourselves in a corner on the second level
from the top, wedged against the side of a large engine
shaft that belches gasoline fumes across the deck; it's a lot
more carcinogenic, but a bit less crowded. Across from
us, an ancient woman with tattooed hands sits cradling
her scabbed and swollen feet. My friends and I don't talk
much. If we do, it's about the heat, or the flies, or where
we should go that's private to drink from the bottles of
water in our packs, without offending those who are
fasting. No one mentions the eyes that turn to stare at us.
I do my best to bury myself in a book.

Nothing moves. The only activity on the deck is a
barber a few meters down who sits with his tools spread
out before him on a blanket. I find myself staring at
him as he changes the blade in his razor between clients.
He takes a full three or four minutes just to lather each
new face, first with the brush, then with his fingers,
brushing the shaving cream to a thick foam. He shaves
with short, deft strokes, effortlessly paring away days of
stubble and dirt, even as the ferry churns its way out into
the Red Sea. He looks like a hell of a barber. One of our
group tries to convince me to get him to shave my head,
but I can't stand the thought of the attention it would
gather—all those glazed eyes, all turned on me.

"I'm a little scared of what's going to happen when the
call to prayer sounds," another friend says to me as eve-

ning draws near. "This whole boat's going to light up like a Christmas tree." I look around, suddenly worried: when the sunset call to prayer signals the end to the day's fast, it is a mathematical certainty that everyone on the boat is going to immediately light a cigarette. I shudder, sniffing at the gasoline fumes billowing out of the grate behind me. If the boat hasn't blown up on any other day of the year, I rationalize, it probably won't today either.

After another hour, dusk is gathering, and a couple of us get up and walk to the railing to watch the red ember of the sun settle behind the mountains of the Sinai. Instead, I find myself looking down at the sea of packed bodies on the deck below. One of our friends in Amman likes to refer to Egypt as a mother with too many children, who can't feed all of them, and looking down from this high deck the metaphor seems vividly real.

The sun is beautiful as it sinks into its cradle of rust-colored stone.

And then I smell something. The faint, tantalizing scent of...roasting garlic? And vegetables? And bread?

And in a moment that seems to last an hour, I suddenly realize how many things I have just gotten wrong. The deck below us has come alive with people, human figures suddenly animated, like marionettes whose strings have been pulled taut. They are sitting up on their blankets, chatting, laughing, eagerly fingering bottles of water and packs of cigarettes. The shapeless bundles they had carried have been unrolled into picnic blankets piled high with food. From nowhere, old Bedouin women are producing boxes of figs and dates, whole wheels of cheese, bags heavy with thick bread; men push past each other in the tight passages carrying plates piled with fresh vegetables, beans, hummus, and *foule*.

Across the deck, families are cooking over tiny fires, while below us mothers divide up portions for those gathered around, and children's fingers tear eagerly at their bread, anticipating the droning sound of the call to prayer that means they can begin their *iftar* meal.

And so I finally, finally get it. Many of the people on this boat are poor, yes—but they are not hopeless, or helpless, or lost in an abyss of poverty and despair. They're just tired. They've been traveling all day and haven't eaten or taken a drink or smoked a cigarette in twenty hours. Because it's Ramadan, that thing that I'd forgotten.

"Hey there!" a man calls up from the deck below. "Where are you from?"

"We're Americans," I say, fearing the worst, but feeling trapped.

"Very good," he shouts back. "Welcome to our country! Welcome to Egypt! I wish you pleasure!"

"Oh God," mutters one of our party, who has lived a long time in the Arab world, "run!"

"What, are they gonna stone us now?" I ask.

"No," she says, "but if we keep talking to them, they're going to invite us to dinner with them, and they can't afford it."

Smiling and waving back at the man below, we turn away from the railing and retreat to where our friends are sitting by the engine, gratefully swigging water as the call finally sounds. But it's too late: here's the barber, leaning over us with a smile, holding out a huge tub of dates, passing it around and gesturing for us each to take some, then smiling and passing it around again.

We had packed food for the trip, but it spoiled, stowed in the hot luggage compartment of our bus, and we have nothing to offer in return. So, suddenly, we are the ones being looked at pityingly by the feasting Egyptians, who offer us olives and water and sugared dates. One old woman hands us an entire round of cheese.

And then the barber is back, with his friends, smiling as he presents us with a bag stuffed with thick, crusty bread, which he shoves into our hands with a smile. He doesn't speak a word of English, and my Arabic is meager, but he repeats over and over the phrase *Ahlan wa sahlan*—Arabic for welcome.

We thank him as best we can, in broken sentences, and he goes back to his family. There is nothing more to say. My friends and I sit in silence on the freighter's grease-stained iron deck, and share our dinner. It's one of those nights.

~≈ ~≈ ~≈

Nicholas Seeley is a features writer and sections editor for JO, *an English-language magazine in Amman, Jordan, that covers social issues, art, and culture. He moved to the Middle East in 2004 after studying journalism at Northwestern's Medill School of Journalism in Chicago, and theater at Cornell University. In his spare time, he writes fiction and manages a theater company in Amman.*

※ ※ ※

The Barber

When a shave is not just a shave.

THE FIRST TIME I THOUGHT ABOUT TRAVELING TO Vietnam was thirty-some years ago, and what I thought was that I didn't want to go, even though the U.S. government would have paid for the trip. At that time, the Vietnam of my imagination wasn't the land of saffron sunlight, purple clouds like eggplants in the air, and cool, damp, crumbling concrete it is for me today. Rather, the Vietnam of my anxieties was an asylum of sucking, gray mud and olive drab, a place where I'd get my ass skinned. I couldn't imagine a kid like me in a hellish place like that. What would I do? Whatever would I do?

I'll never know the answer to that question, a fact brought home to me when recently, rifling through a box of memorabilia, I found my draft card, and even after all these years it rattled me. Thankfully, I was never called

up, as I'm sure I wouldn't have had the imagination then
to say no, though I've since outgrown many of my infan-
tile assumptions, including that bourgeois conceit, the
righteousness of authority. In the same box I came upon
a Vietnamese 10,000 dong note I had squirreled away,
not a lot of money by American standards, but meaning-
ful to me for its picture of sailing junks on one side and,
on the other, a portrait of Ho Chi Minh with the thready
beard he wore in old age. I looked at the portrait, noting
Ho's distant gaze, the gaze of a strategist, of a man who
considers eternity from the point of view of the past, and
wondered briefly what my wife would say if I grew my
own beard out.

My goatee and shaved head perplex many Vietnamese
because in their country beards are for venerable old
men like Uncle Ho and bald heads for monks, and I
am neither. Their confusion revolves, as so often with
Americans in Asia, around my role in life and what
deference I am owed. We Americans as individuals are
inevitably paid more of this intangible currency than we
deserve (a transaction I am uncomfortable with) because
America itself is economically powerful. To the good,
however, in Vietnam my beard and clean skull afford
me the opportunity to visit a barber and undergo rituals
of grooming that, in their unfamiliar way, are beautiful
and revealing since they are both personal and not my
own.

I discovered this a few years ago on the outskirts
of Hue when, cycling through a quiet neighborhood
beneath the dappled shade of overarching trees at the
height of the morning, I stopped for a rest and a shave.
The barber I happened upon, unused to foreign customers, eyed me in alarm as I lay my bike on its side in

the leaf litter beside the road, but quickly recovered his composure and indicated that I should wait my turn outside his shop, a three-sided shack of woven bamboo matting with a concrete floor and tin roof, economically appointed with a pair of high chairs upholstered in red naugahyde and a turquoise sideboard and mirror combination. A collection of photographs of young women modeling different hairstyles, vintage early '80s, hung above the mirror, and an electric fan, switched off, squatted desultorily to one side.

As I waited, a small crowd gathered in the street to watch. By the standards of that quiet neighborhood, I was conspicuous: overly large, fair-skinned, and disreputably dressed. Suddenly self-conscious, I thought about moving on, but no one seemed to mind my being there, so I stayed. People were merely curious, except for the barber, a young man, immaculate in gray slacks, a white, short-sleeved shirt, and sandals, who glanced at me from time to time with a look of foreboding.

When he had finished with the client he was attending, the barber beckoned me to his chair and draped a green towel across my chest. In the mirror, I watched his hands, fine boned and gentle, flutter about my head like a pair of birds. He looked inquiringly into the eye of my reflection, and I, dragging the flat of my hand across my stubbly cheeks and pate, showed him what I wanted. He hesitated and then gave a single nod, and as he stepped to the sideboard to prepare a straight razor and soap, I noted that the nail of his left little finger, long and sharp as is the style in Vietnam, was trembling. When he was ready, the barber reclined the back of my chair and, standing behind me, touched the bottom of my chin with his fingertip. Obediently, I arched my neck and closed my eyes and felt the cool tongue of his badger brush lick my exposed throat and his thin steel against my skin.

Half an hour later, snapping the green towel smartly, the barber released me from his ministrations. With a craftsman's hand, he had assiduously scraped my skull, my cheeks and jaws, as well as my brow, my neck, my nose, and the rims of my ears, which he had also laboriously cleaned with a tiny metal spoon. As we stepped together into the glare and shocking heat of the street, I indicated my appreciation with signs and gestures, and for the first time, he smiled. I asked him how much I owed him. I can't recall the exact amount, but it was pitifully little, so little, in fact, that I was embarrassed to pay it. Instead, I gave him a one-dollar bill. He looked at it in astonishment, then into my eyes, and his smooth, young face began to crumple. He took both my hands in his and thanked me for the boon. I didn't know what to say. A dollar, nothing to me, was everything to him, and when the impact of this incongruity hit me, I felt a lump begin to form in my throat.

As I write, I have laid my souvenir 10,000-dong note and an American dollar bill side by side on the table next to my computer. One is green, the other printed in red. From one, George Washington, the successful revolutionary, now contented and well fed, looks me directly in the eye as if between us there is an understanding; on the other, a hollow-cheeked Uncle Ho gazes into the distance, ignoring me completely. In 1907, when he was a student activist in Hue, Ho Chi Minh roved the city with his friends giving haircuts, often received involuntarily, to passersby who still wore the traditional bun that had come to symbolize Vietnam's feudal past, chanting:

Comb in the left hand,
Scissors in the right,
Snip! Snip!

Cut out the ignorance,
Do away with stupidity,
Snip! Snip!

Looking at Ho's portrait, I think about the American wars in Southeast Asia, thrust upon all of us by five cynical administrations that to some degree believed in a communist conflagration they had themselves lit in our imaginations, then stoked with lies and secrets (many now a matter of public record) in efforts to win elections. And I think about the incongruity of this fantasy when laid side by side with the crystalline idealism of Ho Chi Minh. And I think about that young barber. How little had passed between us—and how much. We had not spoken, but had for a brief time been melded, hand to head, and between the soft pads of his fingertips and his keen blade, he had taught me the unambiguous economics of his heart, which unlike mine understood the razor's edge. I think about what he had asked of me that morning, what I had given, and the disparity between what it had meant to him and how little it had cost me. And I think about how powerful I was, with my dollars and my ability to insinuate myself into his neighborhood halfway around the world.

And then I think about who had held the razor to whose throat, and how thin the line, the thin, red line is between eternity and a close shave, and I am humbled.

୬ଟ ୬ଟ ୬ଟ

Dustin W. Leavitt contributes articles and essays on subjects including travel, social commentary, and art criticism to books and periodicals. Much of his travel writing visits Asia and the Pacific, where he has lived, worked, and wandered at various times in his life. He teaches at the University of Redlands, near Los Angeles.

≈ ≈ ≈

Sunday Dinner

Don Quixote would understand.

GREGARIOUS AND FRIENDLY THOUGH THEY MAY BE, the Spanish are nonetheless slow to invite friends into their homes, let alone strangers, so it is the rare foreign visitor who sits down to table for a Sunday afternoon family dinner. A pity, because the Sunday afternoon family dinner is Spain in exaltation. It is a mini-fiesta in which fireworks are sure to go off. All the traditional elements of Spanish life—the drama of the bullfight, the passion of flamenco, the solemnity of the Procession, mysticism and tragedy, hot blood, the gaiety of sun and sea, the pomp of a parade, and exquisite Mediterranean cuisine—are compressed and packed into a small dining room with tacky furniture.

The first time I meet my girlfriend Carmen's parents, Pep and Antonieta, is at Sunday dinner in their home in the barrio of Collblanc, which borders Barcelona. Carmen's sister, Ana, is also in attendance. Like many Spaniards, they are made shy by the presence of a foreigner, yet their welcome is touchingly naïve and exceedingly warm. All the same, they remain puzzled. The position of *el novio de mi hija,* "my daughter's boyfriend," has been mentally filled by—first and foremost—a Catalan. He speaks Catalan, he thinks Catalan, he is Catalan. He is also a good boy from a good family, a businessman of some type, probably without any vices whatsoever, an amorphous person present only in a vaporous sense, causing not the slightest ripple in the tranquil pond of Catalan family life. He is also—let's come out and say it—very rich.

In short, I am not what Pep and Antonieta have imagined for their daughter. On the other hand their daughter is not what they had imagined for themselves. As we tour the white-tiled apartment, they try to prove precisely this point. In every room we pause to examine family photographs and in each there is Carmen—at four, eight, ten, twelve years old—dead serious or terribly sad, her soft brown eyes glinting like bullets.

"Look," Antonieta says, "never smiling."

Her tone enjoins me to imagine what it must have been like to raise such a daughter. I nod, for I know that even back then this little girl believed in abnormal, anti-Spanish concepts like silence, solitude, and foreign travel. (What can any parent do with a kid like that?) Gazing at the same photo, Pep shakes his well-groomed head.

"Strange," he says.

The figure of Don Quixote is not only a literary character and advertising logo for tourism campaigns but a Spanish personality type, one that can be found in every fourth bar—(likewise the short, stout cohort)—and Pep is quixotic. He is part knight-errant, part absent-minded peacock, part dapper minister arriving in church without his sermon. He dresses far better than anyone in the family, better than anyone in this working-class barrio, and he sees danger everywhere. An insurance agent, he worries about the way we drive the motorbike, cross streets, crack open eggs, cook them. When Carmen and Ana were children and the family went on outings in the car he used to arm his daughters with tiny hammers. The two little girls sat in the back seat, hammers on their laps, secure in the knowledge that if an accident occurred, they could break open the rear window and escape.

"Strange," Pep repeats.

"And this is the bathroom?" I ask, pausing in the middle of the hallway.

Antonieta and Pep trade a look. How odd foreigners are. Imagine, stopping to poke your nose into the bathroom.

"*Es...un baño cualquiera...*," Antonieta answers uncertainly.

Yes, it is like any bathroom whatsoever, or at least like most, but I just want to have a little look because I know something about this bathroom. I know that the unhappy child in the photos used to lock herself in here to get away from the routine noise levels thrown off by a Spanish family. Many of her tragic expressions simply depict her failure to find sanctuary in this chamber. Pep and Antonieta used to pound ceaselessly on the door. "Foolish girl! Come out right now!" *No, please, papa, I want to be alone only for a minute!*

It is said that when Franco died, Barcelona drank itself dry of champagne. This tale may be apocryphal or exaggerated but it is certain that the first person in line at

the local *colmado,* plunking down her pesetas for a few
bottles of celebratory *cava,* was Antonieta. A Catalan
nationalist of fervent zeal, she becomes incensed hearing
any word—*franquicia* (franchise) or *francófono* (French-
speaking)—that even sounds like Franco. Humorous
and charming, she is at the same time a domineering
presence who will have her way. In the dark and murky
depths of mother/daughter relationships few views are
clear but here, perhaps, is the key difficulty with the
little girl in the photos: she would not bend.

Carmen, a doctor, takes her family in small doses, a
self-medication plan begun long before she wrote pre-
scriptions of any other kind. Many are the hard-nosed
company CEOs in Spain who lack the backbone to beg
out of Sunday dinner and our frequent absence is not
well regarded. But what is offensive at the start becomes,
as the years fall away, normal, at the worst, eccentric.

Thus, we arrive in Collblanc at two o'clock and for
an hour or so nibble on *tapas.* Then we sit down to table.
As always, I take my seat fiercely resolved that no matter
what transpires in the next three hours, I will not permit
it to distract me from the unimaginable banquet about
to be served. Of the top thirty meals I have eaten in
Spain, the first twenty-nine were prepared by Carmen's
mother.

It is regional cooking at its best, centuries of Catalan
culinary art passed down from grandmother to mother
to the occasional uncle or aunt, on to another mother, to
a daughter, and then onto this table. Recent large-scale
immigration has brought numerous ethnic restaurants
to Barcelona but twenty years ago it was hard to find a
place that served pizza, let alone Asian or Indian fare.
Regional cooking was simply too good to admit com-

petition and nowhere was it better than in this humble home. The first course might be *esqueixada,* a mix of tomatoes, white beans, red peppers, onions and olives, upon which salted cod is shred; or a classic Catalan salad. Nearby is a plate of *pan con tomate*—bread rubbed with tomato, salt, garlic and olive oil—and perhaps some prawns and *allioli* in which to dip them, or a traditional romesco sauce energized with garlic and cognac. We usually drink a Penedès or an El Priorato, sometimes a Rioja. Later we toast with champagne. Always there is something to celebrate.

Unfortunately, conversation does not rise or even aspire to the artistic level of the cuisine. It could, because on any given day Carmen has between five and ten fascinating patients, a liver transplant victim on the way to Russia to adopt a child, or a team of mountain climbers off to scale some peak in Pakistan. Ana is a registered nurse in the Intensive Care Unit of Bellvitge Hospital and every night she takes part in life and death drama. In addition we all have opinions on art, politics, cinema, and music. But we speak of none of these matters. Instead we discuss recent remarks made by the neighbor or the price of tomatoes at the market. The meal still enjoys a radiant sense of communion. Endearments and tenderness nourish us in concert with the food. Laughter can become so effusive napkins dab at eyes more often than they wipe mouths.

As the years pass, Ana acquires a new boyfriend, Javier, another non-Catalan. Of all places, he hails from Andalusia. Then children appear, Berta and Elia, *las pequeñas reinas,* the little queens. The amount of loving affection they receive in the course of a normal Sunday dinner would be enough to sustain a dozen emotionally deprived foreign children over a decade. A kiss here, a caress there, a tickle and hug as voices rise and tears fall, as arguments ensue, doors slam, and the second course is served. Perhaps it is chicken with shrimp, or *sarsuela,* a seafood mixture cooked in a fried onion, tomato and garlic sauce; or duck with pine nuts and prunes, baked slowly in an earthenware pan to coax flavors into full maturity.

Part of every meal, without fail, is Pep's speech. It occurs just at the moment that emotions have peaked, that the conversation has somehow strayed beyond tomatoes onto some less fruity topic. All at once Pep's eyes well up and his thin lips tremble. What he has to say is so pressing, so acutely visceral he must rise from his chair. His silver hair, combed back sleekly, catches the light. He inflates his chest and raises his forefinger, a lance aimed at a windmill. He hesitates, seeking the exact grandiloquent phrase to commence his oratory. The dining room trembles on the cusp of a great moment.

But his excessive delay has caused a traffic jam. Other mouths have filled with words and can wait no longer. Ana fidgets, twisting her napkin. This scene reminds her of other scenes in restaurants when her father is overcome by similar grand passions and must rise to congratulate a waiter on his smile or interrupt fellow diners to bestow a compliment on a cherubic child. Then Ana squirms in the grip of one of the most crippling emotions any Spaniard can feel—*vergüenza ajena,* shame for another.

Now she twists her napkin tighter. Antonieta is no less impatient. She has not yet finished telling us how much tomatoes used to cost. Pep still hesitates, his forefinger still points at the windmill, his lips still tremble.

Finally his mouth opens. He is about to utter the first word of his speech.

"Papa, sit down!" Carmen says. "You don't know what you want to say."

"He never knows!" Ana says.

"Don't talk to your father like that," Antonieta scolds.

"Don't yell at my sister," Ana snaps.

As the three women squabble, Pep appears stunned: a gigantic blade has just detached from the windmill and whacked him upside the head. His body goes limp. He collapses into his chair. His forearms plop down onto the table and his lifeless eyes peer into a haze of defeat, his dignity obliterated, his life in ruins.

This sight squeezes my heart and I encourage him to continue, to have his say and explain his important point, but now he can do nothing except stare over the remains of the paella, the wine corks strewn across the tablecloth, the crumpled napkins and discarded toothpicks. Before long his eye settles on a half empty plate of prawns. Listlessly, he selects one, peals off the semi-transparent shell—*crickle, crickle*—puts it into his mouth, bites, chews. After a moment his nose wrinkles, his forehead furrows and he mumbles:

"These prawns are overcooked."

Finally he has found a place to stick his lance. The effect of this simple phrase upon Antonieta, who never over- or undercooks anything, who only cooks to perfection, is so profound, so coronary-inducing, that everyone must leap to the defense of the offended prawns. Carmen gives me a kick under the table. If I do not now eat several prawns in quick succession, noisily smacking my lips and sucking my fingers, she and Ana will soon be administering cardiopulmonary resuscitation to their white-faced progenitrix. I eat quickly and things calm down. Antonieta recovers her color. She swears she does not know how this could have happened—perhaps Jaume at the market slipped in some rubbery prawns when she was concentrated on opening her purse. Next time she will be more vigilant. *"Està bé,"* Pep says.

A pause before dessert. If it is summer, Carmen, Ana, and Antonieta wave hand fans, employing a detached eloquence only Spanish women can pull off. A flick of the wrist sprays open the fan, another flick snaps it shut. The three fans flutter like hummingbirds above the table, hovering over dessert. Perhaps it is *música,* a portion of nuts and dried fruits served with sweet muscatel; or goat cheese and walnuts drizzled with warm honey; or my favorite, *crema catalana,* a creamy custard dish with a glazed top. We wash down dessert with champagne. The bubbling liquid and the fluttering fans delight the air. I watch Carmen and Ana, thinking that in place of fans they once held tiny hammers.

On one particular Sunday I myself wish I had a hammer, or any device offering the hope of escape. Carmen correctly accuses me of cowardice and I accuse her of postponing the inevitable. For the last several weeks she has withheld information from her family. She claims she has done so to reduce hysteria and mitigate suffering but now the moment for hysteria and suffering has arrived.

As dinner begins, she summons her most cheerful voice. She could be announcing some triviality, a decision to take the bus to work instead of her motorbike. While others pour wine, ladle out soup, unfurl napkins, not really listening, she goes on perkily. Then, out of nowhere, she happily announces that tomorrow morning at six o'clock she will board an airplane—alone—and leave for two months in Burkina Faso.

Thus, she succeeds in creating the silence she so longed for as a difficult child. Never has the apartment been quieter. Mute faces digest her crazed words. A wine glass hangs above the table, a fork clicks down onto a plate. Berta and Elia scan adult faces searching for the emotion they are now required to feel. Nobody knows where this place is—Burkina what? Faso where?—but the sound of such tribal syllables is troubling, about to create panic.

Today there will be no talk of neighbors or tomatoes. Nor will there be any laughter. This will be the only meal in which Pep does not rise from his chair to attempt a speech. Over the years I have been tacitly excused from family arguments. My hearty appetite, my foreign birth, and general uncertainty over how much Catalan I comprehend, have bequeathed me the status of "only partially involved guest," but that is now revoked. Today I will pay a higher price to eat.

Berta and Elia normally rejoice in the thunder of emotions. At five years of age the little one, Elia, not only eats escargot with aplomb (insouciantly plucking the meat onto her thin, double-tined snail fork and dipping it in a white wine and garlic sauce) but knows how to pitch a classic fit of pique. When roused, she can shove forward her plate, toss her napkin, kick back her highchair, and storm out of the room, ruffled pride and little chin held high. But today's emotions are way beyond anything these little girls know. Their mother, Ana, perhaps the most emotional member of an emotional family, has just slipped on a pair of sunglasses; from behind the dark lenses fat tears roll down her cheeks. Looking from face

to face, trying to make sense of the tragic grimaces and
yammering voices, the two little queens understand only
that their beloved Aunt Carmen is about to vanish from
the face of the earth. They cling to her sides, each grasping an arm, kissing her shoulders.

The meal has only just begun and I am already wrung
out. Carmen has anticipated this moment—or says
she has—and now offers assurances to all objections.
For example, two former patients—two good Catalan
boys—professional adventurers who run a safari opera-
tion in Burkina, will pick her up at the Ouagadougou
airport. These strong, powerful, trustworthy men owe
a malaria-free existence to her and will protect her
with their lives, or at least carry her backpack. But two
platoons of crack foreign legion troops would not be
sufficient for this mission and three hours of dinnertime
turmoil follow. The food remains uneaten. Dessert is
not even served. No one dares uncork the champagne.
At the door I pry fingers off Carmen's arms and back
us into the elevator, blocking the entrance. As the cage
descends, we listen to the cable playing out, the gears
grinding, the cries echoing down the shaft.

At four o'clock the following morning we are in the
backseat of a taxi, heading for the airport. Yesterday's
emotions still grip me by the throat. Many things were
said but many more were not. This journey may not
be exactly the holiday picnic Carmen has described.
Among other things, she will be giving vaccinations
near the Sahel region. Will it be dangerous? Probably
not, but I am aware she is not skipping off to Madrid for
the weekend.

I hold her hand and stare at the dark road ahead,
watching the white hash markers unzip the future. I

see many unknowns and only one certainty: it will be at least two months until the next Sunday dinner.

Carmen caresses my hand, whispers in English that she will be fine, then repeats it in Spanish. I nod, smile, press her hand. Then, at the same moment, the taxi driver, Carmen, and I see the impossible. We are on a freeway, north- and southbound lanes separated by a divider, but—*it cannot be*—bearing down directly on us is a set of headlights. At the last second our driver yanks on the steering wheel, the taxi veers off and the other car sails past, missing us by inches.

"*¡Madre de Dios!*" our driver cries.

Mother of God indeed. I am so rattled I sputter at the driver in English. Carmen sits beside me as rigid as a syringe. We do not have our tiny hammers and the undertaker has just come calling. Finally I summon the presence of mind to reach forward, place my hand on the driver's shoulder and squeeze. This able man has just saved our lives.

By the time we reach the airport he has received a report on his radio. The National Police have already made an arrest at a roadblock set up near Plaza España. The man is a *conductor suicida,* a suicide driver, drunk, drugged, or demented, but now in handcuffs and on his way to jail. I pay our taxi driver, telling him I will not give him a tip. He nods, saying he would not accept one. Our lives are worth so much more.

Carmen and I enter Terminal A. She checks in and I kiss her goodbye, then watch as she disappears through Passport Control, her face still pale.

Two months later in the same airport terminal the Arrivals door slides open and she emerges, her olive skin burned the reddish-brown of fine leather. She has lost a few pounds and now wears a colorful African shirt. On the way home she tells me she is fine. She had one or two bad moments in Burkina but nothing to match our scare in the taxi.

The following Sunday we arrive at her parents' apartment. Carmen passes out presents: a tribal mask for Ana and Javier's living room wall, soaps and scented spices for Pep and Antonieta, beaded bracelets and trinkets for the little queens. Carmen has also brought back several fine traveler's tales from Africa. In a remote village she administered vaccinations and the chieftain, in token of respect and gratitude, gave her two half-dead chickens. Later a deputy regional governor invited her to inspect his barefoot troops. Traveling out in the bush, she has seen antelopes, hippos, and enormous flocks of vultures.

But she will tell none of these tales. It is sufficient for everyone to know that it was hot in Africa. Instead of going into it any further we will discuss recent price increases at the market.

Nonetheless, everyone is well aware that this dinner is special. Antonieta began preparing food yesterday and has cooked a meal that threatens to demote others from my top thirty. Today there is truly splendid reason to uncork the champagne. The prodigal daughter has returned, the family is reunited, and we may partake of communion, exulting in the celebration of the Sunday afternoon family dinner in Spain.

Emotions swell and Ana must put on her sunglasses. The little queens shake their arms, rattling their new bracelets. Finally Pep can contain himself no longer. On the ballast of rising passions, he levitates upward from his chair. He lifts his champagne glass toward the ceiling. Bubbles pop as he feels his way forward, putting the final embellishments on an opening phrase. Finally he is about to speak. The dining room trembles on the cusp of a great moment.

❧ ❧ ❧

Patrick Pfister is the author of the books, Pilgrimage: Tales from the Open Road *and* Over Sand & Sea. *His stories have appeared in* Travelers' Tales: Food, Greece, *and* American Southwest. *For the last twenty years he has lived in Barcelona, Spain.*

MICHAEL ENGELHARD

⚛ ⚛ ⚛

Blood Ties

Wolves and people go way back.

There was a girl who met up with a wolf, back in Distant Time, when wolves were human. The wolf wanted her for his wife, even though he had two wives already. When he took her home his two wives smelled her and knew she was human. After a while she had a child—a boy—and the wolf decided to kill his other two wives. He did that, but afterward the spirits of those two wolf wives killed his human wife and ate up her insides. Since then, women are never supposed to kill wolves, and they should not work with wolf hides until the animal has been dead for a while. They must follow these rules until they are too old to have children.
— A KOYUKON TALE

My cross-country skis hiss against the surface glare, slicing mile after mile of the snowy back-of-beyond. Only the panting of huskies and the crunching of sled

26

runners augment their noise. We are on our annual spring break trip, this time tracking the drifted-over road to Wonder Lake into the heart of Denali National Park. Twilight overtakes our dog team and skiers early on this brisk March day. When the cold starts to bite through thick layers of wool and down, and all color drains from the land, we pull over to camp in a copse of white spruce.

After dinner in our wall tent—kept cozy by a small wood-burning stove—I step outside. By now, the ghostly, cold fire of northern lights plays overhead, fluttering in curtains of neon-green gauze. They easily blot out the scatter of stars. I stretch my sore shoulders, and my senses strain into the calm. The alleged purpose of this venture is to scout a route for a National Outdoors Leadership School course; but I really hope for a run-in with the most secretive denizen of these frozen wastes: the Alaskan gray wolf.

In all my time in the Big Dipper State only once has a wolf graced my life with its brief presence. I was solo-kayaking the Noatak River, gliding through blankets of brush fire that pulverized tundra and shrouded silt-and-clay cutbanks. As the smoke screen lifted momentarily, I glimpsed a large canine standing still, blending in perfectly with the surrounding ashes. It appeared like a northern mirage: a creature like smoke itself. The solitary wolf on the riverbank gazed at me without curiosity or concern. He then turned and trotted away, quickly dropping from sight. I had felt strangely abandoned.

A high-pitched wailing pulls me back into the present. It wavers, rises and falls, in sync with the splendor above. It seems to come from nowhere and all places at once—piercing the night and my soul. The lone voice is soon joined by others, meshing with the pack's desire.

These must be the wolves of the East Fork of the Toklat River studied by Adolph Murie, a Minnesota wildlife biologist, between 1939 and 1941. This pioneer of wolf studies found that like humans, packs too, develop their own "culture," a culture that survives the death of its individuals. Thus the Toklat bunch has occupied the same dens and hunting grounds, possibly since long before World War II. It also has learned to remain largely invisible.

Our sled dogs briefly raise their heads, but stay eerily silent. They curl up again—noses buried under tails— disregarding the song of their wild cousins. A breeze has picked up, ruffling the fur on my parka hood. The ruff is a strip from a wolf pelt, much coveted, since it does not frost up easily when breathed upon. It is silken, and rich with memories.

Years ago, I attended a memorial potlatch in the Koyukon Indian settlement of Huslia. The entire village had gathered in the octagonal community hall built from logs. The women wore shawls and colorful calico dresses in the traditional style, many of the men knee-high mukluks made from the leg skin of caribou. Scores of children were zipping around the hall. After a series of speeches to honor Sophie Sam—an elder who had passed away a year before—the singing began. Men and women took turns at the microphone, with songs composed for the occasion. The rhythm, hammered out on a hand-held frame drum with a padded stick, filled the enclosed space, vibrating in the pit of my stomach. The falsetto singing was marked by fierceness, by a passion defying the finality of death. Afterwards, the family of the deceased gave gifts to the crowd. They handed out beaver skins, rifles, blankets, beaded buckskin gloves, and assortments of household goods. I received one of many strips cut from a wolf pelt, which my mother later sewed onto my parka hood. This token not only embodied the sharing of grief, but also joined two species in their mortality. It made visible deep bonds between wolves and a human community.

The evening ended in a form of communion; long tables bent under homemade casseroles, stews, bread, and muffins; "Eskimo ice cream" had been whipped into a fluff, from sugar, oil, blueberries, and pounded whitefish. Most important though, were meat and fish taken from the land, the true foods ascertaining Athabaskan identity: moose, caribou, wild sheep, and salmon—baked, boiled, jerked, canned, or smoked. According to tradition, the elders were served first.

I had learned much about wolves from one such elder, Stephen Moses in Allakaket, north of the Arctic Circle. When I visited for the first time, I had found his mudroom cluttered with the implements of a bush life. Hip waders slumped next to foul weather gear, snow-machine parts, dip nets, a shotgun, beaver skin mittens dangling from a nail, and a motor saw with a chain that needed tightening. Two wolf pelts flowed from the rafters—complete with tail, legs, ears, and muzzle. Before I knocked on the inner door, I had reached out and stroked the silver-tipped fur. The gaping eyeholes and the hides' flattened appearance had left me slightly unsettled.

A dead beaver lay on the kitchen floor half-skinned and placed on a piece of cardboard, to keep the meat clean and blood off the linoleum. Stephen invited me to sit. But before I unrolled my maps on the table, we snacked on caribou jerky dipped in seal oil (a delicacy traded from coastal Eskimos). His wife Minnie meanwhile busied herself quietly with a pot of caribou tongue soup bubbling on the stove.

The National Park Service wanted to know which areas of Kobuk River and Gates of the Arctic national parks these hunters and gatherers had traditionally used. If they could prove prior use, the Koyukon would still be entitled to hunt there, and even to trap wolves.

Stephen pointed out the routes of his hunting and trapping expeditions. His forays had taken him way above timberline, into the snowy crags of the Brooks Range, and as far south as the willow-choked banks of the Yukon River. In the mountains and plains to the north, bands of semi-nomadic Koyukon had hunted Dall's sheep and caribou for thousands of years, in friendly competition with packs of wolves. The meanders he drew on my maps, with felt pens of various colors, resembled the tangle of wolf wanderings and territories wildlife biologists chart on their maps. Stephen's eyes veiled with distance, as if he were re-living each mile on the trail. His crinkled, leathery face relaxed.

"That *teekkona*, he keeps caribou strong." An ecological understanding rivaling that of Western science found expression in these few words. A lifetime observing the animals under natural conditions had made this man a wolf expert and better hunter. I sensed admiration for the sleek and efficient predators under his words. With a callused finger, the elder tapped on their den sites, and on those of bears, black and brown. He shared that the quality of pelts—fox, mink, marten, lynx, otter, beaver, wolverine, and wolf—was best in January and February, when temperatures plummeted and the animals grew coats dense and shiny. Though he was too old now to go on long trips, Stephen remembered how to intercept wolves near their kills, which bait to use, and how to set and disguise traps. "They are smart, just like us," he chuckled.

In soft, lilting village English laced with Koyukon phrases, he recalled a rare black wolf he had caught more than four decades ago. He had traded its pelt together with other furs in Kotzebue, at the Bering Strait coast, for his first decent gun. Wolf pelts are still valued highly. They can bring $450 or more at the fur exchange in Fairbanks or Anchorage, cash that is needed for outboard motors, rifles, four-wheelers, and snowmachines.

Stephen spoke at great length about respect. He told me about the web of taboos surrounding this animal, an animal whose spiritual power is only rivaled by that of wolverine and bear. I had read in an early ethnographic account that in pre-missionary days, Athabaskan hunters honored a killed wolf like a chief. They carried it to camp on their shoulders. Then they brought it inside the hunter's home, propped it up as if alive, and a shaman would set a potlatch-style banquet before it, to which the entire village contributed. When the wolf-guest had eaten its fill, the men took their share.

When I mentioned practices and beliefs I had come across in my research, Stephen became serious. He nodded, in recognition of an age-old kinship. Currently passing on his knowledge to a grandson, he stressed the rules that guide contact with wolves. A rifle used to shoot one should always be left in the front of the house and for four days afterwards. To appease the departed spirit, a chunk of dried fish should be put into the dead wolf's mouth, or a choice piece of caribou backstrap fat burned as an offering. "If you don't do this," he concluded, "he will turn on you." Disregarding the rules of conduct will unfailingly bring bad luck, injury, disease, or even death, to the hunter or his family.

According to another Distant Time tale, the pact binding Koyukon and wolves is ancient: long ago, when such things were still possible, a wolf-man lived among humans. He shared their lives, participating in their hunts. When he left the people to return to his own, he promised that wolves would sometimes leave kills for them. They would drive caribou toward human hunters, in exchange for favors received while they were still human. And thus, to this day, Koyukon men who come upon a fresh wolf kill feel entitled to take what they need.

These days my old down parka is stored away in a box. Its wolf ruff has turned a bit ratty. I no longer live in Alaska, but in a state where the last wolf was killed more than seventy years ago. In my new home state, a debate rages about the reintroduction of wolves. Brother Wolf is ensnared, once again, in the agendas of game managers, ranchers, hunters, politicians, and environmentalists.

Winter nights in the Wasatch Mountains can be crisp and clear and studded with stars, like up north. But they lack the serenading of wolves. No longer can tan-and-gray mists be glimpsed from the corners of your eyes. No longer does the air crackle with the presence of large carnivores, causing your skin to tighten. No new stories take shape, renewing blood ties between us and them. Like grizzlies, wolves have been banned from their native range. The price of a few cows and sheep—or even deer—seems small compared to the loss pervading these forests.

There is reason to hope, though.

On November 27, 2002, a black male wolf was trapped near Ogden, Utah. Tracks of a mate were found nearby. The radio-collared animal turned out to be a stray from a Yellowstone pack 200 miles north, seeking to expand its territory. After an absence of nearly a lifetime, wildness had returned.

At times I feel tempted to relocate to Alaska, to a place where the voice of the forest can be heard in the night. I still stay put, believing that perhaps, like the Koyukon, we can learn to live with *teekkona*.

~ ~ ~

Michael Engelhard is the author of Where the Rain Children Sleep, *as well as the editor of two anthologies. He is currently finishing a book of Canyon Country vignettes (*Redrock Almanac*) and commutes between Alaska and the Colorado Plateau. Since writing this story, he has been blessed with more wolf encounters.*

GARY BUSLIK

❧ ❧ ❧

My Military-Industrial Complex

Leaving Cuba takes an expensive turn.

THE LINE AT JOSÉ MARTI INTERNATIONAL WAS FOR tourists what every other line in Cuba was for Cubans: long and languid and as listless as a boa constrictor after eating an agouti on a sweltering afternoon. We had barely moved for almost two hours—sitting on our suitcases, reading, playing blackjack, muttering obscenities, occasionally standing to regain circulation and nudge our bags with our feet, playing Name That Tune on the zippers and Hang the Butcher, with the Butcher having a full beard, smoking a cigar, and wearing guerrilla fatigues from the 1950s. But, like the Dow Industrial Average, in all that time we had gotten absolutely nowhere. One crummy check-in agent for a couple of hundred sunburned, bunion-throbbing, pissed-off Yanquis. Eventually the python began to bulge here and there and then break apart like that New Hampshire revolutionary flag, "Live Free or Die."

When I couldn't stand it anymore, I moseyed outside and found a kid—Jorge, nine years old—selling stale coconut fragments and gave him ten dollars to come inside and stand in line for me.

Let me explain something. In Cuba you can bribe anyone to do anything for a U.S. dollar. One night we went to the Museum of the Revolution, only to find it closed for "remodeling"—a term that is to Cuban economic reality what "International" is to Cuban airport. Well, fine. One dollar, and the security guard not only let us in and turned on the lights for us, he invited us to help ourselves to whatever mementos we might like, such as *Granma*, the boat on which Castro and one hundred of his men sailed from Mexico to launch their revolution. "Go on," he said, waving, "just take it."

If you got sick on hotel food and—the Cuban doctors being among the world's best—they diagnosed you with needing an entire upper-body transplant, and there were 3,000 desperately ill Cubans on the upper-body waiting list, a buck would do the trick, and you'd be flying home with a spanking new thorax.

So in offering Jorge a sawbuck, I was not only giving him at least a thousand times more than necessary, I was also single-handedly reviving the Cuban gross domestic product. Unfortunately, my wife didn't see it that way.

"What's the matter with you?" she hissed.

I explained about the Cuban economy.

"He's not standing in line for you. It's demeaning."

"Not as demeaning as constantly losing at Hang the Butcher. What the hell kind of a word is *sphygmomanometer*? You made that up."

"Not you. Demeaning for *him*, you twit."

"Now there's a word I can wrap my brain around."

"Send him back out there."

"He's selling chunks of old coconut for a nickel. He'll be dead before he makes ten bucks."

"Then let him keep the ten dollars."

"It's not slavery. He wants to work for it. Look," I said, "if you send him away, he'll think it's his fault. Anyhow, what's so demeaning about standing in line?" I glanced around at our fellow travelers. "I'll bet they wish they'd thought of it first." She magnetized my molecules with her MRI glare—usually reserved for when George Bush says something idiotic, as if I, personally, had been responsible for the low oxygen level in his incubator. I patted Jorge's noggin. "Hey, we all work for someone."

"Not standing in line for spoiled Americans," she said.

A fat Canadian with a ponytail in front of us shook his head—in disgust, if I wasn't mistaken. "Right on, sister," he muttered. Instead of a respectable, bourgeois suitcase with gimpy wheels, he nudged a backpack across the floor, the kind usually seen on the bony shoulders of pimply college undergraduates, not middle-aged men shaped like Shamu the whale. I knew he was an escapee from the Great White North because his passport was tucked into a strap on his backpack, as if he wanted to make damn well sure everyone knew he wasn't an American. You can pick out a Canadian passport from across a room, because its cover features a gold-embossed portrait of Queen Elizabeth eating a bacon sandwich. You can tell it's bacon by the curlicue tail sticking out of the bread.

I happen to like Canadians. Many years ago, my best friend, Steve, and I spent a week at a fly-in fishing camp in southern Ontario, on a system of lakes that, had Livingston been fishing there, Stanley would not have found him in a bazillion years. The landscape was so unremittingly wet and featureless and bland, even Canadians considered it boring. It was like a Hamm's Beer bar sign had fallen off the wall into the sink, and the bartender accidentally left the cold faucet running overnight, and a storm came and blew the roof off the bar, and the bartender, who had fallen asleep drunk in the storeroom, drowned.

The lakes were so easy to get lost on that we were supposed to wear bright orange ponchos so the seaplane that had dropped us off would be able to find us in a week, and if we heard the plane but didn't see it, we were supposed to make a fire and, if necessary, burn all our clothing to attract attention. The problem being that we and all of our belongings were so thoroughly soaked to the bone—if our belongings had had bones—that we could have doused ourselves with kerosene from our sleeping-bag warmers, had we not run out of kerosene four days earlier, and had our sleeping bags not fallen out of our capsized canoe, along with our food, tent, clothes, and ourselves—and they still would not have caught fire.

So we wound up fishing naked, which we found very liberating and glorious and spiritual, until my accident with the lure. Then we had to call in for an air ambulance, which cost three thousand dollars Canadian—sixty-five U.S.—but which at least supplied us with dry hospital gowns. They flew us to Winnipeg, where they surgically removed the lure and related minnow, and, after a massive dose of antibiotics, we saw an American movie with Canadian subtitles and went to a "massage" parlor where we could be with actual women, as opposed to walleye pikes dressed up like women. My "massage therapist" was a nifty brunette named Margo, who at the time reminded me of Jill St. John, but in retrospect more resembled Herbert Hoover. In any event, there I was lying on my back, "massage" towel draped over groin, and Margo dribbling warm "massage" oil into my navel while we engaged in a bit of preparatory idle chit-chat. Then she asked me if I would like her to remove the towel, and I said sure, and when she saw what was underneath she screamed and asked what the hell was that. I told her it was a fish-hook accident, but I don't think she believed me because she blew a whistle, and in ran a seven-foot-tall Canadian with a hockey stick who threatened to slap-shot me stupid if I did not scram and take my weird-looking groin and my friend Steve with me. Or it may have been the other way around.

So you might wonder why I like Canadians, and I will tell you. A couple of years later the Blackhawks made it to the Stanley Cup playoffs versus the Maple Leafs, and who should turn out to be Toronto's star defenseman but Matt Chevalier, Margo's seven-foot bouncer. I had just met Janice, my future bride, and I wanted to impress her on our first date, so I asked her if she wanted to go to a playoff game, only to find out that tickets were pretty much impossible to get. So in desperation I found out what bar the players hung out at, and I took a chance and cornered Chevalier, and after very little prodding he remembered that I was the fish-hook guy whose arm he had threatened to tear off and beat me with,

and I bought him a Labatt beer, and we became new
best friends. He got me two front-row seats, and Janice
thought I was some kind of CEO or something, and I
asked Chevalier not to mention the Margo/lure incident
in front of her, and he never did. So we fell in love—me
and Janice, not me and the defenseman—and I thought
she was a Republican, so I married her.

And she was a Republican, too, until George W. Bush
got elected, at which time she became a communist, and
now she blames me personally for everything that comes
out of his mouth, including the hay. Somehow or other
it was *my* fault that we didn't find weapons of mass destruction in Iraq, that the levees failed in New Orleans,
that there was a volcanic eruption on Montserrat, and
that Karl Rove is the moral equivalent of smog. I am
not allowed to watch Fox News while she is in the room
or turn off any TV while set to that station, in case she
should be the first to turn it on again. She is suddenly
gung-ho for Hugo Chavez, reparations for blacks,
and changing Chief Illiniwek's name to Chief Rotten
Imperialist Pig. She now believes that *The Wall Street
Journal* is an example of ideological state apparatus; that
the military-industrial complex dictates our personal
hygiene; that maybe Thomas Jefferson wasn't such a
great guy after all, considering he liked brown booty;
that Fidel Castro is the second coming—assuming there
had been a first, which she doubts—and if George Bush
had his way, Havana would be a Wal-Mart and the rest
of Cuba a parking lot, as though the previous fifty years
have been a figment of the earth's imagination.

Reminding her that she had married me under possibly
false pretenses fell on "audibly disadvantaged" ears, and
she replied that if I wanted a divorce, fine and dandy, and

if Bushy nominated one more evangelical Christian lunk-head to the Supreme Court, she had her divorce lawyer, Adolph Hitler Mendelbaum, ready to file, so I'd better pray for the justices' continued good health.

So, yes, I did like Canadians, but the muttering for-mer hippie in front of us at Jose Marti "International" was a tad suspicious-seeming. For one thing, I had sel-dom seen a fat Canadian—they worked off their bacon by cleaning fish, I guess—and, for another thing, all the hippies I had ever known pretty much grew out of it in their twenties, when they traded in their roach clips for Audis and condos. The last time I had seen a ponytail on a man the age of this so-called Canadian was when they found that Green Beret alive in the Cambodian jungle, having survived there for thirty years and never know-ing the war was over or that Nixon had resigned and that America had matured to the point where we would teach creationism again in our public schools, and all he could eat for the next year was capybara poop, until after long and intense psychotherapy, in which he was gradually introduced to current movie prices and *The O'Reilly Factor*.

So right off the bat I didn't like this corpulent, time-warped freakazoid, although based on what you already know about my wife, you probably thought she would have answered his clearly provocative, anti-American crack, "Right on, sister," with a raised-fist, black-power salute, like those putzes in the 1968 summer Olympics whose names no one even remembers, and that she would have given him a hippie handshake and trucked-on-down with him to the airport lounge, where they would have shared carrot juice and a toke, and they would have ex-changed notes on how to blow up oil tankers.

You would think so, but you would be as wrong as a naked fisherman trying desperately to reel in a twelve-hook, guaranteed-kill-or-your-money-cheerfully-refunded, Godzilla-brand lure that happened to be snagged on a sunken Canadian log. You cannot get more wrong.

Because here is an interesting thing about Janice. On the one hand, she will make a mad dash to Michael Moore's latest movie with the enthusiasm of one dog's nose up another dog's backside, and she will return home spewing all manner of liberal claptrap to her emotionally needy, Bush-voting husband who desperately wants a bit of nooky before bedtime. On the other hand, you can't make a sow's ear out of a silk purse, and I knew, just *knew*, that when it came down to it, if some foreign, Jefferson Airplane-loving weed-sucker dared to say peep against her country, she would de-spleen him with the efficiency of mongoose on snake.

And sure enough, recognizing that murderous, patriotic gleam in her eye, I both feared for the unsuspecting, pony-tailed lard bucket and, at the same time, braced myself for some yuks.

But, oddly, she pinged him with only a grazing look and said nothing. Instead, she turned to Jorge, folded his hand around my ten dollars, so he knew he could keep it, then pointed to the door and smiled maternally. "It's yours, honey. Go."

The kid looked at me, confused. "No change," he stuttered—probably a phrase he had learned phonetically.

Janice shook her head. "It's O.K., keep it."

Again, Jorge, frowning, glanced at me.

"No problemo," I said, loud and slow and showing my palms. "Keepo itto."

The Canadian clacked his tongue, flicked his ponytail, and rolled his pork-loving eyeballs.

Okey-dokey. Now he was really in for it. True, Janice had been perfectly willing to deal him a beginner's good hand. It had been his lucky day. He had pulled a pair of tens. But with that clacking he had pressed that luck, split his pair, and was about to get his head handed to him. He was about to be blonded.

I held my breath. This was it. Cobra, prepare to die.

She turned to me. "Fork over a twenty."

"Twenty what?"

Her eyes bulged. I whipped out my wallet and found a double sawbuck. She snapped it nice and loud—to irritate our Canadian enemy, I assumed. She handed the money to Jorge. "For you," she said. "You don't have to do anything. We have lots."

"We do?" I whispered, making a sound like a sneezing hamster.

She motioned for my wallet again.

"Um, don't you think this is the kind of thing we should discuss as a couple?"

She thrust out her palm and wiggled her fingers malevolently—again, undoubtedly for the benefit of our northern friend.

I handed her my wallet. She went right for the hidden pocket, where I kept my bail money. She handed Jorge two crisp hundreds. "For you to do whatever you want, sweet boy. Don't forget the rest of your family."

The Canadian said nothing. Evidently humiliated, demoralized, and defeated, he had returned to his crossword puzzle.

Janice took out two more hundreds from their imitation-leather lair, creased them lengthwise, and tucked them into the lad's pocket. "We're rich," she told him. "Wealthy Americans. Very spoiled." She turned to me. "Aren't we, dear?"

I cleared my throat. She handed me back my wallet with three dollars in it.

Did we show that Canadian, or what?! *These colors don't run!*

She patted Jorge's head. "Have a nice day."

The boy turned to me. I could see what was left of his lunch on his back teeth.

"Yeah, have a nice day," I said. "Try real hard."

Janice tilted her head at me. I held up my hand. "O.K., I'm not saying another word."

"And you're going to keep me company in line and not get any more bright ideas?"

"You bet, and no way."

"Deal the cards, bright boy."

I did, and she drew twenty-one, and I busted. We sat on two suitcases and used the third as a table, and every now and then we'd scoot along and continue playing, and after about an hour I dealt her a ten and a six and was waiting for her to indicate stay or hit, and when she didn't I glanced up and saw her looking around the hall, her mouth twisted weirdly, her eyebrows gnarled, and I followed her gaze and saw it, too. I was the last one to see it, but that's the story of my life.

Jorge had put out the word, had rounded up a horde of his young *compañeros*, or whatever they're called, who were now stampeding the waiting line with offers to stand in for passengers at a U.S. dollar each. In a few minutes Janice and I were pretty much the only non-Cubans still in line— the Canadian having been one of the first to fork over his buck, no doubt so he could rout up a pork sandwich.

It all worked out, though. I taught the urchins how to play blackjack, and when they lost their money, I explained about what we call in English the "learning curve" and made them repeat the phrase several times until you could hardly detect an accent, and after I won back my bail money, I let them play on credit, and when they continued to lose I was willing to let them work off their debt by walking on Janice's and my backs, which were killing us from having waited so long in line. At first she didn't like the idea, but when I pointed out that I was teaching them the evils of gambling, ancillary to the evils of capitalism, she, too, saw it as a life-lesson master stroke and flipped over on her tummy.

∽ ∽ ∽

Gary Buslik teaches creative writing at the University of Illinois, Chicago. He writes short stories, essays, and novels, and his work appears in many commercial and literary magazines. His most recent novel is The Missionary's Position, *an Eastern-Caribbean romp. This story is from his book-in-progress,* A Rotten Person Travels the West Indies.

CAROLYN A. THÉRIAULT

~ ~ ~

Confessions of a Water Pipe Smoker

Local culture travels well through the
chambers of the *sheesha* glass.

I AM A DR. FRANKENSTEIN, A CREATOR OF SORTS; I HAVE harvested liberally from the defunct bodies of my less fortunate water pipes in order to generate, or perpetuate, the life of one. I look upon my sole remaining progeny and confess that it has a face only a mother can love. In spite of, or rather because of its spurious legitimacy, I dote on my gaudy green water pipe, made (so its faded label tells me) of the finest Bohemian crystal, its chipped body stained and sticky from overuse and inadequate cleaning, its now tarnished stem and valves pathetically bereft of a tin of Brasso. I have plugged its many airholes with bits of cellophane and cardboard in an effort to facilitate airflow. Its faded leather hose has become dangerously brittle and its many resultant cracks repaired with duct tape. The dapple-gray plastic mouthpiece has broken twice but is still serviceable when used backwards. It is truly a thing of beauty, but then again, love is blind.

When my water pipe was but a twinkle in my eye, I secured a position as an archaeological site supervisor in Upper Egypt for several months. I flew into Alexandria, believing that it would be a logical transitional point between East and West, mitigating the inevitable culture shock awaiting me in Cairo. Within hours of my early evening arrival and imbued with a heady cocktail of jetlag, adventurousness, and naïveté, I veered off the beaten path and found myself lost among the myriad alleys that split from the main thoroughfare like the legs of a centipede, half-heartedly illumined with sallow neon lights and bare bulbs suspended by lone wires.

Like so many alleyways in Egypt, this one was also a makeshift tea stand where wobbly chairs (no two of which shared a common ancestor) stood precariously along each wall, where men in suits or djellabas came to discuss the events of the day over a glass of tea and a *sheesha* (for such is the water pipe called in Egypt). Behind me I could hear "Alex," as many locals and ex-pats refer to this city, freshly-awakened from its siesta, its traffic and promenading youth shaking off the fug of the afternoon heat, gathering momentum and volume. Before me, men sat in huddles, gesticulating with the mouthpieces of their water pipes, voices raised in mock rage or laughter, while boys ran up and down the length of the alley, deftly bearing trays of glasses, foodstuffs fetched from other shops, or shavings of live embers to refresh a pipe.

The alley was filled with the din of conversation, the clinking of glassware, and the sound of a lone lovelorn woman, her recorded voice rendered warbled and tinny by the archaic cassette player that stood in an open doorway, doubling as a doorjamb. I stood at the mouth of this Aladdin's cave and gaped like an idiot.

I wanted in. But I was an *agnabeeya,* a female foreigner, and before me were none of my kind, neither females nor foreigners. Would I be allowed to sit? Would I be offering offense, sowing discord by my very presence? Would I be transgressing some age-old code of male solidarity?

Gathering what little resolve I had, I passed over the outstretched legs of a number of men who, startled, shifted awkwardly to make way for me until I found a vacant chair. Immediately a young man in track pants and a t-shirt appeared with a small table and a glass of water. I asked for a glass of tea, looked about me, and then paused. He paused. I pointed to my neighbor's pipe and attempted to win him over with my pigeon Arabic.

"Mumkin sheesha?" I asked feebly. Can I have a *sheesha?*

"Aiwa! Aiwa!" he cried. Yes! Yes!

My neighbors who had been watching me covertly up until that point made no attempts to hide their interest and apparent delight as my waiter told everyone in earshot that I had asked for a *sheesha*. Chairs scraped as they were repositioned in my direction. All eyes were on me as my waiter carried the *sheesha* over. I was the stage show. God, I was the headliner! From a brass dish he deftly removed the sizzling embers breathing fire into the quickening night, positioned them on the clay cone that was filled with the treacle-sticky tobacco and stood back a few paces. The cone sputtered and hissed from the marriage of cool, moist tobacco and glowing charcoal; within seconds a sweet perfume of smoke serpentined before my eyes. I took my first drag. I heard the intake of many breaths. Heads were cocked to watch me closer. I closed my eyes. I inhaled; I exhaled.

I neither coughed nor hacked up a lung; instead, I experienced The Rapture as the first rich hit of unadulterated molasses-flavored tobacco began to undulate within my body. I felt myself billowing, if not swaying, in an ineffable awareness of bewildering peacefulness: two days' worth of traveling stress was suddenly washed from my body. I opened my eyes and smiled.

"Good?" my nearest neighbor asked me in thick English, with a co-conspiratorial look in his eye.

"*Kwayyis!*" I answered in Arabic. "Good!" The men about me broke into peels of approving laughter. My neighbor slapped me on the back with a bear paw, which nearly sent me reeling onto the pavement.

"*Tamaam!*" I added. "Excellent!" and I was a hit.

I spent another hour or so drinking tea and chatting in the patois of travel: bits of whatever tongue worked, be it Indo-European, Semitic, or body language. Fresh tea was served, more embers added to my pipe. When I eventually got up to leave, I realized that I had somehow lost my land legs so that the act of standing and balancing was not as simple a task as I had remembered it to be. Nobody seemed terribly concerned about my condition and I did manage to stagger out of the alley without falling. As I rounded the corner, I lurched against a wall and retched uncontrollably; remarkably unperturbed, I kicked dust on my roadside offerings and went on my way.

From Alexandria to Aswan I whiled away many the hour in swank coffee houses, impromptu tea stands, hotel patios—wherever a *sheesha* glowed and the kettle was clanking on the fire. Men unquestioningly shared their water pipes. With the exception of that first *sheesha* in Alex (you always remember your first), none were sweeter than the *sheeshas* I shared with the site caretakers and staff at our excavation site. In their gracious company, we talked and laughed, and smoked languidly at the door of the dighouse after their evening prayers. In the lengthening shadows of the Temple of Karnak, we would watch desert fox course the outer mudbrick walls, nighthawks and owls careen through the tall grasses, and listen as donkeys laden with fodder appeared out of the charred night, their drivers offering up a litany of greetings to us all. Sometimes they would sit and join us; more often than not they continued on, their donkey's little hooves never missing a beat.

On the penultimate day of my Egyptian sojourn, with only a hundred or so last-minute errands to run, I ventured into the Khan el-Khalili market, once the largest caravanserai of the Islamic world and now Cairo's largest tourist mecca, (second only to the pyramids at Giza). I had neither the time nor the inclination to comparison shop or negotiate for my "best price." Nevertheless, thirty minutes later, after a considerable amount of haggling, I left the Medieval-era district with three *sheeshas* (one to use and two for parts), and a goodly supply of tobacco which, when wrapped up and placed side by side in my suitcase, looked suspiciously like bricks of hashish.

My *sheeshas* are still with me in spirit although only one survives, a hopeful monster, an amalgam of my original three. My furniture is irrevocably permeated with the smell of Egyptian tobacco. I unabashedly enlist anyone I know traveling to Egypt to bring me back tobacco, which is, unfortunately, the weak link in this narrative. Shops here in Canada that do carry *sheesha* tobacco tend to sell the fruitier blends (apple, banana, and strawberry, mint and, horror of horrors, cappuccino and licorice), tantamount to offering Juan Valdez a cup of butter pecan coffee. I am a purist: it is *maasel*—tobacco sweetened with molasses—or nothing. I sourced out Egyptian merchants in Montreal who will occasionally sell me a few packages of the unadulterated stuff clandestinely in their back-rooms, and every once in a while I am able to track down a rogue shipment to a local Lebanese food store. It is all so sordid, yet so worth the effort.

I fear that my sources will eventually go up in smoke—I know that I must return to Egypt with a couple of empty suitcases for the mother-of-all tobacco runs. If successful, I could follow the trend of larger cities and open up a *sheesha* bar—but how would this jibe, I wonder, with our smoke-free sensibilities? Perhaps I would qualify for some level of government funding as long as I didn't use tobacco in my advertising. I'll have to look into that a bit deeper. In the meantime, a new Egyptian restaurant has opened in town. I should pay a visit to the owner.

≈ ≈ ≈

Holding a questionably practical graduate degree in Egyptology, Carolyn Thériault has worked and traveled throughout North Africa, Europe, and her native Canada in an effort to avoid debt and responsibility. She currently resides in Morocco, whose sheeshas, *she is sad to report, pale in comparison to their Egyptian counterparts. Her work has been published in both literary and academic journals, most recently in* Gastronomica, Glimpse Quarterly, Transitions Abroad, The Suitcase Generation, *and* The Square Table *magazines and is a co-founder of Urban Caravan Photography, a website that features her travel photography.*

ANTONIO GRACEFFO

❧ ❧ ❧

Kick Boxing for Pride
and Peanuts

Muay Thai fighters duke it out
in the "sticks" of Thailand.

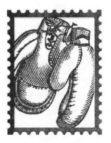

WHEN I WAS A YOUNG BOXER IN THE UNITED
States, the most I ever made for a fight was
$150. And I only got that much because the promoter
let the fighters have half the money from the tickets
we sold. I have a big family and they all bought tickets.
For that paltry sum, I had trained and sparred countless rounds, and fought literally hundreds of challenge
matches for free.

When the big night came, I climbed into a ring, faced
a man I did not know and had nothing against, and we
pounded each other for three long rounds. The recov-
ery time necessary after a fight like that is two to three

weeks. That gives a small-time boxer an income of about $300 a month. (In Thailand I would later discover that there are Muay Thai boxers earning $12 a month.)

My story is rare for a fighter, because eventually, I got an education, and began to make a life for myself as a writer. Most of my training partners from those days were not so lucky. Many wound up physically wrecked, hooked on drugs or alcohol, or in prison. At the very least, they drifted away, into obscurity. In retrospect, it was easy for me to feel sorry for myself and the scores of poor boys who, like me, saw boxing as a way out of poverty.

But on a chilly night, in the small, northern Thai city of Chiang Rai, I got my first glimpse of what it meant to be a minor-league professional Thai boxer, coming up the hard way, and dreaming of a payoff that would likely never come.

While foreign boxers are commonplace in Chiang Mai and Bangkok, they are rarely seen in rural Thailand. I was the first foreigner to train in this jungle camp, sixty kilometers north of Chiang Rai. At first glimpse the hill tribe boys here were not much different from the poor kids back home in the United States. They were uneducated and from broken homes. Many of them had brushed up against drug addiction and the law. No one expected them to get any further than their parents, and their parents hadn't gotten very far at all. Fighting was their only chance of amounting to anything.

My first impression was that they could have been fighters anywhere in the world. But as I learned more, I saw that these disenfranchised youths of the Thai-Burma border faced even more problems. Most of them were officially stateless persons. Having been born in remote villages where illiteracy is the norm, their births had never been recorded, meaning they were never entered into the Thai system. They had no passport and no identity card. It would most likely be impossible for them to get papers, so they could never take a traditional route out of poverty by becoming policemen or soldiers, or holding a legitimate job. And even if they possessed the relevant skills, the doors of the state universities were closed to them.

The only bright note was that the boys' world was so small that they didn't understand they were stateless. They had never needed identity cards, so didn't feel the loss when it was denied them.

The loss they did feel, however, was the absence of family. The boys living in these types of camps are loosely referred to as orphans. But in the strictest sense of the word, they aren't orphans at all. Often one or both of their parents are still alive. They are simply unwanted and parents will often deposit discarded sons at the nearest temple or Thai boxing camp.

So aside from the fact that Thai boxing training is infinitely more painful than coaching for Western boxing, by the time these boys even got in the ring they had endured more than their share of hard knocks.

My team was to fight on two consecutive nights, as the main entertainment at a rural fair. On the first night, the promoter noticed me, the only Western face in the crowd, and asked me if I would come back and fight a match the next day. I quickly agreed. He made me strip off my shirt in the cold night air and shadow box in the ring while the crowd cheered. For many of them, mostly farmers from remote villages, it was probably the first time they had seen a foreigner at all, much less seen one box. I was immediately given the fight name "Toni Farang."

On fight night, I watched my friend and training brother, Payong, decimate his opponent. At twenty-one, Payong was the oldest fighter in the camp. He'd been abandoned by his mother when she remarried but he was the kind of guy who was always laughing. No matter how low my mood, Payong could cheer me up with his antics. But when the bell rang, there was no trace of the comical, good-natured guy who shared a bamboo hut with me. Instead, the once peaceful Payong had been replaced by the most vicious fighter I had ever seen. I have fought in hundreds of matches around the world, yet I'd never witnessed the crude violence that Payong unleashed on his opponent. The fight was stopped in the middle of the second round, when both the referee and the corner felt that Payong's opponent had endured enough.

I couldn't help wondering if the anger he displayed in the ring was the result of his abandonment. Was there some deep specter of pent-up aggression lurking inside him?

Meanwhile, I was quite a spectacle. People were coming up to me, grabbing my calf muscles and feeling my biceps, discussing which way they were betting in the Toni Farang fight. Small-time fighting is always pretty disorganized. People crowded in on me, making it impossible to breathe. By the time I realized that my name was being called, my opponent was already in the ring waiting. No time for a warm up or a rub down. I just began stripping off my clothes as the crowd pushed and dragged me to my corner.

Luckily, my trainer, Hote, an ex-Thai boxer, was

able to fight his way through the crowd, and stick some gloves on my hands, or else I would have had to fight bare-fisted.

The ring announcer was shouting for me to get in or get disqualified. Half the crowd was trying to push me up the steps, the other half was still feeling my muscles and trying to get me to pose for photos.

"No weigh-in?" I shouted to Hote over the din.

"Now boxing," he cried back, desperately trying to pull me into the ring.

"What about hand wraps?"

"No time," he said.

I had visions of nursing broken knuckles the following day. Even after I climbed into the ring, people were still holding on to my legs. Someone else was trying to force something like a huge bathtub underneath me. It nearly knocked me off my feet. After bruising my calves, they gave up and began dumping ice-cold water all over me. Apparently this is something they do in Thailand. But I was so cold to begin with, my muscles began cramping. And the ring was now wet and slippery.

A bell rang. I wasn't sure if it meant come out fighting or come out and get the instructions. The referee was shouting at me in Thai. The crowd was shouting. There were instructions coming over the loudspeakers. I looked to Hote, asking what to do, but he just shrugged.

"Thanks, man," I said. A good corner man can make or break the fight for you. And in small-time fighting you get small-time corner men.

I tried to take a step, but people had climbed up on the ring apron, and were still holding on to my ankles. I ripped my legs free and walked, warily, to the center. This was the first time I saw my opponent. He was the biggest Thai I had seen. At that moment, he seemed like the biggest man I had ever seen. He was at least a head taller than me, and easily twenty kilograms heavier.

One thing about small-time fighting is that the fighters have been through so much, you don't usually get an attractive opponent. This guy was no exception. He had a forehead so big that it blocked the sun. He looked like he had just stepped out of Darwin's walk of man, somewhere between Cro-Magnon and Neanderthal. He wasn't just ugly, he was circus ugly. Small-timers fight constantly to make a semblance of a living and he had open cuts all over his face when he walked in.

I was intimidated by his battered appearance, until I remembered a scene from the movie *The Magnificent Seven*, where they are looking to hire good gun fighters. They see a man with scars all over his face, and someone says. "We should hire him. He is very tough." Yul Brynner says, "No, we should hire the man who gave him those scars."

I breathed a sigh of relief. My opponent smiled, revealing a mouth devoid of teeth. A mouthpiece is optional in Thailand. I guess they are optional everywhere, if you have no teeth.

The fight went really well for me. I whirled and kicked and punched and hit my opponent about 300 times. He hit me about 6 times. But the real battle was always in the corner, where people kept grabbing me and yelling at me. Whenever the bell rang to go out and fight I felt relieved. It was all so confusing. At the end, I didn't know who had won. I just knew that my opponent left, and they asked me to stay in the ring and take pictures with my arms over my head.

Later, lying in our hut, Payong and I talked about our fights, too excited to sleep. "You were great," I told him, pantomiming all of his excellent kicks and knees.

"Toni was great," he said, and swung his fists like a mad man.

We joked about my opponent's lack of teeth and had a good laugh imitating how Payong's opponent was knocked down twenty-five times.

"Payong is happy," he told me. "Mother and father happy." Payong's parents had shown up at the fights. I had heard that many of the parents did this, coming around to take most of the winnings from their son. In this case, Payong had won 300 baht (less than $2).

"Mother-father say Payong can go home now," he told me with boyish delight.

My stomach turned. They kicked him out when they had no use for him. But now that he looked like a moneymaker they wanted him back. I lacked the Thai vocabulary to tell Payong what I was thinking, and wondered if it was right to interfere in the first place.

Suddenly, his face turned sullen. "Is Payong good?" he asked, sounding like a hurt little boy.

"Of course Payong is good," I said. "Payong was fighting like this," I said, kicking and punching frantically.

He became very quiet, and again asked in a timid voice, "Is Payong good?"

It hit me what he was asking. He wasn't asking about the fight. Ultimately, he seemed to be asking me, "Is Payong a good enough person that he deserves better than to be abandoned by his family?"

I cursed my minimal language skills. Hoping my tone would convey what my words could not, I said. "Yes, Payong is good."

He looked at me for a moment, as if deciding whether or not I was telling him the truth. Then a smile spread across his face and he burst out in his usual laughter. "Payong is good," he chuckled. "Payong is good."

≈ ≈ ≈

Antonio Graceffo is the author of The Monk from Brooklyn; Bikes, Boats, and Boxing Gloves; The Desert of Death on Three Wheels; *and* Adventures in Formosa. *Keep track of him at speakingadventure.com.*

~≈ ~≈ ~≈

Rilke Was Miserable Here

The muse, she is a bitch.

"IN THIS HOTEL," THE PLAQUE READS, "MODIGLIANI lived and worked. Here the Spanish painter Picasso created his masterpieces, painters Pisarro and Degas derived inspiration. The famous Kikki of Montparnasse held court and modeled for the famous artists of her day. Man Ray and Henry Miller came from afar and did their best artistic work here in these very rooms. And the poet Rainer Maria Rilke was miserable here and wrote *The Notebooks of Malte Laurids Brigge* while, poverty stricken, he worked as a secretary to the greatest sculptor of his time, Auguste Rodin."

The Hotel Istria, located on the Rue Campagne-Premiere, stands, a modest brown facade, sandwiched next to an extravagant art deco glass-fronted pile of ateliers, lavish studios through the windows of which can be seen mountains of bookshelves, complete with books and ladders with which to reach their orderly largesse, and, through other glass, the twisted reverse curves of chrome and white furniture. Although one has waited in front of the massive door to these ateliers, one has never seen a human enter or leave. Instead, large groups of earnest French architecture students or sometimes elderly French tourists, can be seen, gathering in expectant knots, notebooks in hand, a smartly dressed guide at their head, discussing the architectural ramifications of this almost transparent building.

But in front of the abutting Hotel Istria, nothing happens. No one waits, notebook in hand. No one lectures to a throng. The misery has taken place inside, not out on the street for everyone to see. Poets, painters, photographers squirreled away like rats record their misery in private. The rooms, one surmises, are as small and brown as in any two-star hotel room anywhere.

Wind sweeps down the cold street of the first Campagne, so named because of some connection with Napoleon and with the countryside, that fictional presence maintained so faithfully by Parisians. It is just as cold here as on all the other streets of Paris, for it is December, and although proud France has better public relations than any other country, it seems to nevertheless suffer the exact same dreary climate as does London, a glum city with a poorer self image.

The presence of so many great artists of the past, streaming from all corners of the earth into Paris, the continuation even now of that tradition, brightens the soul. The artists who put Montparnasse on the map when they moved away from what they considered too-high-priced Montmartre into shabbier digs still breathe along this now-modest street. There is the Camelo, a neighborhood cafe, the Post cafe, opposite the post office, a dry cleaning establishment now almost supplanted by a self-service laundromat, a lovely restaurant Natacha, and one before which one hesitates to enter, named La Mere Agitee. The Agitated Mother, indeed.

There is a deserted school at one end and two small stores run by Arabs of indeterminate origin, all stocking the same tired carrots and potatoes, often frequented by the street's inhabitants too exhausted or too lazy to make a big production out of shopping.

Hidden away from the street, behind the shutters and heavy doorways and closed gates, down twisted alleys and little secret ways next to the garbage cans, are the remnants of old studios, now cut and subdivided and divided again, so that, for the price of a whole house in the United States, one has the privilege of squeezing into an upright coffin, the ceiling three times as high as the allotted floor space. Maybe, if you are lucky, a small window, a hot plate, a toilet down the hall, a communal shower. Only foreigners, writers, or international students sent to the city to learn French, or foolhardy types engaged in playing "artist" would tolerate this set-up; the French themselves are much too smart for this squeezed living: their inheritance and practicality have assured them this.

It is not hard to imagine, as one shrinks oneself, with a sense of stepping into a much loved image of living in Paris, that many artists worked here, fell in and out of love, struggled with loneliness and drink and self doubt and in the case of at least one, Modigliani, leaped to his death. Darkness, despair, depression, all take on a jubilantly grim overtone in Paris: Artists "were miserable here." We, too, are unhappy: hooray, we are part of a great tradition!

The nearby Closerie de Lilas, where so many artists and writing wannabe's gathered, is as beautiful as ever, garlanded with vines and flowers. The piano player still plays for tea and the evening cocktail hour, but the prices are now so high no artist could ever afford to enter: $6 equivalent for a cup of coffee, $10 for a glass of sour house wine. Lots of atmosphere and history and pretty chandeliers and gleaming wood. The soft red lampshades glow softly in the beautiful old interior. Earnest yuppies come here after work. It is said that publishing and movie moguls find their way, with the occasional Kikki look-alike clad in black: black fringe, black velvet ribbon around the neck, dark eyes sparkling and a tight black dress. Perhaps they too are miserable in another way, but the high-priced whine of computers humming all over town, barely perceptible to the ear, is sufficiently anesthetizing. The past recedes.

An appointment, even for lunch, is a subject for endless negotiation. Everyone is so busy in this yuppie yippee world. One must endure the repetition by the initially invited lunchee, of his or her schedule for the upcoming month. "Let's see...on Monday I have my analyst. On Tuesday I have a meeting. With someone very important." You try not to grovel as you court and outwait this impossibly busy, and, let's face it, impossibly self-important Parisian personage into finding a spot for you somewhere. "Wednesday. Perhaps Wednesday. No, no, that is quite impossible; on Wednesday I must see my mother. Maybe Thursday. No, not Thursday. I have an important deadline. Perhaps Friday. Well, can you call me later in the week?"

You are grinding your teeth with frustration. "Bien sur. Of course." You have no intention of telephoning again next week to inquire politely if perhaps, just possibly, your friend might not have already filled her calendar with other more pressing engagements. The little omelet you had in mind at the Raspail Vert, the small café at the other end of the street, seems unimportant after all.

Behind its blank face, rue Campagne-Premiere conceals its hidden alleyways and gardens. A tiny number, 8 bis, half concealed on a mildewed wall, indicates a driveway behind a large gate. It curves past the post office parking lot. And then, as one rounds the curve, flowers appear; a magnificent old tree, gnarled and flourishing, neatly rimmed with its own little wall.

And overlooking this, a sprawling stucco barracks of a building, divided and subdivided into a rabbit warren of studios, small dank apartments, and here and there, something a bit larger, shared by several foreign students. Always the clatter of shoes going up stairs, the entries smelling of damp and cat piss, and the few old ladies bravely dragging their shopping carts, their canes tapping "make way, make way." "*Bonjour Madame*," you will have learned to say, relatively impersonally. For by now you have rented the rabbit warren: Was there ever anything so cold and dark? You have put down a deposit, put down key money, both of which you will most probably never see again, signed a lease, paid three months in advance, and moved your few possessions in. Unfortunately, every French person trying to rent must undergo the same unreasonable process. That's why so many of the young adults still live at home, necking like mad in the subways and parks, desperate for a little privacy somewhere. Still, "you're paying much too much," the concierge tells you. You cross her palm with silver and hope she will not throw away your mail.

For you are, after all, an American, toward whom the French have an array of ambivalent behaviors. Well, honey, learn their language—but not too well. It is said that Modigliani lived in your entry. Picasso also. Naturally. If one were to believe the reports, these artists lived everywhere, blessing the numerous semi-habitable addresses with their fictitious presences.

In the five years that you have lived and worked and forever returned to Paris you have moved at least as many times. You have sublet tiny barely heated flats, only to have the owners return unexpectedly under emergency conditions. Illness in their families, maybe a death. Sometimes the apartment in which you have established a temporary existence is sold. Or the landlord needs it for his daughter. Everyone is terribly courteous and apologetic, yourself included. So you leave, starting the whole stomach-aching process of searching yet another damp and dark and overpriced studio room. "This is Paris," you tell yourself. You experience a permanent sense of dislocation. You move your two suitcases and boxes of books again. "Keep it light, keep it simple." You try to keep warm.

In the past five years you have moved through this great City of Light, hauling your boxes of possessions from one location to another. You have sublet on the Rue de Seine, your introduction to Paris. There in the heart of tourism you lived a dream of Paris, Paris of images, of movies. And you have also lived on the rue Charles Beaudelaire, around the corner from the magnificent Marche Alligre, overlooking a tiny gated park with a pergola and an organ grinder and a bakery right out of a rainy Paris fantasy with an oblong black sign, "Boulangerie," across the square. You could see it from your window. You lived next to a lingerie store with bold advertisements and models in the window that would make Frederick's of Hollywood look tame. You rented the flat on rue Charles Beaudelaire sight unseen, taking it for the name only. It is the one street on which, you later find out, Beaudelaire never lived, although during his short life he moved forty times, occupying forty different addresses on forty different streets.

Most bourgeois Parisians, you learn, never move at all. They stay on in the buildings into which they have been born, quarreling and not speaking to and having interminable Sunday dinners with their families of origin.

On rue Campagne-Premiere the cobblestones gleam at night in the rain and the corner rings with laughter and birdlike voices calling to each other as they part. You are an outsider here, living in a dream of a past so obviously not yours. The nights of Paris call to you and your chest resonates with an answering ache of longing. For what? For a past which has colored your imagination all your life, a past where art and literature are worth living and dying for, or for a present which treasures its cultural past? No matter that France neglects most of its actual living starving artists—we have read about that, heard it portrayed in opera and song; even that neglect has become "romantic" in the world's eyes. There are always the few artists and writers sanctioned by the Establishment and by the State, linked inextricably. But perhaps it is better to be neglected in France right now, which at least gives lip service to valuing artistic heritage, than in your own native land, which appears to despise it. France still spends fortunes on art exhibits and theater and subsidies for dance and music. Writers appear on television, reading their favorite classics aloud. Paris hosts a large Salon de Livres each year where publishers and booksellers and booklovers come together—all subsidized. When its artists die, France is proud of them. Streets, city squares, and plaques on individual buildings all remind of the proud artistic and historic heritage. The "Patrimonie."

Seen from the vantage point of this graceful culture, you cannot help but reflect on your own. And in the obvious ways, your country, young and bumptious, with its increasing lack of appreciation for both education and the arts, appears, in its public image, to be an artistic and cultural wasteland where violence alone is king. One has only to look at American movies—one winces at the quality that we export—television, at the values reflected inherent in our violent visual imagery, to understand the predominant big money values driving the nation, and the negativity with which we are seen. Yet, at the same time, in the U.S, for the arts that still manage to survive, there is an amazing vitality. France is a country of history, and manifests deep pride in what is seen as "pure French." That means traditional, mandarin, elevated. By contrast, you come to value the multicultural diversity of your own country, mainly grassroots, largely regionally sponsored, reflected in its art and in its literature, in its poetry readings and poetry slams and energetic dance performances and drama. There is a vitality to literary and artistic production in the United States today that is remarkable, raw though it may be. And, because we are a new country, there has been, since its inception, a sense of freshness; we are not yet worn out by our classics. We will have plenty of time to lie back on our divans: but first, we must create our body of great literature. This sense of possibility, these many multicultural voices speaking out from all over the United States, is something one misses abroad. Where smaller countries respect mostly their mandarin writers, in the U.S, each region is alive with voices reflecting our immigrant populations, voices which find their way to be heard, regardless of "budget cuts" and other details that try to impede their expression. While big publishers, and big money, tethered together in giant conglomerates, attempt to dominate the marketplace, beneath this monolithic domination are other ways of being heard. So our encouragement of variety and vitality is appealing, the other side of the impressive and exquisite French literary and artistic Pantheon. Europe and the United States stand like two poles, emblematic of the tension between tradition and the present tense. Always one reflects on what one has left. There is always a price for the choice.

Sometimes melancholy, the solitude in the midst of a crowd, burns like a sickness in your body. Forever an outsider, you keep exploring your foreignness as one explores an aching tooth. How strange, this hole in one's formerly complete existence, how dark with possibility, this ache.

Homesickness, a longing for family left behind, for friends, for one's own language and setting, for the familiarity of natural surroundings that comprise that complex concept "home," is the subtext of living elsewhere. So many writers and artists have flocked to Paris over the centuries; some are political exiles, but many come because they are cultural exiles in their own lands. How to explain this, the feeling of alienation at home, the feeling of recognition of self that one finds in France. The Muse, whoever she is, lives and breathes on these humid streets, circling you in a death grip, her cold breath rising. You want to sob out your heart; you don't know why or to whom. Instead you spill that fullness of emotion into your art, onto the canvas or the page. The Muse encircles you with promises: culture, literature, the fellowship of your own kind. You look at the many other exiled artists here, past and present, and they are your family now. Like them you are forever both participant and observer at the same moment. You have no choice but to accept and embrace that which has always been at the heart of your own existence: alienation, marginality, the soaring moments of pure epiphany, a yearning to create meaning out of difficult truths, the joy in doing so. Your life's endeavor.

❦ ❦ ❦

Kathleen Spivack is the author of many books, including The Break-Up Variations, The Beds We Lie In *(nominated for a Pulitzer Prize),* The Honeymoon, *and a novel,* Unspeakable Things. *A protégé of Robert Lowell, she has written and published extensively on Lowell and the group of poets around him: Sexton, Plath, and Bishop. In Boston, she directs the Advanced Writing Workshop, an intensive coaching program for advanced writers. She is a (one semester) Visiting Professor of Creative Writing/ American Literature at the University of Paris.*

❧ ❧ ❧

Bad Country

Always watch the waves.

I SCREAM AND THE BUS COMES TO A STOP. NO ONE flinches or is startled and the normalcy of everyone aboard is amazing. But it's not their fault. Two-thousand colones to the driver and a glance over my shoulder and I jump off. The bus leaves in a cloud of dust and exhaust. On the other side, fifty yards back, a mangled *motocicleta* is crushing a human being. The driver mumbles something. All I hear is indifference and he shuts the door.

No one follows. *Pero no tienen la culpa*. It's not their fault.

Running back up the road I can't help but question myself. It's in my blood. My mind. I should've stayed on the bus and pretended nothing happened. How can I enjoy the rodeo now? I probably won't even go. Shit. SHIT.

Hue puta.

Standing above the tangle of motorcycle and man I'm helpless. The darkness and moonlight come together and turn the blood deep purple. Or maybe I heard once somewhere that the purple blood is the heart's blood. The last pint you lose is not red, but purple. It's the royalty of blood. That's it. Whatever the case, it's everywhere—all over the bike. All over the man. Creating royal mud beneath both with the fine, dry dust.

Hijo de puta.

It's not indifference but fear that keeps me paralyzed. A few moments at least. Then I crouch butt to heels and reach for his hand. I hesitate. It's fear. Fear. Then his bloody hand is in mine. It's still warm. Some part of me wanted that hand to be cold, dead. But it's warm. Now my responsibility really comes to mind. *Do something.* I breathe.

It's dusk and I'm on the side of a dirt road between two towns thirty-seven kilometers apart with nothing in between. There's a dying or dead Tico [Costa Rican] at my feet. No one around, no headlights coming. My heartbeat steadies as I walk around to the other side of the *moto.* I pull the bike up by the handlebars and it's not as heavy as I anticipated. If it was a Harley or something akin, I would be helpless. But it's not. It's a ninja or crotch-rocket or whatever these whiny things are called. But the only thing that matters is the life at my feet. Or maybe the death.

I feel for a pulse and his skin is smooth like satin for the blood. Warm, royal skin. He has a pulse and at first that too frightens me. But then I'm calmed. There is no terror here. Just two organic lives, one of which is leaking a lot of blood. I revel for a moment in my newfound composure.

Be practical.

Be of use.

I notice he has no helmet. His jeans and legs are shredded to pieces. I look back up the road and follow his skid marks. They must go for twenty meters. But that doesn't matter. This is not a crime scene, this is a deathbed. Play doctor. Mom's a nurse—what would she do? I take the shirt off my back and make a tourniquet around his left leg because it seems to be bleeding the worst. And then there's the gash in the right side of his head. I can't make a fucking neck tourniquet.

Direct pressure. That's it. Stop the bleeding.

I take the sweatshirt out of my backpack and press it firmly to the royal gash in the side of his head. In a moment of vanity I realize it's my favorite sweatshirt. It's of a band. *The Weakerthans.* On the front is the silhouette of a fallen cowboy. You know it's a cowboy because the man has a full-brimmed hat, a lasso, and spurs on his boots. A fallen cowboy. The irony hits me hard. The tears well up and I begin to cry.

Some minutes later I am still applying pressure and I see headlights coming from the west. I come to my senses almost instantly. Hope! The tears stop. From the west, I think. That's a good thing—the closest hospital I know is east of here. I reach down for his royal pulse.

Nothing.

And the skin is cold.

It must be true what they say. The last pint of blood is not red. It's purple. And royal.

I stand and thumb the pickup truck now closing in. The driver sees me at the last moment and comes to a stop ten meters down the road. I pace up to the truck and hop in the back. There is a spare tire, a shovel, and a few empty bottles of oil. One patch of the bed is rusted all the way through and I can see the road below. The driver slides open the back window.

"*¿Que paso?*"

"*Accidente.*"

"*¿Se murio?*" Did he die?

I nod.

"*Asi es la vida,*" he says. Then he lowers his eyes and shakes his head.

I nod again and look away.

"Mario," he says.

"Joaquin," I reply, still gazing away. "Quincho."

He chuckles and shuts the window and begins to drive down the bumpy road. Joaquin is not my name but I use it for the difficulty the Ticos find in saying my real name. In Costa Rica most of the popular names have specific nicknames. For Jose its Chepe. For Joaquin it's Quincho. I prefer Quincho.

As we drive off and the rising cloud of dust and exhaust helps to erase the moment, I smile. Twenty-three thousand people die each day because they can't find a single thing to eat. Agony, I imagine. Your body consuming its own self. At least the *motociclista* fell in an instant. And he was unconscious or comatose, or whatever. Hopefully, he could think but feel no pain. That must be like a sliver of heaven. Maybe the only. I think about the moment. Not the moment that just passed, but the moment between the body's death and when the mind finally halts. I shiver.

It's bumpy and rackety in the bed of the truck, and noisy for the wind. The window slides open again and Mario holds out a beer, an Imperial. A part of me smiles. To royalty, I think, as I twist off the cap. *Here's to Royal*

Blood. I take a swig and lie out flat to look up at the sky. So many stars. The Milky Way sparkles like a lens to the larger picture. I sit up and take another swig as we hit a pothole and the beer spills down my naked chest. I lie back again, my head thumping with the road against the bed of the truck. I remember the rusted-out hole and inch the other way.

Imperfection, I think. Imperfection.

Two weeks later I'm chasing a northwest swell down the Guanacaste Peninsula. I caught super good waves for three days up at Roca Bruja. Stiff winds and courteous tides. And the camping was nice, mosquito-less for the winds. I'm hoping to catch the last of the swell down in Mal Pais, at the tip of the peninsula, and I'm lying down in the back of a pig truck, or chicken truck, or something. It's empty, with plenty of sunburned straw to cushion the bumps. The sides of the truck bed are rotten planks of wood that have been haphazardly tied to the four metal posts rising from each of the corners. The planks rattle and maybe loosen with each pothole, but they seem to do their job well enough. Still I feel sorry for the pigs or chickens or whoever. Or is it me? I hold the corner post a little more firmly. Safety, I think. And I laugh at my own stupidity.

The thought reminds me of the fallen cowboy. Both fallen cowboys actually, because I'm cold and that was my favorite sweatshirt, my only sweatshirt. I didn't think I would hear of either cowboy again, but I did—sitting in a little *soda* two mornings later in a town called Liberia. I picked up a *periodico* and found a small article on the fourth page. There was no picture, but the article said the man had considerable traces of alcohol in his blood, presumably on the way to the rodeo in Playa Brasilito. I remember reading the article with a bit of indifference. I remember thinking again that he was lucky to not have been one of the 23,000 who die of hunger. I shake off the memory. It doesn't matter anymore.

The truck is slowing down and I picked my head up to look over the side. We come to a stop and the driver, an old and weathered man, leans out of the window.

"*¿A la derecha?*"

"*No, sigo a Mal Pais.*"

I grab my board and backpack and hop out of the truck, catching a splinter in my palm on the way over. I slap him 500 colones and he returns a warm toothless grin.

"*Que le vaya bien.*"

"*Igualmente.*"

I smile and turn away from the dust, looking down at my palm. A small prick. I wipe the blood on my shorts and sigh. The sun still has some time in the sky but I realize I might be stuck. I'm on the road less traveled—the Coastal Road that stretches from Playa Carillo south, all the way to the tip of the peninsula. Really it stretches north all the way to Tamarindo but the stretch south from Playa Carillo is different. Only a handful of coastal towns and miles and miles of empty coastline. Emerson would be proud. Secret spots, I now know, are plentiful in this region. And reachable mostly by boat, or committed hike. But that doesn't matter right now.

I'm basically in the middle of nowhere. Traffic is rare. Bittersweet, I think. More sweet than bitter. I pick up my board and start walking south.

I remember the first time I traveled this stretch. My dad was driving, boards strapped to the racks, I was thumbing through my brand new *Webster's Spanish-English*—the one that's still with me now, five years wiser and more weathered.

"You know what *Mal Pais* means, Dad?"

He bit his lip for a moment, shook his head.

"Bad Country."

We looked at each other, exchanged grins.

Twenty minutes later we were lost as hell, my dad complaining about unforeseen forks in the road. Then, WHAM-PHHT, flat tire. It took us four and a half hours to make the forty mile stretch south from Carillo. But, credit to him, it usually takes about two. Somehow we ended up looping inland and circling back out near the ferry docks and through Montezuma.

A faint drone interrupts the memory. An engine maybe. An engine. Thumb goes out and I turn north. It comes in sight.

White Rav4. Rental, definitely a rental. I whistle and extend my arm farther. Boards on the racks—I'm stoked. Definitely heading to Mal Pais. A gringo with no passengers. A cold shoulder and dark glasses make for no eye contact. He blazes right on by, not even a brake light. All windows up, AC blasting. I look up at his boards hoping to gain something to commit to memory

Two longboards. Red rails on both. Prick thinks he's Curren. That's kinda funny. Red rails. *Verjas rojas.* Got it.

I walk on. The road starts to ascend and curve back out toward the ocean. Just before I reach the top I remember the bluff that awaits. You can see south all the way to the tip, and there's a tiny *pueblito* below with a two- or three-mile stretch of white beach and shifting sand bars. It's hard to judge the waves from so far above, but every time I see them they look decent. I always find something strange about the whole picture though. I think it's the town, though I've never been.

I reach the top and the enormity of the view takes me over once more. I grab a loose log and drag it to the edge of the bluff. The uninterrupted stretch of beach is still there. So are the endless beach breaks. I look below and to the north at the *pueblito*. I take a few moments and take it all in. The big always helps with the little.

The town still creeps me out. I reach behind me for my backpack. Two PB&J's and I lick the plastic knife clean. Zip up the bag. The Pacific is welcoming the sun and the clouds ahead are gaining orange. The ones behind, pink and purple.

I might as well find out about this little town once and for all. Besides, what's strange is usually what's foreign. And what's foreign, strange. I realize I can probably still sneak in a little session and that brings me to my feet. I head for the turnoff that runs out and down to the little town.

Another engine. A big engine. From the north. Still a chance.

It's a Dos Pinos truck, the *leche* and *helado* distributor. Milk and ice cream. I soften my expectations and throw out a thumb anyway. He's coming downhill—another negative for the hitchhiker. The driver meets my eye, smiles, and passes. There's someone sitting shotgun as well.

Brake lights. It takes him a while to stop and he waits at the bottom of the descent. I guess me and that odd *pueblito* will meet another day. I trot down the hill, shoeless. The passenger hangs his arm and head out the window, turns.

"Mal Pais?"

"Mal Pais."

He swings the door out, hops down, and leads me around to the back of the truck. As he unlatches the hinge locking the two back doors he pauses and turns to me.

"*Un poco frio*," he says. He speaks slowly, imagining cultural ignorance. His skin is dark with years of *sol* and his eyes are hidden by a pair of sporty Oakley rip-offs with bright yellow frames, the kind that are sold dime a dozen streetside in Tamarindo.

"*Esta bien con migo.*" Fine with me. I smile. He smiles. I recognize some species of understanding.

The doors swing open and steam bellows out into the warm evening air. Cold steam. Really cold steam. Cartons and cartons of *leche* fill both sides of the truck.

"*Hue puta frio*," I mumble.

He laughs. We laugh. And now I sense, more than understanding, a bit of respect. I climb in and he lifts my boardbag and backpack up to me. He starts to close the doors and I ask him to hold on for a second. It's fucking *frio*. I unzip the boardbag and slip out my board. I wedge the board between two rows of crates, hoping it's stable. Then I drag the boardbag toward the front end of the truck, opposite the doors, where there's a handle or something similar extending from the wall. I climb in the bag, zip myself inside. My last sight is of the man with the yellow *gafas de sol* shaking his head in laughter.

I yell, "*Listo*," ready, as the doors close.

"*Buena suerte,*" good luck, he replies.

It's not dark. It's black. The kind of blackness that scares little kids. Completely black. And completely cold. Freezing cold.

The truck starts to rumble along. Then it speeds up.
It speeds up some more. A little bit more. Hairpin turns
no problem. Finally it's driving the way trucks drive in
Latin America. *Loco.*

Another thing about this stretch of coastal road is its
remarkably rough condition, illuminated by the name-
sake destination of those heading south. Mal Pais. I
instantly find pleasure in the fact that my boardbag has
considerable padding. Padding that's intended to soften
the blows of those heartless airline bagger fucks, but
that's now comforting my aching bones in the freezer of
a speeding milk truck.

The bag is zipped all the way up, save for a small hole
at the top where my right forearm and wrist extend to
hold the handle on the wall. With a Tico at the wheel it's
not a hold but a life grip. Is that even a word? No. I decide it's more a feeling. Then I'm feeling cold, extreme
cold. What if this was the ice cream freezer? There's a
question. One I'm not sure I'm willing to answer being
cold as hell in the milk freezer.

Chills. More chills. Bone-to-skin, head-to-toe
CHILLS. I have to concentrate. Relax. Calm.

I take a few deep, methodical breaths and they seem
to warm my little board bag coffin just slightly. But they
warm it. Or at least I think so. So I take some more. I
concentrate on the breathing. Four in, six out. Four in,
six out.

But somewhere, somehow, the breathing remains my
focus. Four in, six out. Four in, six out. I find warmth,
let my mind wander to tomorrow's *olas*. A destination or
purpose or reason. Or all three in unison.

Squealing breaks and a violent swerve defy the
peace. Then more breaks. Slowing. We're there. That

was quick. Then the accelerator. Fake stop. Guinea pig duped.

The truck hums to a halt some time later and the slamming of doors insinuates freedom. And warmth. Hot, sticky, equatorial warmth. The very thing I would otherwise be trying my best to avoid.

I wonder, if only an instant, what it would be like to be forgotten back here in this milk truck. Another hour, maybe two, or overnight. There's chatter outside from a number of voices. Would they forget? *Imposible.* They couldn't. Who would forget a gringo in the freezer of a milk truck?

A Tico, that's who. Then the latch jingles.

"Buenos dias."

It could be morning, I think. The dim lights of the night are as bright as day. My senses come to and I find maybe a dozen Ticos hooting with laughter. Applauding. Or maybe they're mocking. Not sure. Don't care. For the moment I'm more concerned with my right hand. Blue. Numb. Shaking. No longer clutched to the handle but nevertheless fixed in life grip.

I hop to a crouch, dislodge my board from between the crates and slip it back inside its home. The amused Ticos lose interest and start away, leaving the man with the yellow glasses alone at the foot of the truck.

"¿Donde estamos?" I ask.

"Frank's Place."

Perfect. The place I want to stay is a two-mile hike back the way we came. Yellow Glasses helps me with my bags and I jump down. Two naked feet meet unfriendly rocks.

"Te invito. Una cerveza." I'll buy you a beer, he says.

"Tuanis." Nice.

The thought of a beer soothing my aching body sounds damn good, cold or not. We take a seat at the bar and he orders *dos* Imperials. My memory stirs and I turn to him, half in jest, half in sincerity.

"Hey *carrepicha,* what happened back there halfway through—you guys trying to kill me or what? I got tossed around like a *hue puta* ragdoll!"

He laughs and throws down 800 colones with a nod to the bartender, Frank.

"Some gringo fool swung his truck into the ditch."

"Yeah?"

"Looked like two flats. Mabe a snapped axle."

"White car, boards on top?"

He nods, a bit beguiled.

I shift to Spanish, eager for assurance.

"¿Verjas rojas?"

"Verjas rojas."

I smile and we tap beers.

"Salud."

⊰ ⊰ ⊰

J. Spencer Klein is a surfer and a traveler at heart who is currently posted on the north shore of Oahu.

꙳ ꙳ ꙳

Argentina on Two Steaks a Day

You'll need all your teeth for this place.

THE CLASSIC BEGINNER'S MISTAKE IN ARGENTINA IS to neglect the first steak of the day. You will be tempted to just peck at it or even skip it altogether, rationalizing that you need to save yourself for the much larger steak later that night. But this is a false economy, like refusing to drink water in the early parts of a marathon. That first steak has to get you through the afternoon and half the night, until the restaurants begin to open at ten; the first steak is what primes your system to digest large quantities of animal protein, and it's the first steak that buffers the sudden sugar rush of your afternoon ice cream cone. The midnight second steak might be the more glamorous one, standing as it does a good three inches off the plate, but all it has to do is get you up and out of the restaurant and into bed (for the love of God, don't forget to drink water).

The afternoon steak is the workhorse steak, the backbone of the day. It's the steak that gets you around the city, ensures a successful nap, steers you into the bar and (most importantly) gives you the mental clarity to choose the right cut of meat in the restaurant that night. Misorder the first steak and you will either find yourself losing steam by eight o'clock, when no restaurant is open, or scampering to find an awkward third bridge steak, to tide you over until dinner.

All you need to know about the quality of pasture in the pampas is that cows went feral in Argentina. You can still see them grazing pretty much anywhere there is a horizontal patch of grass, all now firmly back in the hand of man, but still with a happy grassy glint in their eye. This most docile, placid, and passive of large herbivores stepped off the boat, took one nibble at the pampas, and made a run for it. It knew that it wanted to spend the rest of its life eating the pampas grass, without outside interference. And the settlers, once they caught some of the early escapees, began to feel the same way about the beef.

Eating steaks in Argentina feels like joining a cult. You find yourself leaning on friends to come visit, and writing "YOU JUST DON'T UNDERSTAND" in all caps more often than feels comfortable. Argentine beef really is extraordinary. Almost all of this has to do with how the cows are raised. There are no factory feedlots in Argentina; the animals still eat pampas grass their whole lives, in open pasture, and not the chicken droppings and feathers mixed with corn that pass for animal feed in the United States. Since this is the way of life a cow was designed for, it is not necessary to pump the animal full of antibiotics. The meat is leaner, healthier and more flavorful than that of corn-fed cattle. It has fewer calories, contains less cholesterol, and tastes less mushy and waterlogged than American meat. And the cows spend their lives out grazing in the field, not locked into some small pen. You can taste the joy.

When the meat is cooked, it is roasted in thick pieces over open coals by obsessive meat chefs who have been cooking meat all their lives, for other people who have been eating meat all their lives, in a country that takes its meat extremely seriously. You are not likely to be disappointed.

Steaks here are ridiculous—not so much in diameter, since they rarely overhang the plate by more than an inch or two—but in thickness, having roughly the proportions of an American canned ham. But what the Argentines have really mastered is flavor. Strange cuts of meat that would be ground into flavorless paste up north come to your table here infused with a delicious texture and flavor, provided they are cooked right. And they are invariably cooked right. The waiters are solicitous about asking (in English) how you want your meat done, but if you let them make the call, you get a two-inch-thick slab of meat that transitions seamlessly from carbon to bright pink and back.

As you would expect, there is a forbidding amount of terminology around beef-eating—*bife de chorizo, asado de bife, churrascos, lomo, vaco, bife de costilla, ojo de bife,* various more exotic portions of the animal. However the basic principles are simple. Meat is prepared in two ways, either on a *parrilla* (charcoal grill) or an *asador* (a system of iron crucifixes circling an open fire). The crucifix shape is suggestive and amusing. An excellent essay on Argentine history by Martín Caparrós may give a clue to its origin:

> Juan Díaz de Solís, a Sevillian and a gentleman, arrived in the Freshwater Sea in February of 1516, when none of this existed yet. He voyaged in three ships, as is fitting, and when some shameless natives made him a signal of welcome, he readily leaped onto the shore with his cross and his sword, only to land without further ceremony on the coals of a banquet: he was to be the main course. His companions, who watched him slowly tranformed into a dish from the boat, then told the world of those who bury their dead that Argentine history had begun as an *asado* of their captain, skin and all.

Surely Solís was wearing one of those crucifixes that shows Jesus actually hanging from the cross. It must have been a simple mistake on the part of the natives, who saw him as a friendly gift from the visitors on the boat, complete with a serving suggestion suspended around his neck. In any case, you will now see crucified lambs and calves in the front window of many a larger *parrilla*, roasting for hours in front of unfazed diners.

At dinnertime, meat is served in a state of nature, which means you don't get any default potatoes, salads, or side dishes—not even a sprig of parsley. The Argentine steak stands alone, towering over the plate. Daytime steaks may be more coy. While the parsley sprig as garnish is unknown in Argentina, you will sometimes encounter a fried egg, an olive, or a strip of pickled red pepper, sometimes even a combination of all three: This gorgeous specimen is called a *lomito*; it's a standard lunchtime steak, clearly so thin that the Argentines are embarrassed to send it out into the world without a protective wrapping of ham and cheese. An American who didn't know better might greet the *lomito* as an old dinnertime friend—the choice sirloin—but it bears about as much resemblance to a full Argentine steak as a rubber duck does to a battleship.

Steaks come with a condiment called *chimichurri*, which is intermediate on the condiment spectrum between salsa and Worcestershire sauce, and can appear in any viscosity from liquid to little diced cubes. *Chimichurri* is made from garlic, hot peppers, oregano, parsley, and vinegar, in varying proportions. Some of the best I've had resembles pesto, with barely any hot pepper and thick bergs of garlic; other *chimichurri* is much spicier and red in color. It is there to help you—something about the sauce helps the steak go down without fuss—and you should let it do its job. The same goes for Argentine wine; it is excellent and designed to get you safely through the large portions of beef.

There is a darker side, too, to Argentine condiments, and it is called *salsa golf*, the unholy alliance of ketchup and mayonnaise. This will sneak up on you when you least expect it, including in eight-star restaurants and the most delicate of seafood dishes. Any trip to an Argentine supermarket should give you fair warning: you can find yogurt, for example, in little containers ranging up to about 200 milliliters in size, but mayonnaise is sold in foil bags (bags!) of up to two liters in size. These are great fun to drop off your balcony.

The Argentine meat obsession is intense but completely democratic. Steak is a staple food here, and you
don't have to contend with Peter Lugar-style snob-
bishness. You are dealing with a food of the people.
Argentina is number one in world beef consumption,
weighing in at 65 kilograms (about twelve steaks) per
person per year, half again as much as Americans eat.
There are amusing reminders of this everywhere. The
one-touch settings on the microwave oven in my kitchen
are marked:

Ham
Chopped meat
Chicken (whole)
Pork
Beef (rare)
Beef (medium)
Beef (well done)

As you might expect, vegetarians will have a somewhat rough time here. For most people in Argentina,
a vegetarian is something you eat. One's diet will ac-
cordingly lean heavily on pastas, gnocchi, salads, and
(for the less squeamish) fish. Vegans will not survive in
Argentina. However, even egg-, milk-, and cheese-lov-
ing vegetarians should be careful not to get cocky. Two
vegetarians have visited me here during my stay, and
from both I had to listen to many glowing words about
the quality of Argentine fries, unable due to my impec-
cable upbringing to ask what they thought it was that
made the fries taste so wonderful, or why they looked
so deliciously yellow. On even the most innocent box of
crackers, in the slot where you would normally expect

to find "partially hydrogenated vegetable oil," it reads simply "beef tallow." The homemade cookies bought in the minimarket downstairs taste of steak.

It should be no surprise that the land of beef also has excellent milk and butter. The milk comes in plastic bags that would give any American marketing department a heart attack. They proudly advertise "GUARANTEED 100% BRUCELLOSIS AND HOOF-AND-MOUTH FREE." One brand even brags that its bacteria count *never* exceeds 100,000 per milliliter, and prints daily statistics to prove it (only 82,000 bacteria/milliliter on Monday! *Mmm*!). Meanwhile, the butter here either has a different name than in the rest of Latin America ("*manteca*" usually means "lard"), or else Argentine lard is the best I have ever tasted.

You might think that fruits and vegetables would get short shrift in this animal paradise, but they are actually delicious. Tomatoes, for example, have odor, flavor, and are colored red, an intriguing novelty. You can get excellent salads in any restaurant, although just like with the steaks, you get only what you ask for. Celery salad is a bowl of celery, with nothing else; carrot salad is a bowl of shredded carrots. You need to be explicit, and you need to be firm in rejecting Mazola in favor of olive oil as a dressing. Most places offer it, but some waiters have the superstitious Argentine fear of seasoning and will try to dissuade you.

There is a strange duality to dining in Argentina. By every measure the food is wonderful, yet foreigners who have been here for a while will get a strange, glazed look when you try to rave to them about the cuisine. After you've spent some time here, you realize this is because the entire country operates off of a single master menu:

ARGENTINA MASTER MENU

APPETIZERS
Empanadas

MAIN COURSE
Grilled Meat
Milanesas [Schnitzel]
Salmon or Trout
Pasta
Gnocchi
Pizza

SIDE ORDERS
Salad
Fried Potatoes
Boiled Potatoes
Scalloped Potatoes
Mashed Potatoes
Golden Potatoes
Sliced Potatoes
Grilled Potatoes

DESSERT
Flan
Fruit salad
Ice cream
Don Pedro (ice cream and nuts in a bowl of Old
Smuggler)

This menu is delicious, but with rare exceptions it is all you are going to get. People coming for more than a few weeks are advised to bring a discreet bottle of Tabasco sauce.

With any order from the master menu comes the Bread Basket, which should be treated as you would treat a basket of wax fruit, that is, as a purely decorative ornament. It is considered bad form to actually eat anything from the Bread Basket, as this will force the restaurant staff to send someone down into the cellar for a replacement roll before placing it on the next table.

In fact, you won't find good bread anywhere in Argentina. You can buy day-old baguette segments in a plastic sack, or else purchase the large sheets of white American-style bread used to make their triangular canapes (sandwiches *de miga*). The latter are actually punched out of the bread sheets like cookies from rolled dough—I would not be surprised to see *miga* bread being sold on a giant roller, paper-towel style.

Other dangers lurk in the Argentine pantry. Worst and most puzzling in a country settled by Italians is the horrible ground coffee. Most cafés and restaurants serve good espresso, but you are in the wilderness as soon as you try to find something you can brew at home. The idea of purchasing beans to grind seems to be a great novelty—it took several days of hunting to find both a grinder and something to put in it. Grocery store coffee is inevitably sold pre-ground and roasted with sugar, giving it a dark color and the taste and aroma of burnt socks.

It's possible that coffee, like Argentine yogurt, is just meant as a delivery mechanism for sugar. The sugar cubes here are the size of Lego bricks, and when you order an espresso you are given three packets of sugar the size of a small wallet. Every pharmacy has an aisle devoted to artificial sweeteners, for those who must do without, and there is a general inability to imagine a dessert that does not make your teeth hurt. Items are preventatively glazed with sugar whenever there is be the slightest doubt as to whether they are supposed to be sweet or savory; this is what prevents the otherwise excellent Argentine croissants (*medialunas*) from being the king of breakfasts.

There is a more serious kind of confectionary panic that goes beyond glazing, and it brings us to the true dark side of Argentine cooking. I am talking about *dulce de leche*.

Dulce de leche is a culinary cry for help. It says "save us, we are baffled and alone in the kitchen, we don't know what to do for dessert and we're going to boil condensed milk and sugar together until help arrives." This cloying dessert tar is so impossibly sweet that you wish you were ten years old again, just so you could actually enjoy it. It is everywhere. There is a special *dulce de leche* shelf in the supermarket dairy case, and the containers go up to a liter in size. Even the *churros* are stuffed with it—the *churros, montresor!* For anyone who has had pastries in Europe, the added horror is that *dulce de leche* is identical in color, texture, and consistency to a number of much less sweet, tasty fillings, like the earthy chestnut material the French call *crème de marrons*, or the tart kind of plum butter popular in Eastern European bakeries. You see a thick layer of dark brown jam-like material and think, this couldn't possibly be caramel, there's just too much of it. And so worldliness leads you to great giant bites and then disaster.

Thank God, therefore, for the ice cream. When the Italians came here at the start of the century, they took one swig of the fine pampas milk and knew what they had to do. The ice cream in Buenos Aires is easily the best I have ever eaten, and the parlors that serve it are everywhere. The secret seems to be an insistence on making it from scratch in each *heladeria*, since the only remotely similar ice cream I've tasted was the kind our chemistry department in college used to make from liquid nitrogen in its annual bid to attract new majors. Liquid nitrogen ice cream (recipe: heavy cream, walnuts, liquid nitrogen, sugar. Stir.) is delicious because the ice crystals it forms are so very small; this also makes the ice cream melt very fast. The same is true for Argentine ice cream; there is no guar gum to contend with, when you get a cone you have to work fast.

I spent a considerable amount of time trying to figure out how meals work in Argentina, and they remain a mystery to me. Dinner is clear enough: people tend to go to restaurants beginning at ten o'clock (for those with small children), with the main rush around eleven, and dinner is pretty much over at one or so in the morning. And breakfast—or rather, its absence—follows as a logical consequence of eating a steak the size of a beagle at midnight. But I have yet to figure out whether people eat some kind of meal in the afternoon, and if so, when. Wander into any bistro or restaurant between eleven and six and you will be served a delicious lunch-sized meal, but you are likely to be the only person there, with the waiter mopping floors in the corner and the *parrilla* stacked with raw meat for the midnight dinner rush.

I've come to think the culprit in the missing Argentine lunch scene is *yerba mate*.

What Tim Horton's is to Canada, *mate* is to Argentina —a national obsession whose appeal is inexplicable to

outsiders. Where the ignorant foreigner may see just another kind of herbal tea (*yerba mate* is a very unassuming
shrub that grows in the northern parts of the country),
the Argentine sees a taste treat of unimaginable subtlety,
and a tonic for all his problems. The Wikipedia article
on proper *mate* preparation should give you a warning of
the level of obsessiveness attainable here (the Urugayans
are even worse). To the virgin palate, *mate* tastes like
green tea mixed with grass clippings. The beverage is
traditionally drunk out of a little gourd, through a metal
straw called a *bombilla*, with hot (but not boiling!) water
poured into it (without wetting the surface! clockwise!)
from a thermos. What distinguishes *mate* from coffee
and tea is the social context—two or more people share
a gourd, with a designated pourer in charge of refilling it
with hot water after each turn. The ritual is low fuss but
indispensible. You can buy *mate* gourds and thermoses
in any grocery store, and get your thermos filled with
hot water at any convenience store or gas station, but
you will never see *mate* served in restaurants or sold in
little disposable paper gourds, to go. It's not that people
refuse to drink *mate* alone—anyone working a solitary
shift will have a gourd in hand—but that the concept
of being served *mate* by someone who does not share it
with you seems impossible.

Mate aficionados will tell you that *mate* contains a
special compound, mateine, that serves as a tonic and
mild stimulant, promoting alertness without making it
hard to sleep, reducing fatigue and appetite, helping the
digestion and serving as a mild diuretic. Scientists will
tell you that mateine bears a suspicious resemblance to
a chemical called caffeine. *Mate* aficionados will then
grow indignant, explaining that mateine is really a

stereoisomer (mirror image) of caffeine, with different effects, which will in turn irritate the scientists, who will snap that caffeine doesn't have a chiral center, so it can't have a distinguishable mirror image, and why don't the *mate* aficionados just put a sock in it.

Since I am writing this from Argentina, I will just diplomatically state that *mate* includes a constellation of chemicals, whose presence may affect the way the body absorbs caff...er, mateine, giving it a unique physiological effect.

The national love affair with *mate* doesn't just affect lunch. It has the dire effect of making Argentines less than enthusiastic about booze. The wine here is very good (something has to stand up to that steak), but Argentina has no liquor to call its own, relying on whiskies like Old Smuggler and the low-maintenance Don Juan cognac to carry the flag.

Beer is ubiquitous and comes in a bewildering variety of sizes, although there is a skittishness about the full-on liter. Things level off at 970 milliliters. In my case, it means I end up drinking 1940 milliliters of beer as a kind of personal protest, and all is well with the world. To make up for the abundance of sizes, beer comes in only one variety, Quilmes, which inevitably comes served with a tripartite platter of snacks—nuts, salty cylinders, and aged potato chips. On rare occasions, you may even get a four-leaf platter (olives), this is considered lucky.

Once you have had your afternoon *chopp* and its accompanying beer snacks, there is nothing better in the world than switching on the television to watch one of the many cooking shows that seem to be so popular here. You can take your pick from superhip (filmed at an angle, chef has sleeveless t-shirt) to extremely low-pressure shows for frazzled moms (today's dessert: whipped cream!), but they all pale in the face of the program called *Dulces Tentaciones*, starring the Swiss radical nun Sister Bernarda. This fantasy grandmother shows you how to make tarts, tortes, and other Old World desserts, carefully cleaning her work area in between recipes while classical guitar or flute plays in the background. It is the most relaxing television program ever created, better than any drug, better than any steak.

⊰ ⊰ ⊰

Maciej Ceglowski is an oil painter and computer programmer now living and working in Beijing. Born in Warsaw, Poland in 1975, he grew up in the north Chicago suburbs. He graduated from Middlebury College in Vermont in 1997 with a degree in Russian and studio art, and since that time has alternated between working as a full-time artist and part-time software developer. He writes a travel-related weblog at www.idlewords.com.

TANYA SHAFFER

≈ ≈ ≈

The Girl Who Drank Petrol

Just where is home anyway?

W*HEN I THINK OF HANNAH, I ALWAYS SEE HER
in the same spot. She's near downtown Accra,
striding along a red dirt path above the beach. Flecks of
ash dance in the air. Beside the path a woman sits on a low
stump, roasting plantains on an iron grill, while far below the
raggedy silver ocean laps at the pale sand. Hannah walks fast,
feet turned out, cheeks pink with exertion, curly golden hair
bouncing, chest and chin up, bright green eyes fixed straight
ahead. She is purposeful and oblivious, at home in her city,
her Ghana, her world.*

The first time I saw the Dutch volunteer called Hannah,
she was sitting on the sun-bleached wooden steps of the
volunteer hostel at high noon, surrounded by African men.
I'd arrived in Ghana from Ivory Coast the night before

and was making my first tentative sojourn into the achingly bright day. The assembled men shouted boisterously, cheerfully one-upping each other, vying for Hannah's attention. She reclined against the top step, all pink cheeks and yellow curls, flirting and sassing like some kind of postmodern Scarlett O'Hara. I was just about to scoot past her onto the footpath into town, when she turned to me abruptly and said, "Did you know I almost died?"

"Really?" I asked uncertainly.

"Yes!" she said brightly. "Only two weeks ago! I had malaria, but it was the kind where you are not aware that you have it, and you become more and more...how do you say...like a slow and creeping worm? You walk like this," she stuck out her arms like a zombie, "and laugh all the time like this," she demonstrated a vague, high-pitched giggle, "and you have no desire to eat anything. I ate no food for five days. Then when I went to the hospital, the doctor said if I had waited one day longer I would have died." Her accent was soft and rounded, difficult to place.

"Our sistah was looking sooooo skinny!" one of the African men chimed in. "We make her chop *fufu* six times a day now, so she will be plump and beautiful again." He poked her in the side.

"Chop *fufu*?" I said.

"Chop," said Hannah, gesturing toward her mouth and chomping her jaw up and down. "*Fufu* is Ghana food—you must try some very soon." The man poked her again and she giggled, "Stop it, Gorby!"

"Gorby?" Everything felt bewildering in the hard, flat light.

"My camp name," he said, extending a strong, slender hand. "Claude Mensah, a.k.a. Mensah Mensah

Gorbachev, at your service." He grinned at me with such genuine warmth that I giggled in response.

"But we just call him Gorby," said Hannah. "Don't we?" She rubbed her hand across his close-cropped hair. "And he is my dear, dear friend. Gorbachev is his camp name. And this is Ninja, Momentum, Ayatollah, and Castro." I shook hands all around, dizzied by the wattage of smiles. "At camp, the Africans take foreign names and the foreigners take African names. Have you been to camp yet?"

I shook my head. "I just got here last night."

The work projects, which took place in the rural areas, were called camps. Foreign volunteers paid $200 for a year's membership and then participated in as few or as many camps as they chose during that time. At camp, the volunteers were given room and board. When not at camp, they were welcome to stay here, in the Accra hostel, for as long as they liked. The hostel was a low-ceilinged wooden building, painted olive drab like a military barracks, which housed both a volunteer dormitory and the organization's offices. The dormitory was a long, low-ceilinged room, which fit about thirty bunk beds. Each upper bunk had a hook above it on which the volunteer could hang a mosquito net. Those on the lower bunks attached their nets to the metal lattice of the bed above. The overhead fan worked sporadically, and the rough wooden floor bestowed many splinters on tender pink soles. Sunlight filtered in through small, screened windows. In midsummer, when the hostel was packed with volunteers, the bunks were supplemented by mattresses on the floor.

The hostel was for foreigners only. Ghanaian volunteers were expected to live at home when not participating in camps, although they were welcome to visit during the day. Ghanaians who complied with certain criteria could participate in the camps free of charge. No one seemed to know exactly what those criteria were, but all the Ghanaian volunteers were literate, spoke good English, and had families that were financially able to spare them. With a few exceptions, they were city youth, getting a taste of the countryside. Some of them seemed as alien to the lives and customs of the villagers as we foreigners were.

A few local young men who were not volunteers hung around the hostel during the day, practicing their English and hoping to develop friendships with foreigners that would lead to marriage, employment, or at the very least sponsorship for a journey abroad. These men were clean-cut and solicitous, and many of the foreign women were all too eager to take advantage of the opportunity for roadside romance (and if that's all it turned out to be, the men didn't seem to mind too much either). As a brunette, I didn't get quite the attention the blondes did, but I got enough. Too much, even. I was still far too confused about the relationship I'd left behind to think about flirting. Michael's and my letters had slipped back into a tone of such intimacy it was as if we were still together. On my stronger days, this felt like a burden—I worried that my homesick heart was writing checks my itinerant body wouldn't keep. But on days when I felt most unrooted, it was a tremendous comfort to know that he was there.

Periodically throughout the day, Mister Awitor, the head of the organization, emerged from an inner office to chase away nonvolunteers with harsh words in one of the local languages. He often added in English—presumably for our benefit—"If I see your face here again, I will surely telephone the police."

"We don't mind them," the foreign volunteers insisted, but he simply shook his head and walked back inside, murmuring under his breath that we would surely mind when our costly cameras and sunglasses went missing. The young men always reappeared an hour or two later anyway. Though Mister Awitor's tone was menacing, they'd learned by now that the threatened phone call was never made.

Some foreigners participated in one camp and simply stayed on at the hostel for the rest of the year, bumming around Accra and smoking potent local marijuana, called "bingo" or "wee." Hannah, however, had been in Ghana for three months and already participated in four camps.

"We must choose your name!" Hannah clapped her hands with delight. "What shall we call her, Gorby?"

"We must call her Korkor," he said, "like my baby sistah."

"Korkor," I said. It sounded like kaw-KAW. "What does it mean?"

"It means second-born, in Ga," said Gorby.

"Are you second-born?" asked Hannah.

"To my mother I am." I was about to explain that my father had older children from a previous marriage, but Hannah interrupted.

"Perfect! Gorby is...how do you call it...soo-kick?"

"Psychic," I said.

"Psychic! Gorby is psychic!"

"What's your camp name?" I asked Hannah.

"Mine is Abena," she said, "Tuesday-born in Fanti. Everyone here has a day name. But then there are also nicknames and family names and Christian names. Africans have so many names, it is very confusing."

"Not to us," said the man called Momentum.

"Only to girls from Holland," added Gorbachev. He flashed her an adoring grin.

Later Hannah confided in me that back home in Amstelveen, the suburb of Amsterdam where she grew up, she'd never considered herself attractive. She had not been popular in school, she told me. She was always isolated. Boys picked on her, girls whispered about her, and she had few friends.

"But you're so beautiful!" I stammered. "Not to mention smart, and sweet, and vivacious. You would've been very popular at my high school, I can promise you that."

She looked at me warily. "I don't think I should thank you for telling me lies. I may be smart, but I am not beautiful."

"You're—"

"Stop it," she said sharply, and something in her tone prevented further protest. "I know what I am. Anyway, it is all past. I am not in Holland now. I am in Ghana, and here I will be a new Hannah, a completely new girl."

I never found out what the old Hannah was like, but this new girl was a charmer. She insinuated herself into my brittle heart the way a child might, and in fact she was like a child, begging for attention, pouting when she didn't get it, pointing out her own best attributes at full volume, basking in the world's love. Among the volunteers, she was the favorite daughter of Africans and foreigners alike, doted on and pampered. She was a baby, really, not even twenty, and though there were others around that age (I was practically the grandmother of the group at twenty-six going on twenty-seven), there was something about her that made you want to protect her, to take care.

Hannah had a flair for drama. Once she leaned over in the night to take a swig from her water bottle and got a big swallow of gasoline instead. She ran to the bathroom and spent the rest of the night vomiting. The burning sensation lingered in her throat throughout the following day.

"I drank petrol!" she crowed to the group on the steps the next day. "You must tell your children and grandchildren this story, so that the girl who drank petrol will become a legend. You must tell them that after that day this girl had the power to light a fire with only her breath."

In Accra I initially was put off, as I had been in Abidjan, by the gaping holes in the sidewalk, the open sewers running down the sides of the streets, and the curbside food stands swarming with flies. The fumes of gasoline, human waste, and charred meat nauseated me. I was beleaguered as well by boisterous strangers who accosted me on the street, shouting, "What is your name? Let me be your friend! Give me your address! Bring me to your country!" I wondered sourly whether these overtures constituted the legendary Ghanaian friendliness.

But within two weeks I no longer noticed the sewage or the flies, and I was gobbling up street food like it was going out of style. I relished it all—the dark green *kontumbre* with its texture of creamed spinach; the thick, savory groundnut stew (Ghanaian for peanut) with sticky rice balls; salty *jollof* rice flavored with bits of egg and fish; tart, juicy pineapple; sweet oranges stripped of their peels but still clothed in their white felt underskins; starchy cocoyams; *kenke*; *banku*; *shitoh*; *akieke*.... All the stews were heavy with palm oil, its drowsy flavor reminiscent of coconuts and cashews. But far and away my favorite street food was *keli-weli*, a spicy-sweet concoction made of small chunks of plantain fried to a crisp in palm oil, then sprinkled amply with ginger and chili pepper for a sharp, tangy bite.

Simply put, I loved Accra. While embracing the amenities of running water and electricity, it maintained a character all its own. No New York-style highrises to be found here. Instead it unfolded, neighborhood by colorful neighborhood, a curious mixture of African and European influence, opening outward from the center like an elaborate tropical bloom. Accra was alive. Every city block pulsated with energy, from the solid cement buildings of the downtown area to the tin-roofed shacks of the poorer neighborhoods, from the sweltering maelstrom of the Makola Market to the crumbling castle that housed the government offices. In any one of these places, you were as likely to see a man dressed head to toe in full African regalia as you were to see a woman in jeans, tube top, and high-heeled shoes. And the colors! Brilliant shades of orange and red, turquoise and lilac, fuchsia and teal. The African fabrics would make a flamingo look drab. The prohibitions against combining reds and pinks or circles and stripes were absent here. Fabrics of every description lived side by side in delirious dissonance, a dizzying visual feast. The hairstyles too were astonishing. Some adorned the women's heads like helmets, with sharp spikes sticking out in every direction. Others were elaborate multi-tiered sculptures, their interlacing layers balanced against each other like houses of cards. Still others were interwoven with beads and ribbons, which complemented the colorful outfits with extra splashes of light.

On top of all this, I'd fallen completely in love with the people. Strangers still waylaid me daily, but what initially felt like aggression I now saw as vitality tinged with humor. I understood that the people on the street didn't actually expect to go home with me. They enjoyed engaging for its own sake, and while they were at it, they figured they might as well take their shot. This was the quality that struck me the most about the Ghanaians: for better or worse, they *engaged*. Riding across town in a *tro-tro* (Ghanaian for minivan), I often found myself in the midst of a rowdy argument, with people on all sides shouting at each other in the local language. These arguments were almost always good-natured, ending with laughter and backslapping when the participants disembarked. I recalled sadly that in the United States I had once taken a Greyhound halfway across the country without speaking to a single soul.

There were nights when Hannah, Gorbachev, and I, along with Ayatollah, Momentum, and a shifting group of European volunteers, would smoke bingo (purchased from a mysterious man called Bush Doctor who hovered around the path near the hostel) and tear ravenously through the streets of Accra at midnight, searching for food. Eventually we'd find one of the few stands that hadn't closed down for the night. The nodding attendant, usually an old woman, would wake with a start and make us egg sandwiches on thick chunks of white bread smeared with Laughing Cow cheese. We'd each down two or three sandwiches and a cup of Milo, a warm chocolaty beverage, before setting off for the hostel, our laughter echoing through the night streets, our running feet keeping pace with the rats that darted in and out of the sewers.

"A rat stepped on my foot!" Hannah shrieked one night. "I am marked by the King of Rats! Like, do you know, 'The Nutcracker'? Now you must tell people, I knew a girl who—every night at midnight exactly— she would get down on the ground and squeak like a rat, or no, a girl who had power to change a bad person to a rat."

Hannah's need to mythologize herself touched me. It was what we all yearned for, I thought, to be seen, recognized. We all wanted to be heroes or martyrs, to create lives worthy of legend. She just wore her desire a bit more nakedly than the rest.

Our volunteer efforts were a mixed bag. While some of the projects ran smoothly, others were woefully ill-conceived. The idea was simple enough: We'd go into a village, start up a project, and leave behind materials so that the villagers could finish the project after we left. The problem was that in many cases no one seemed to have consulted the villagers in advance. Unless there was a committed individual in the village to galvanize the community into action, the hospital or school might easily remain unfinished, while the building materials were slowly spirited away to patch failing roofs or add adjoining rooms to people's homes. It was also unclear why certain villages were chosen for projects several years in a row, while others nearby remained unvisited. Since the presence of so many foreigners brought a lot of energy to the local economies, I suspected personal connections might be involved.

One of the more disheartening stories I heard involved a camp in which the volunteers dug a foundation
for a schoolhouse right next to an identical foundation
that another group had dug and abandoned. When
the volunteers asked why they couldn't simply build
on the existing foundation, they were told that it was
forbidden to interfere with the work of another group.
Another tale involved a village to which a group had
returned several years in a row and done nothing but
make bricks. As the story went, the village was so over-
run with bricks that the local people were using them as
tables, chairs, even bassinets.

Most of the foreign volunteers I worked with in
Ghana fell into one of two groups: those who came with
an already ingrained sense that the work we were doing
here was futile (but doing it was marginally better than
doing nothing at all), and those who arrived filled with
hopeful romanticism about their own ability to "help."
Members of the second category were often terribly dis-
illusioned when their projects hit a snag, and tended to
resemble the members of the first category by the time
they left. Members of the first group, on the other hand,
were occasionally jolted back to the second by the sheer
exuberance of Ghanaian life.

Outwardly, I allied myself with the jaded camp—I'd
done enough volunteering in the past to know that it
often benefited the supposed help-*ers* more than the
help-*ees,* but my cynical veneer was ridiculously thin.
Beneath my world-weary affectation, I longed with my
entire being to be knocked over the head by a driving
sense of purpose. I approached each new project harbor-
ing a shameful secret: a vast, uncool reservoir of hope. In
the guise of offering service, I came to the construction

site seeking nothing less than redemption. Perhaps we all did.

Whenever I returned to Accra, I looked for Hannah. She alone seemed peculiarly free of either grudge or expectation concerning our role here. She soaked up everything with unbiased delight. I envied her capacity for simple enjoyment and secretly hoped that if I spent enough time with her, some of it might rub off.

A few months after our initial meeting, I came back from a project on the northern coast to find that Hannah had gotten romantically involved with a Ghanaian volunteer who went by the camp name of Rambo. Rambo was devilishly handsome, with silky skin the color of polished walnut, pronounced cheekbones, and striking gray-green eyes. He dressed to fit his nickname, in Western tank tops that exposed his enormous biceps, camouflage pants, and heavy-soled boots. He was studying mathematics at Legon University and was rumored to be a brilliant student. He came from that minuscule portion of the Ghanaian population that could be called middle class, meaning he had been raised in a home with both a television and a phone. His father had some mysterious government post, which Rambo cryptically described as "near the top." He spoke flawless English in a deep, purring voice, and was famous for his ability to drink any European under the table when it came to *apeteshi*, the strong home-brewed liquor that was popular in the Ghanaian countryside.

Throughout the steamy afternoons and into the balmy evenings, Hannah sat beside Rambo on the steps of the hostel. She listened intently as he talked to the other African volunteers in Fanti, Ga, or Twi, his arm slung heavily across her shoulders or hooked around her neck like a boa constrictor. Often she leaned over to kiss his cheek or nibble at his ear. He allowed this briefly before pushing her away with a murmured reprimand.

She began to wash his laundry on a regular basis. As I sat in the dirt courtyard behind the hostel with my plastic bucket, wringing the dust from my own grungy socks and shirts, I'd see her laboring over the heavy camouflage pants or scrubbing away at a spot of dirt on a white tank top. When I suggested to her that Rambo could just as easily do his own laundry, she shrugged.

"How do you say, when you are with the Romans?" She giggled nervously.

Hannah had little time for her old friends.

"I have known this man," Gorbachev grumbled to me privately, "and I have not liked him. I am very sure that he seeks only to marry a white sistah so that he may leave this country. He wants to be a doctor in Europe or America, where he can make a lot of money and own many cars. Our sistah Abena, she is so innocent. She trusts every person."

A week later I returned to the empty hostel from the Makola Market in the middle of the day. The Makola Market was the largest in Accra, and its endless rows of outdoor stalls provided the ideal place to revel in the beauty of African fabrics. I was laying out my pur-chases—three exquisite batiks dyed in richly saturated blues, purples, and greens—draping them across my bed to admire, when I heard a strange, stifled sound, like someone choking. Looking around, I saw, through the gauzy veil of a mosquito net, a huddled lump on Hannah's bed, covered by a sleeping bag. Alarmed, I rushed over.

"Hannah? Is that you? What's going on?"

In one violent motion the sleeping bag flopped flat on the bed and there she sat, shaking and red-faced.

"He will marry her!" she screamed. "He is all made of lies! He will marry *her!*"

"Who? Who will marry who?"

"Rambo," she sobbed, throwing herself at me through the mosquito net. I ducked beneath the netted shroud and wrapped my arms around her. She heaved and wailed against my shoulder.

"I'll kill him!" she cried. "I will give him petrol to drink. I will turn him into a rat. Then I will make him marry only me, after he is *dead.*"

"Hannah, Hannah, sweetheart…" I murmured. She sobbed in my arms for close to an hour, occasionally breaking away to hurl accusations at Rambo and his unnamed bride.

Eventually, the story came out. That morning, while Hannah was still in bed, a former volunteer named Isabella had arrived from Spain. Rambo had introduced her to the omnipresent crowd on the steps as his fiancée. He'd been anxiously awaiting her return, he said; they would be married at the end of the month. Hannah heard the commotion and wandered out in her oversized t-shirt to find Rambo liplocked in the sort of public display of affection he was never willing to engage in with her. When he came up for air, Rambo met her eyes for a long, cool moment, then looked away. She ran and threw her arms around him, shouting that he was hers. He pushed her away, and told the astonished Isabella—whom Hannah alternately described as ugly as a rhinoceros and beautiful as Sophia Loren—that this crazy girl had been hanging around the hostel bothering the volunteers and would soon be shipped back to Sweden or Germany, wherever she came from.

"But that's ridiculous!" I sputtered. "She'll hear the truth before the day is out. She'll know he can't be trusted."

But Rambo and Isabella had taken Isabella's things and left the hostel. Hannah had run after them, trying to grab the luggage out of Rambo's hands. Several of the assembled men held her back, chuckling and clucking, trying to soothe her. Now she no longer wanted to live in the hostel, no longer wanted to see the faces of those men.

Hannah had long ago befriended Sistah Essi, the feisty, sparkly-eyed young proprietress of a tiny beachside restaurant called The Last Stop. Located about a quarter mile from the hostel, The Last Stop was a favorite volunteer hangout, a breezy open-air shack with sand underfoot, located a short sprint from the ocean. Essi lived with her two daughters, ages one and three, in a room adjoining the restaurant. She assured Hannah it would be no problem for her to pitch her tent on the beach, and offered Hannah meals in exchange for helping out in the café.

Hannah's good nature returned after a week or so, but her eager-to-please, puppy-dog energy had been replaced by something calmer and more distant. That was when she began her walking. At any time of the day or night you might see her, striding through the streets or along a red dirt path above the beach, chin and chest thrust forward like a woman on a mission. She walked that way for hours, unafraid and unapproachable, perfectly poised on the crust of Africa, perfectly alone.

"Where's she going?" one volunteer or another would wonder aloud as we sat on the balcony of the Wato Bar, another favorite hangout, watching daylight turn to dusk. As the cloth wicks on the kerosene cans took flame one by one in the streets below, we'd crane our necks just in time to see Hannah slip quickly between the food stands and disappear.

As time went on, she became fluent in Fanti, which she practiced with Gorbachev and the other African volunteers while serving us our food at The Last Stop. There were over sixty languages spoken among Ghana's 18 million people. Fanti belonged to Akan, the dominant language group, which most Ghanaians understood. Hannah's English, too, sounded increasingly Ghanaian, her accent, sentence structure and turns of phrase growing more African with each passing day. Her relationship with the African men had changed, too. She no longer flirted the way she once had. She was friendly, even affectionate, but a distance remained.

"Why don't you go out with Gorbachev?" I asked her once. "He's such a sweet, gentle man, and you know he worships you."

"*Eh!*" she clucked. "Ghana men and me, we are finished. Ghana men are *weak!*" she shouted, echoing a common insult the African volunteers threw at each other in the camps. "Now I want only Ghana. Ghana here," she pounded the table. "Ghana is sooo sweet. Amsterdam was never my place. Ghana here, this is my place."

When the rains came, Hannah began spending nights in the small room attached to The Last Stop, with Sistah Essi and her two girls. Hannah and Essi had become very close, and often when Gorbachev and I went down there for a midday meal I could hear them giggling behind the kitchen partition while they chopped vegetables and stirred the stews. Sometimes I had to call out three or four times before Hannah would come out and greet us with a friendly, "*Eh!* Sistah Korkor, Brothah Gorbachev, you are welcome!"

Essi's husband, Kweku, was in the army and came home every month or two for a few days. He was known around the hostel as an odd character and a heavy drinker; the Ghanaian volunteers were reluctant to visit The Last Stop when he was in town. Whenever he appeared, Hannah moved back to her tent and, as though by tacit agreement, her relations with Essi became stiff and formal. Kweku was suspicious of her motives for working at The Last Stop, and one night she heard him shouting through the walls, while the two little girls whimpered and wailed.

"They are so rich," he shouted in Fanti, "to come here, from so far away, and stay for many months, doing nothing, buying whatever goods they please. Why then should she work like this, eating our food?"

Hannah could not make out Essi's reply, but when she heard what sounded like a hand striking flesh, she put her head under her sleeping bag and counted to a thousand. She offered to leave the next day, but Essi begged her to stay.

"Sistah Korkor, Essi hates that man," Hannah said. "If I were her, I would surely find a way to kill him." We were sitting on one of The Last Stop's uneven wooden benches at dusk, wiggling our toes in the cooling sand. A gentle breeze rose off the ocean, and a pale sunset tinted the foam pink.

"I know," I said. "It's awful. And I have the feeling it's pretty widely tolerated, too." The previous day, I'd overheard a Ghanaian volunteer telling one of the foreign men that if he himself had a sister whose husband beat her, he would not accept her back into the family. Her husband wouldn't beat her for no reason, he explained; she'd had to have done something wrong.

"I wish Essi would throw him out," Hannah said. Tears stood in her eyes. "She and I, we can run the restaurant. For what does she need him? He takes her chop money and buys *apeteshi*."

I sighed. "She'd probably leave him if she could. Who knows what her options are? We can't really see the full picture."

"I see her! She is afraid, that is all. But I will help her. I will stay with her and help to run the café."

"How long do you plan to be here, Hannah, really? Aren't you going back to Holland, to school?"

"No, no, no!" She started to cry. "For what do I go back to that place? I am Ghana woman now. That place has nothing that I need."

I left the next day to go to another camp, and didn't see Hannah for almost a month. When I returned she was still staying with Essi, and she seemed more entrenched in her "Ghana woman" image than ever. She generally refused to speak English now, though she'd relent and engage in fragmentary conversation with me when pressed.

"Our sistah from Holland is now more Ghana than we Ghanaians!" Gorbachev quipped.

One Saturday night, Hannah, Gorby, and I went with a few other Ghanaian volunteers to Labadi Beach, on the outskirts of Accra, for a dance party. While a tight-knit interracial group danced beneath bright white spotlights and the disheveled silhouettes of palm trees, the three of us walked down the beach to a quiet place where we could smoke our extremely potent *wee*. Buoyed up by a giddy high, Hannah and I stripped off our skirts and charged into the water, which was scarcely cooler than the air. We stood holding hands, with the waves licking our waists, and looked out toward the horizon. There was no moon, and I could see no line between ocean and sky: just blackness, with sporadic zigzags of white that vanished as soon as they appeared. A thrill of danger raised goose bumps all over my body. I couldn't see what was coming—I never knew the size of a wave until it broke around me. For all I knew, the next one would crash down on top of our heads and sweep us out to sea.

It was three in the morning when we crammed into a shared taxi back into town with three other Europeans. We were sopping and exhausted, hangovers already on the way. Gorbachev and I walked Hannah down to the beach by The Last Stop, but when we got there we experienced a jolt of disorientation: Hannah's tent was nowhere to be seen.

"Did you move it?" I asked Hannah.

"No." She shook her head in bewilderment, looking around her in a kind of daze.

"Thieves?" said Gorbachev.

We walked toward the spot where the tent had been. I stepped on something squishy, and when I reached down I felt fabric, slick and synthetic, with feathers leaking out of it. Exploring further, I found a zipper.

"Oh no," I said softly. Taking another step I tripped on a slender plastic pole.

"This…this is…someone has…Gorbachev sputtered, as we discovered pieces of clothing, paper, and plastic, ripped and scattered around the beach. Down near the water I stumbled over a mass of nylon, sopping wet. It was Hannah's tent.

Hannah began to cry. Gorbachev was shouting, "Who…. Who has…"

A burst of light exploded from The Last Stop. A male figure leaped out into the night with a flaming torch in his hand.

A torrent of abuse came from his mouth in Fanti, interspersed with sporadic words of English. Amid the torrent the words "spy," "thief," and "CIA" jumped out at me, and then, later, "white witch" and several times, "my wife."

"She's not your wife!" Hannah shouted suddenly. "She doesn't love you! She hates you! She loves me!"

After that, everything blurs together. Kweku lunged toward us with the torch, and then Gorbachev was holding my hand and the three of us were running blind along the beach. At some point we turned uphill, staggering toward the porch light of the hostel, which glimmered feebly on the horizon. Hannah, on Gorbachev's other side, screamed a string of Fanti words into the wind as we ran, stumbling and gasping, toward the light.

The next morning, Hannah was gone. At my panicked insistence, Mr. Awitor made inquiries and learned that she had called her parents in Amsterdam, who had arranged for a ticket home the same day. By the time I awoke, she was already at the airport. I don't know whether she got up at dawn and went to the beach to salvage her possessions. Some volunteers went down there to search, but they found nothing. She would at least have needed her money and passport, I pointed out, but Gorbachev said that Hannah always carried those things with her, in a money belt worn under her dress, "like a foreigner."

For me she left no note, nothing. And I never found out whether she'd said goodbye to her beloved Essi. I didn't go back to The Last Stop for many months. When I finally did, Essi chattered cheerfully, avoiding my eyes, and I couldn't bring myself to ask.

"She loved Ghana so much," said Gorbachev sorrowfully. "And this horrible man, he must drive everything to ruin."

"But why would she just leave like that?" I asked for the hundredth time. "She could have found another place to live. And she could have visited Essi when Kweku was away."

"Sistah Korkor," said Gorbachev, looking at me sadly. "Our Sistah Abena, you know, she was a very kind girl, but she was not strong like you. It is very good fortune that she was born in this world to parents who were able to send for her."

Later, when I was back in the States, I got a letter from Hannah. The tone was exuberant, filled with exclamation points. It sounded more like the girl I'd first seen on the hostel steps than the woman run off the beach by a friend's irate husband. She was now in nursing school, she said. One day, she'd gone for a long walk in a part of Amsterdam that was unfamiliar to her and stumbled onto a Ghanaian restaurant. She went inside and was amazed to find all her favorite foods: *fufu* and pepper sauce, *kenke*, garden egg stew, groundnut soup, even *apeteshi* to drink. Imagine the waiters' surprise and delight when she began speaking to them in Fanti!

Soon she was going there every day. They invited her to parties, and she discovered a whole community—a little Ghana in Amsterdam. For the first time in her life, she felt almost at home in her hometown. And that feeling reminded her of what she'd nearly forgotten: how right it all was before it all went wrong.

"Oh, Sistah Korkor!" she wrote, and I could hear her voice as clearly as if she were standing before me, flushed and tremulous and filled with hope.

"I remember now how very sweet Ghana was! How tender the air, the nighttime smell of ocean. Also Essi, her laughter too loud at my ear. Now I know what I must do, and school is no longer boring! I want to study and learn, so I can take my degree quickly and soon, so soon, I can leave this place forever and go home."

~≫ ~≫ ~≫

Tanya Shaffer has toured internationally with her original plays and solo performances, including her solo show Let My Enemy Live Long!, *which was based on this story. Her latest play,* Baby Taj, *based on her travels in India, was chosen by the* San Francisco Chronicle, *the* Oakland Tribune, *and the* San Jose Mercury News *as one of the Top Ten Shows of 2005. Her stories and essays have appeared on Salon.com and in numerous anthologies. This story was excerpted from* Somebody's Heart is Burning: A Woman Wanderer in Africa. *The book was selected as one of the* San Francisco Chronicle's *Best Books of 2003 and profiled in* USA Today *and* Vogue, *which called it "perhaps the best of recent adventure travel books written by women." Visit her online at www.tanyashaffer.com.*

~ ~ ~

Mr. Hat's Neighborhood

Lake Wobegon has nothing on Pagoda Alley.

WHAT IS IT ABOUT A PANAMA HAT? OTHER THAN the fact that mine is probably the only one in the country. The local Vietnamese here in Saigon (guess I'll never be able to think of it as Ho Chi Minh City) call me Mr. Hat, for the ol' Panama. Well, the expat community is relatively small here, especially among the writers, photographers, and artsy-fartsy types. Even people who have never met you eventually hear of you. So I'm now "the guy in the Panama hat," to the expats. I have walked past clutches of them sitting at their beer, and one of them will look at me knowingly, maybe she'll nod. I'll pass one in the street and he'll do a double-take. A guy across the street will wave at me and point to his head to indicate his awareness of The Hat.

At least the foreigners know it's a Panama. The locals,

universally, call it a cowboy hat. And I have failed at
every attempt to educate them otherwise. They simply
do not have a place in their consciousness for the idea
of "Panama hat." It's a concept foreign to them. And
when I tell them that a Panama comes from Ecuador,
two countries most of them have never heard of, it only
makes things more confusing. They simply nod politely
and tell each other it's a cowboy hat. So it's official. Mr.
Hat is a cowboy, pilgrims. *Whoopey tay aye ay.* I don't
know how they square that with my English desert
boots and khaki trousers. And I shall not delve into it.
But *yeeha*, nonetheless.

The expat soaks who hang out here in Pagoda Alley
have had a bit of high drama in their otherwise steady
and predictable lives. The well-known Crumpet, known
to the folks here as Miss Argument, has been banished,
at least temporarily, from the peaceful byway. Her offense? Causing an argument, of course! She arrived at
the Phuong (Phoenix) Restaurant with the guy they call
Mr. Boots. (He wears those old style jungle boots we
had during the war. One wonders why a Swede wants
to wear them, but life needs mystery.) All was going
swimmingly when Mr. Bob arrived. (They call him Mr.
Bob because his name is Bob. How lame is that? You got
nothing about you that the locals can pick up on, or pick
on you about? Poor Mr. Bob!)

Turns out Mr. Bob was the Main Squeeze for Miss
Argument. Or at least the Main Paycheck. At least this
month. When he saw her cavorting with Mr. Boots,
there was hell to pay. Invectives flew! Accusations were
hurled! The peace was disrupted! Anglo-Saxon ver-
biage of the coarsest kind (new to some Vietnamese ears)
was liberally applied. Beer bottles and blows were on the

verge of being hurled. Curiously, of the three malefactors, the one in most high dudgeon was Miss Argument herself. She was furious at being caught out, in such a public forum, in front of Buddha and everyone. She kicked over a chair, threw a drink, and I think she spat at somebody. It was all about face and stuff.

Two ladies restrained her. A couple of guys interposed themselves between Mr. Boots and the hapless Mr. Bob. I was sitting on the other side of the alley, which means about five feet away, cheering on Mr. Bob, when somebody told me to shut up, I was being a butt-inski, or words to that effect. The two ladies delivered Miss Argument into the hands of Mr. Boots. He dragged her away, kicking and screaming. I guess it's like that old Texas saying, "Ya dance with who brung ya."

Suzi Q, the bartender who calls me Daddy, is disconsolate this week. She has lost her cell phone, known here as a "hand phone." There are two things one absolutely must possess here in order to be cool, hip, with it, fab, choose your superlative. One is a shiny new motor scooter, and the other is a hand phone. Walk down the street and see that anyone wearing trousers has a rectangular bulge in a front pocket announcing the required hipster's accoutrement.

Suzi Q had both, and she was on top of the world. Scooting about on her scooter, yammering away to all and sundry on the precious hand phone, slinging drinks for exotic foreigners, wearing those tight jeans that scandalize the elders. Life was fine. Then one day last week she was tooling down the avenue on her bright red bike, hand phone proudly to the left ear, when a motor-mounted thief (known as a cowboy, but not the

Mr. Hat kind) swooped down on her and absconded with the prized instrument. She came wailing to Daddy, so I called her number on my own coolness counter, hoping to get a trace on hers. But the wily thief had already cancelled her number. Now Suzi Q is Suzi Incommunicado.

She says it will take three months for her to save up for a new one. I think she's suffering withdrawal. She looks like I did when I quit smoking. I sit at the bar of an afternoon nursing my beer (O.K., I'm guzzling it, who the hell am I kidding?) and she'll come up to me with her puppy dog eyes and say, only half jokingly, "Daddy, you buy me hand phone. I can't call you, talk to you. Can't call anybody."

You haven't seen those puppy dog eyes. Nor have you heard the way she says "Daddy." Pity me, a helpless male of the species, alone in the faraway city. I'm suffering as much as she. I've actually been tempted. After all, hand phones are cheap here. Mine cost less than a round of drinks in San Francisco. But Suzi Q must have one of those expensive phones with all the bells and whistles. She needs all those functions she'll never use, but to be able to boast that she has them. Of course she would use the camera, to send grainy photos of herself to people who already know what she looks like. But fortunately for me, her lust for extra functionality keeps me from giving in.

Heidi is about twelve years old, and more grown up than most people I know. Hmmm, that may be why I like most people I know. Anyway, I first met her as I took an afternoon tea at Madame's Tea Terrace here in Pagoda Alley. She wore jeans, a plain cotton shirt, and a

baseball cap. Her hair hung down to mid back in a ponytail. Slender but not skinny, like most females here. She
had a hand stretched out for money. But she also had a
look on her face that said, "I bet I could beat you at anything fun." It was a playful yet dareful look. I waved her
away, and she stuck her hand closer to my face, and her
expression said, "Run a race, play pool, long jump?"

We repeated this same encounter three days in a row.
No way would I give her money. But I finally invited
her to a coke, which she accepted. We speak only a few
words of each other's languages, so we sipped tea and
coke in silence. But we locked eyes most of the time. We
took each other's measure. I'm sure she looked for weak
spots in my frame in the event of a fight. I wondered
what might scare her. I gave her my business card. She
took it to an English speaker and had that person write
the word "souvenir" across the top. Heidi has become
like Miss Chatter. She knows she can sit at my table, no
matter who else might be with me, and I'll stand her
to a coke. She never asks for more. Not even when she
cleaned my clock at a game of pool a few days ago. Oh,
yes. The twenty-four-hour bar at the end of the alley has
a pool table. Unbeknownst to me, Heidi has been there
a few times.

I finally bought a postcard from Crawling Lady.
Curiously, it was the same day that the Saint Vitus
Dancer made his reappearance after a three-week absence. Saint Vitus's Dance is a genetic nervous disorder
that causes its sufferers to walk in crazy postures, with
pained expressions, arms akimbo, tongue sticking out,
eyes bulging. I don't mean this unkindly, but it's a bit
like a Monty Python silly walk. Our dancer had reached

the middle of the alley and paused, frozen in his pose, statue-like. Because of the position of one of his hands, a passerby thought he was begging and tried to press a small note into his hand. It fluttered to the pavement, and the would-be good Samaritan fled in confusion.

Crawling Lady crawled up to my table and said hello as usual. "Hello, my friend," said I. "I'm happy to see you." I long ago found that Vietnamese people love that phrase, "I'm happy to see you." I'm the only foreigner I know that uses it. And I use it sincerely. And it always brings a smile, even a blush. Crawling Lady grinned, nodded and said "Happy see you, too. You buy postcard?" She always asks, but never presses. The most remarkable thing about Crawling Lady is that she speaks more English than most people in the alley. She's a simple soul and doesn't have a lot to say, but she can say a lot.

I remembered that I needed to send a birthday greeting, so I said, "Yes. Postcard." She took the flip-flops off her hands. Her feet have no use for them. Her legs are permanently bent at the knees, at an angle greater than 90 degrees. She never needs shoes. I'm always astonished at how clean and well scrubbed she is, given her life on the pavement. And unlike other paraplegics here, she wears no scraps of innertube to pad her knees. Yet I've never noticed a hole in her trousers.

I looked at her wares. I selected the card. I paid her the twenty cents. We chatted for a while. And then Heidi appeared. She took her seat, greeted Crawling Lady, and looked at me askance, as if to say, "Why I'm just a girl. I can't play pool." I signaled the waiter, who brought her a coke without being told. Upon receiving it, Heidi first offered Crawling Lady a drink. She took a perfunctory sip, smiled and said "thanks."

The three of us sat there for a while, me drinking tea, Heidi and Crawling Lady sharing a coke, now and then speaking, but not too often. Then a guy at the next table (and the tables are very close together) decided that he must show charity to Crawling Lady. He stood up, and with a grand gesture, offered my lowly friend a bank note worth about a dollar. A tidy sum here. She politely refused. Crawling Lady has never taken charity, and she is sincerely embarrassed when it's offered.

The man urged her to accept, and yet she politely refused, turning her face away. He insisted, and she began to show her ire. He tried to force it on her, and she batted his hand away with her flip-flop. He stuffed the bill into her bag of postcards, sat down in a huff, and told her not to be a fool, take the money while you can! She took it out of her bag, crumpled it into a ball and threw it at him. I could see from her tired expression that she has been this route many times. The man was speechless, almost apoplectic, that his largesse could be so easily dismissed. That so humble a person could so steadfastly refuse him, from so low a posture.

Flustered at the unpleasantness, Crawling Lady turned to go. She pulled her flip-flops onto her hands. She tucked up her bag of postcards. She looked back and thanked me for buying one. "See you later, Mr. Hat," she said. At that moment, Heidi abandoned her coke and without a word dropped down onto the pavement, on all fours, next to Crawling Lady. Just before they began to crawl away together, shoulder to shoulder, like a team of mules, they burst into a fit of giggles. They nudged each other, nuzzled each other, giggled some more, looked back at me and stuck out their tongues playfully, looked at the man and stuck out their tongues not so playfully, then giggling like school girls, crawled together to the very end of my alley.

How can you not love this place?

Valentine's Day came to Vietnam, and the Patron Saint of Love was loaded for bear. Make no mistake, this is still officially a communist country. Officially. The signs of it are everywhere. Daily the masses are exhorted to "build socialism" and to "support the workers' struggle." Yet the big debate is whether or not Communist Party officials should be able to own a private business and have employees and capital. Should wealthy communists be taxed at higher rates than those who simply struggle to get rich? All over town are Soviet-style political billboards extolling the virtues and mighty accomplishments of the Revolution. They are posted, under contract from the Communist Party, by local advertising agencies whose clients include Coke, Levi's, and Vuiton. The Cholon Tuxedo Rental Shop is festooned with flags bearing the Hammer & Sickle. The Commies are playing golf and tennis, and betting on the horses. They talk futures in the same breath as the workers of the world. They are learning to drink wine. I look forward to the day when they learn to drink it without cigarettes.

But, as I say, Saint Valentine came to Vietnam. He even came to my alley. And he followed me around a bit. He was in evidence everywhere. His day is ostensibly a Christian observance, and about 10 percent of the population are followers of Jesus and hence authorized to invoke the Patron Saint of Amore. But the Buddhistas love Love as much as any, and demand to be let in on the action. Even the Commies pause in their steadfast atheism to partake in the special day.

And so big red Valentine hearts fluttered alongside the proud but diminished Hammer & Sickle. Images of Saint V were posted alongside those of Marx, Lenin, and Ho Chi Minh. The florists and jewelers and confectioners did a land office business. So did the hookers. They seemed happiest of all! Just around the corner from the alley is what the locals call "Loving Park." It's about a six-acre green space in the middle of traffic, graced with tall trees and shrubbery. It boasts two of the very few public toilets in town, staffed by amiable attendants. Every night young couples come here on their motor scooters (the vehicle of choice in this country, there is little room for cars on these roads) and park them in long rows at the edge of the green. They sit on a bike, side by side or straddle one facing each other, and talk about their future, and make out, and now and then feel each other up when they think no one is looking, or when the right people are looking.

Miss Jack makes frequent appearances here of an evening. She has several colleagues in other parks around town and they could all bear the name of Miss Jack. She takes up her station in a corner of the park where the shrubbery is about shoulder high. She is visited every ten or fifteen minutes by young men who come to enjoy some of what must be the best exercised fist in the neighborhood. On the evening of the big VD (Valentine's Day) there was a solemn line of young males, ranging in age from about fifteen to twenty-five waiting in silent order at the edge of her domain. Each held his dong (Vietnamese currency) in his hand, worth about twenty-five cents. She called them each in their turn. They stepped up to the plate and she bent to her task. One hopes the shrubbery benefited from the enrichment of the soil. I first saw her that night at about 7 P.M., then again as I passed by at around 10 P.M., and yet again at midnight still plying her trade. I haven't seen her since. I'm sure her arm must be in a sling. And I will never again approach that corner of Loving Park, no matter how well the bushes may grow!

Suzi Q works at the bar I call Regional Head Quarters. Her chief cohort is Sally G, and unlike Suzi Q, Sally G calls me Uncle. There is one more member of the night shift at Regional HQ. I call him Alfalfa. A bespectacled cherub-faced boy of about eighteen, maybe five-foot-four and slender. Always neatly dressed and polite. Not the lisping, mincing rubber-wristed sort, but still about as gay as they come. And he has a crush on Suzi Q's Daddy and Sally G's Uncle. I have a little ritual for my entry into Regional Head Quarters. I whip out the hand phone and call either Suzi or Sally and place my drink order about a minute prior to my arrival. When I walk through the door my beer is poured and waiting for me. Other patrons of the bar are often astonished that the drink arrives before the drinker.

Alfalfa watches the girls as they receive phone calls. If he perceives that it's from me he rushes to fill the order for them, and lets me know that he did so. If he misses that he makes sure to greet me at the door. Sally G doesn't much mind him doing this, though Suzi Q is a bit more territorial. But they all know that he is not al-lowed to call me Daddy, or Uncle, and so Suzi Q is mol-lified. Alfalfa knows well that the girls' Daddy/Uncle is a straight arrow. And he respects that. Though it doesn't keep him from lingering near me after serving me this drink or that snack. "Thank you," I'll say to him. "You go back to work now." But if it's a slow time he'll just sit on the stairs that lead up to the pool room and watch me. I catch him doing so and he doesn't look away. He just smiles. He has such a twinkle in his eye when he does so. He did me a small favor recently, and I told him he was a good boy. That might not have gone over well in the States, but this is Vietnam, where the approbation of one's elders is prized. Especially if the elder is someone you have a crush on. That one comment sustained his good mood for an entire night.

There are roughly sixteen flower girls in the greater neighborhood surrounding Pagoda Alley. They are all between about six and twelve years old. Many of them wear a Catholic school girl type skirt, though they wear different tops. Little Miss Bluejacket is my personal favorite. She has a bad attitude. Most of the girls approach with a sweet smile and an engaging manner. "Mister, you buy flower for lady?" They have taken lessons in charm from their mothers or aunties, and most have learned well how to weedle an extra dong out of the defenseless male. They might rest a head on your shoulder. The littlest ones might even crawl into your lap. But Little Miss Bluejacket, who is now ten, and on her way to being a drop-dead gorgeous teenager, will approach a man with a bundle of roses and say, "You! You buy flower!" Her victim will be polite and say, "Oh, no thank you. I already have one." To which she responds, "You buy flower!" She'll stay right where she is and lock eyes with her prey. And this beautiful bad seed will bend him to her will. She can even exercise this power over women. Perhaps especially over women.

The days leading up to Valentine's Day are good days for the flower girls. As long as they play by the rules.

You see, they have something of a cartel. There is a price below which they agree not to sell their blossoms. One girl might find advantage in doing so, but it would cut into the others' ability to eke out a profit. So the rock bottom price for a rose is about twenty cents.

One night shortly before V Day I was coming out of the little Mexican place in the middle of the alley when I heard a great, high-pitched commotion half way between there and the Phoenix. All the little flower girls in the neighborhood had gathered there for a roisterous pow-wow. Miss Bluejacket was in heated argument with three other girls, and all the others were pressing in upon them. All were shouting at once, apparently calling for blood. Miss Bluejacket had a faction of two, maybe three, girls, but they were vastly outnumbered. Still, she hurled vitriol in exchange for vitriol with several other girls. They got in each other's faces and shouted their curses. As the hostility reached a crescendo, and quite without warning or apparent planning, two girls leaped on Bluejacket. Others shouldered her faction aside and held them at bay. The two assailants grabbed Bluejacket by the arms and pulled them out to the sides as though they would pull her apart. They tugged and tussled, their school girl skirts and their long black hair swaying and rippling with the ensuing struggle. A third girl, urged on by the frenzied tribe of little girls, leaped onto Bluejacket's back and began to pummel her. I could hear the dull thumping sound as each blow landed between her shoulder blades.

Bluejacket knew that she was done for. There was no escape. Her small faction was helpless, as was she. So she just took it, took it as the beautiful little flower girls screamed for more. After a dozen good hard slugs to the upper body they let her go. And she immediately got back in their faces and screamed at them. Of course she had no argument other than her own native defiance. She had been underselling the cartel in the busiest season, the week of Valentine's Day. She had been cutting into the other girls' livelihoods. Justice had to be served. And they savored it. The alpha flower girl made a brief address, jerking her head toward Miss Bluejacket, who stuck out her tongue. The alpha then led the pack away, back into the night; back into the market for fragrant flowers; back to foreign men who were waiting to be charmed by pretty little girls offering blood-red blooms; back to Western women who overpay them in the belief that they are helping to "empower" the girls by promoting their entrepreneurial spirit; back to the soaks; back to work.

The next night Little Miss Bluejacket approached me as I was finishing dinner at the Phoenix. She fixed me with a hard stare as she held forth her individually wrapped roses. "You buy flower," she insisted. In the months I've known her I've never bought a flower from her, just as I've never given money to Heidi, and only bought one postcard from Crawling Lady, and that only when I needed it. But as with Heidi and Miss Chatter, I have bought her a coke now and then, which she takes away to drink on her own rather than share my table. "You got your ass kicked last night, didn't you?" I said to her, indicating the spot only a few yards away where the deed was done. She speaks little English, but my meaning was perfectly clear to her. "You buy flower," she demanded, shoving one into my face. "You buy flower." I think those other little girls had better watch their backs.

In the days leading up to Valentine's Day, all the females I know in the alley and the surrounding neighborhood had been reminding me of the impending event. "You will bring me chocolates, yes?" As with Tet lucky money, they are not shy of asking for it. "But I'm not your boyfriend," I'd say. "But I am woman," they'd counter. "You have to bring me chocolates." I tried to make them understand that V Day is not like Tet. "If I bring you chocolates it means you have to be my Valentine," I told them one and all. "So you will bring me chocolates?" I tried to explain that only their boyfriends should bring them chocolates. But it was like trying to teach them the difference between a Panama hat and a cowboy hat. "You bring me chocolates!"

I resolved to make a day trip to somewhere else on Valentine's Day. Besides, I'd come to know a lot of females in the last three months. There were the night shifts at General HQ and Regional HQ, there were the day and night shifts at the Lucky Café Bar, the girl who brings me the morning paper, Madam at the tea terrace and her daughter, a couple of pool sharks in the 24/7 bar on the corner, plus every female you've read about up to now including Miss Bluejacket. They all wanted chocolates!

So I slept in, then sneaked away. But the whole city had Valentine fever. And it was infectious. Women and girls were all giggling over their chocolates and flowers. Men and boys were beaming. I wanted to participate. So I betook myself to the candy sellers in the Ben Thanh market, about five minute's walk from the alley. There was a bewildering display of candies, many of which I'd never seen and couldn't even guess what flavors. But the only chocolates I saw were in big heart-shaped boxes.

I'd bust my budget for a week if I bought enough to go around. Then I saw my solution. On the floor behind a bin full of what smelled like durian candy was a basket of M&Ms. All plain, no peanut. I scooped up what I thought would be enough packets and then added a few more for good measure. I figured I could give any excess to street urchins.

The day shift at the Lucky was still on duty, so in I walked with my sack of treats. I gave each girl a bag and they positively gushed. And they squealed. It was as though I'd given them each a diamond ring. They tore open each bag and compared their contents to see if they all had the same colors and quantities. And then they ate them on the spot. Two of them traded colors. I was amazed at the power of such a small gesture.

So I made my rounds. Madam hugged me. The girls at General HQ went in together to buy me a drink. One of the pool sharks let me win. Crawling Lady had never received a Valentine before. She pulled off her flip-flops and put her hands together prayerfully and did that Buddhist thing. Heidi looked at me with her special dareful smirk and gestured for a second bag. I pulled her ponytail instead. Miss Chatter, well, you know how Miss Chatter responds to anything. I think she's still yammering on about it. I thought about giving one to Miss Jack, but that would have required standing in line, so I tossed one over a pair of tables at the Phoenix to Miss Argument and ran. I dropped one into the begging bowl of a barefoot mendicant nun. At first she looked confused, but then broke into a grin. Even Bluejacket smiled at me, and punched me on the arm playfully. I think it was playfully; the mark disappeared in a matter of hours.

At length I had three bags left and two girls to go. I headed for Regional HQ. I whipped out the hand phone and told Suzi Q, "Daddy's on the way, Baby. Draw me a cold one." When I arrived the place was empty but for Suzi and Sally. I took my seat at the bar and set my near empty bag on the stool next to me. The girls stood shoulder to shoulder facing me across the bar. They were ever so slightly standoffish, with a cautious look of expectation. I was coy at first. "Did you get lots of candy today?" I asked. "Mmm, some," they answered in unison. After a minute of teasing they knew I had something for them. So I turned to my bag, fished out the last three packs of M&Ms figuring I'd eat one with them. Then I turned back to face my two favorite Valentines, and Alfalfa.

I froze. Where in the Sam Hill did he come from? I thought. The girls' faces were lighting up just like all the others I'd valentined. And so was Alfalfa's! He could plainly see I had three packs of happiness. And there were three of them. Then he saw my hesitation. Now you know the kinds of things that went through my mind. No need to elaborate. But it came down to one thing. If I gave the girls a Valentine and none to him he was going to be crushed. Especially if it happened in front of the girls. Even gay guys don't like to be humiliated in front of girls. If he were to misconstrue my meaning in giving him a Valentine, dealing with that would be preferable to hurting somebody so callously. As I handed each of them, all three, their M&Ms I said, "For my Valentine." The girls went giddy, as the others had. Alfalfa pressed his Valentine to his heart and beamed immense gratitude, and relief.

The girls tore open theirs and gobbled them as the others had done. Alfalfa slowly opened his as though he were unwrapping a gift. He tore it down the seam as some people do with a bag of chips. He laid it down on the bar and spread the bag open to reveal the jewel-like candies. The blue ones really stood out. I'd noticed that throughout the day and night. They were the first ones to catch your eye. It was the same for Alfalfa. He delicately picked up a blue M&M, lifted it to his mouth and slowly chewed, looking at me with such twinkling, smiling eyes that I was taken aback, and even moved. It was as though he had never tasted anything in his life so sweet as a blue M&M.

I stepped into Regional HQ the other day and Alfalfa told me he had just seen Heidi walk by in tears. Suzi Q had drawn my beer as per the usual telephonic ritual, but I laid the price on the bar and told her she could have it. Unlike most Vietnamese women she likes a cold one now and then, despite the fact it's seen as unfeminine. I went looking for Heidi. Anything that could reduce that girl to tears had to be something serious. She is undefeatable and indefatigable. She's Bluejacket's alter-ego; the "good witch." I figured it must be a death in the family. I found her sitting on the pavement talking to Crawling Lady. She was still sniffling a little so I held back. A little girl who can "beat you at anything fun" doesn't want me to see her crying. In a moment she got up and walked away, still wiping her eyes. I approached and knelt down next to Crawling Lady. "Hello, Mr. Hat," she said. "You buy postcard?"

"Hello my friend. No postcard today thank you. You tell me, why does Thuy (her real name) cry?"

"Her bicycle." She need say nothing more. I knew this day would come. And I knew it would come soon. I knew it the instant I saw the bike.

It was a festive night, as so many are here in the neighborhood. I had just turned into the alley on my way home for a shower and shave before dinner. There stood Heidi, proudly gripping the handlebars of a brand new bicycle. It was a girl's bike, natch, painted sky blue and dotted with white daisies. It had a white wicker-work basket hanging from the handlebars and it was full of fresh flowers. The rear fender sported a carrier for either cargo or passenger. Fat new tires on the rims of white-spoked wheels promised miles and miles of pedaling pleasure. One of those shiny, hemispherical, ringy-dingy bells was bolted to the right handle. No girl of twelve ever had a more beautiful bike.

Totally confused, I asked her, "Where did this come from?" She grinned and pointed behind her to a middle-aged man from somewhere in the USA. He didn't look a bad sort. And he didn't seem overly pleased with himself. I'm sure his primary motivation was a simple idea that every kid ought to have a bike. It was his last night in Vietnam, having come for a two-week vacation. Heidi had put the touch on him his first day in town.

Of course he was charmed by her. She's a "good witch." She has a pouch that she carries by a strap over her shoulder. It holds photos and postcards and dedications in her writing book by people she has charmed. They are from all over the world. Some of these people have become her pen-pals. That's the more remarkable for the fact that she must have everything she writes and receives translated, as her English is quite limited. But her kind of charm overcomes language.

So her kind benefactor, in a fit of fatherly type love, or brotherly type love, or maybe something less savory, gave her this rich parting gift. Rich indeed. A rich gift to a poor girl in a poor country. The tuition for primary and secondary education is provided by the state here, but parents must pay for books, materials, uniforms, and everything else. Families are large, and it's not uncommon that they send only one or two of their kids to school. The oldest boy and the smartest girl are the priorities. This is why Heidi is free every day to work the streets and the foreigners. Her family must be poor, indeed, if they have to keep a girl like her out of school.

Heidi was over the moon with the bike. The fact that she didn't know how to ride a bike was irrelevant. She walked it everywhere. She put stuff in the basket, piled cargo on the rear carrier, rang the little bell as she approached anyone she knew. Virtually every adult with the means rides a motorbike here. People park them on the sidewalk and then sit on them as they do at Loving Park. Or they sit on them and just chat with others sitting on their bikes, or just watch the world go by. Heidi would walk her bike to a parking area, drop the kickstand and then sit on her bike like any adult on a motor. I'd walk by her as she perched proudly on that most beautiful bicycle, and she'd ring her bell at me and grin. It lasted longer than I thought it would. About two weeks.

I don't know where she hid the bike at night when she went home. But somehow her parents found out. Or maybe she just copped to it out of filial piety. That's a strong inducement here. I hope that was it. I hate to think that she was caught hoarding such a valuable, easily convertible resource.

So I left Crawling Lady and caught up with Heidi when I figured her tears had stopped. I pulled her over into a sidewalk café, the kind here that are furnished with beach chairs. I sat her down and ordered her a coke, and I had a coke, too. "Sorry about your bike," I said. There wasn't much point in my saying more. She wouldn't understand most of it anyway. But she knew my sentiments. And so we just watched the traffic go by for a while, and sipped our cokes.

Of course at a time like that you want to do more than just buy a kid a coke. I wanted to buy her a bike, of course. So would you. Where we come from every kid ought to have a bike. Where we come from. And I could have bought her one. I could have bought her two bikes. But they would have gone the way of the first. And Heidi would suffer three losses instead of one. I learned many years ago, when I loved a poor prostitute named Fatima, that mucking about with other people's lives is a bad and impossible business. It doesn't work. The law of unintended consequences always applies.

It is said that no good deed goes unpunished. Tonight a generous soul in Sweetapple, Ohio, or maybe Armpit, Texas, or Bumfuck, Nevada, sleeps soundly. He is secure in his generosity to a poor girl in a poor country. He is no doubt happy for the chance to practice charity, to be the Great White Benefactor. His investment pays dividends. He reaps the reward. He isn't the one punished.

We were finishing our cokes. And as we were across the street from the 24/7 bar with its pool table, I suggested a game. Heidi does love to shoot stick. And as you know, she can usually beat me at it. I figured a little victory in life was just what she needed. She noisily slurped the last of her coke through the straw, stood up and wiped her last tear away, and we headed to the table. She was a bit off her game. I mean, hey, that bike was a beauty. But you know what? She still beat me. And it was worth every missed shot. I never lost a better game.

~ ~ ~

I beat Heidi at a game of pool a few weeks ago. But it was too easy. She was very much off her game. I knew something was amiss. Over cokes afterward I asked her what the trouble was. She sucked on her straw, pensively. She pointed upward with her index finger, signifying North. "Hanoi," she said, and her face clouded. Her family was moving back to their ancestral home. Heidi was born in Saigon. She had only been to Hanoi once. But people here can be away from their places of origin for ten generations, and yet they will long for those places. But not Heidi. She didn't want to go. She loves these streets even more than I. As Melville said that his Harvard College was the deck of a whale ship, so are these streets to Heidi. They have formed her. Though she be only twelve years old, they have formed her. This endless carnival of vendors and hawkers, cheaters and liars, hookers and pickpockets, cooks, bartenders, flower girls, and foreigners from all over the globe, have been her world. And she was loathe to leave it. But she is gone now. And she, and I, and my alley are diminished.

I didn't know how to respond when she told me she was leaving. It wasn't the language problem so much, you know. When you love a kid, and that kid knows you love her, language can be circumvented. But it's important in this country that we not come between persons and their families. Sure, it's important where we come from, too. But it's doubly important here. I had to tread carefully.

We sat silently for a while. Then I got up and paid for the cokes. I nodded to Heidi to follow me. Opposite the western end of Loving Park is the Huyen Sy Catholic

Church. Heidi's family is Buddhist, and I'm Protestant, but the Huyen Sy's flower garden is open to all, and it's a peaceful place. We sat down on a bench facing a shrine to the Virgin Mary. Vietnamese Catholics came and went, lighting incense and votive candles, praying, genuflecting and so on. I explained what I could of it to Heidi. She might have understood every third word. But that wasn't what counted. What counted was that she knew the message of my heart. And she laid her head on my shoulder, and held onto my arm. Here in Vietnam people are quite open to various interpretations of the divine. It isn't unknown for persons to attend both church and temple. None would raise an eyebrow at the sight of a pagan and a Protestant finding a bit of comfort in the shadow of the Catholic Mary.

In the fortnight that followed I managed to meet Heidi's parents. She is the second child of five. Her dad is a day laborer. Her mom has a bum leg, but she does what work she can, like laundry. They were living in two rooms on the second floor of an old apartment building that Dickens might recognize. They shared bath and toilet with I don't know how many. It wasn't as bad as it could have been. Per capita income in this country is only about $500 per year. Through Heidi I managed to learn from Dad that they were moving to Hanoi because he and Mom had determined that their luck would be better there. Vietnamese people strongly believe in luck. Astrologers are taken very seriously. Star-gazers had convinced Mom and Dad that luck awaits them in Hanoi.

I had a nagging feeling that Dad's luck (or lack thereof) centered on cards and dice. Maybe Mom's, too. These people are incorrigible gamblers. The official newspaper that I call the "Red Rag" will tell you that soccer is the national pastime, but I tell you it's the lottery and games of chance. And both Mom and Dad had a certain pallor that suggested that Heidi's bike had been reduced, at least in part, to cheap rice whisky. And certainly that bike was financing the move to Hanoi. Now Heidi's benefactor, the Great White Benefactor, who sleeps soundly somewhere in the heartland, had given her a gift that had not only caused her to cry, it was now taking her away. Away from her beloved streets, and away from me, and no doubt from many others. Truly, the road to Hell is paved with good intentions.

I always tell travelers here that if they want to give money to the children they meet and adore, that they should give to a reputable charity, or at least to the kids' parents. It's impossible to make a difference in a child's life by giving the kid money, or a bike. Giving to the kid's parents might make some small difference. Well-run charities, by and large, will see your dollar go farther than any other means.

So here I was about to violate my own rule. I wanted desperately to help Heidi. Hells bells I wanted to adopt her and take her away from want and deprivation! I wanted to buy her ten bikes and tons of ice cream and barrels of coke. I wanted to send her to college. I wanted to see her go to the prom. I wanted to give her away at her wedding. But I couldn't do diddly shit. Anything I gave to Heidi would end up in the hands of Mom and Dad. And anything that they got, who knew where it would go? Not to any college fund, that was for sure. To be fair, they were doing the best they could. But their best just wasn't good enough. They didn't have the power. They didn't have the education. They didn't have the wherewithal. They didn't have anything. Nothing but the money from Heidi's bike and the words of some soothsayer.

I thought about buying her some new clothes. I don't think she has ever had new clothes. But new clothes can be easily resold. There was no question of giving her money. She's a good girl and would turn it over. And so she should, in this culture. Her parents and her siblings have to eat, too. I wanted to give her something of meaning, something that would remind her of me and my love for her. The perfect gift would have been a custom-made pool cue, the kind that comes apart and fits into a leather carrying case. Maybe her name monogrammed on the fat end of the cue. A few cubes of chalk thrown in for good measure. I could get one for fifty bucks. But Mom and Dad could sell it for forty. Almost a month's pay.

They were to make the journey by bus. It would take three days, if they didn't pause. So I bought them food enough for the journey. The day before they left I went to the Ben Thanh market across the street from Loving Park. I loaded up on various kinds of food wrapped in leaves and steamed. Perfect travel fare. I got about fifteen pounds of fresh fruit, including lots of oranges, custard apples, and papayas. I got some Chinese-style ham and sausage, some Laughing Cow processed cheese (they actually like the stuff here). Heidi likes Coke, so I bought twenty-four cans. On the morning of departure I picked up two dozen Vietnamese baguettes.

I brought the food to them in a cyclo (pedicab) that morning, having told them that I would do so. They were all packed up in cardboard boxes and cloth bags. Their place wasn't far from the bus station, but I told the cyclo driver to go get some of his colleagues and pedal the family to the station. As the family loaded up I took Heidi by the hand and asked Dad if it was O.K. for her and me to walk to the station. He seemed confused, but assented.

I always carry a blue-and-white bandana in my hip pocket. Never go out the door without one. Always pack a few when I travel. I pulled out a freshly laundered one, rolled it up lengthwise and tied it around Heidi's neck. Humble gift though it was, it was one she could keep. She fingered the knot. It was a good square knot. I still remember my knots from navy days. I pulled her ponytail one last time. And so we walked hand in hand. And we didn't say a word. And we got to the station and sat on the family bundles waiting to be lashed to the roof of the bus. I'm really not a morning person, you know. Anybody who knows me can tell you. When I'm sitting at Madame's of a morning reading the *Red Rag* I'm barely coherent. I shouldn't be allowed out and about before noon. I'm just no good in the morning. I felt like I was about to get weepy. And I had already gotten weepy on my birthday. Then Heidi slapped me on the knee. And she stuck out a hand as if for money, just the same way as she did that day we met. And she had that dareful look that said, "I bet I could beat you at anything fun." I laughed out loud, and so did she. I laughed and I laughed and I wiped away the tears, and so did she.

And then it was time for her to go. And she boarded the bus. And she took a seat by the aisle, as all the window seats were occupied. But she looked out to me, still fixing me with that dareful smirk, her black baseball cap cocked to the back of her head, fingers on the knot of the blue and white bandana. Until the bus took her away. And she was gone.

I thought after the incident of the brat cat (the one I tossed across the alley) I might be on Crawling Lady's shit list. And to tell you the truth I'd rather be on George W. Bush's shit list than hers. Of course I'm not lofty enough to be on Dubya's SL. On the other hand, maybe we all are. But I've come to learn that CL just doesn't have an SL. She might remonstrate. She might throw money back at you if you try to force it on her. But she just doesn't have time for a shit list. Her life is going to be short. She knows it, and she's wasting no time with chicken shit. Her philosophy, if I may put words in her mouth, is to treat big things like little things and little things like big things. The front page of the *Red Rag* (or any other rag) becomes a little thing, and greeting a friend warmly in the morning is a big thing.

I knew I was forgiven for using the cat for a forward pass not long after the incident. She crawled towards me, sidled right up next to me, and slapped me on the thigh and laughed. Then she tucked her useless legs under herself, leaned up against my leg and stayed a while. Now that's become her habit. Thigh slapping and all. And she doesn't ask me to buy postcards anymore.

A couple of days ago she invited me to lunch. Yeah. Her treat. What do you say to somebody who is as poor as a church mouse, is gonna die young, crawls on the ground with flip-flops on her hands, is diabetic and God knows what else? Oh, and you are the only person who has ever given her a valentine, even though it was just a lousy pack of M&Ms? What do you say? Well, I think you say, "Thank you. I'd love to." But for some reason that's hard to do. Maybe for lots of reasons. Maybe even reasonable reasons. And you can ask yourself why that is, and answer it on your own.

I stood up and I asked my humble friend where we were going for lunch. "No animal," she said. "No problem," said I. She crawled and I followed to a little hole-in-the-wall around the corner. I know the place. I take a coffee there now and then. CL hoisted herself up onto a little plastic stool next to a little plastic table. I sat beside her. She called for iced tea for herself and a beer for me. I wanted to say no to that. The beer would cost more than all else combined. But she knew that. So I took it, and I savored it. Might have been the best beer I ever had.

I had rice and veg, she had noodles and veg. And we talked idly about this and that. We exchanged a little gossip, and wondered about our little love Heidi and how she might be doing, and how we might go together to Hanoi to see her. She followed lunch with a few of her battery of pills. I had to wonder if all of them were real, or just fakes or piracies. That's not unknown here. Maybe that's why she gets sick on them. But how could I know? And who am I to ask? It's her life, and she fiercely defends it, short and painful though it's going to be. But it's all going to be on her terms.

I've recently read *The Tale of Kieu*. Written in the early nineteenth century by Nguyen Du, it is widely considered to be Vietnam's most important piece of literature. An epic poem, its final stanza is:

> This we have learned: with Heaven rests all things.
> Heaven appoints each human to a place.
> If doomed to roll in dust, we'll roll in dust;
> We'll sit on high when destined for high seats.

Does Heaven ever favor anyone,
Bestowing both rare talent and good luck?
In talent take no overweening pride,
For talent and disaster form a pair.
Our karma we must carry as our lot—
Let's stop decrying Heaven's whims and quirks.
Inside ourselves there lies the root of good,
The heart outweighs all talents on this earth.

I'll be back home this week, after six months in the neighborhood, with a few side trips here and there. I've fallen in love, with people and with a place. I've never laughed so much in half a year, nor come so easily to tears. And I'll be coming back to my alley as soon as I can, for as long as I can.

So that's the news from Pagoda Alley, where all the big things are little, all the little things are big, and where, from a balcony on the third floor of the Faifo Guesthouse, the world makes love to you every time you look at it.

And goodnight to you, Miss Jack, wherever you are!

❧ ❧ ❧

Richard Sterling is the author of The Fire Never Dies, How to Eat Around the World, *and several books in Lonely Planet's World Food series. His anthology,* Food: A Taste of the Road, *won a Lowell Thomas Award for Best Travel Book, and he is also the editor of* The Adventure of Food *and coeditor of* The Ultimate Journey: Inspiring Stories of Living and Dying.

❧ ❧ ❧

Dervishes

A traveler is mistaken for a wandering Dervish in
Pakistan and finds out why some people believe the
dervish has "nothing to do with Islam."

"**D**ERVISH ARE AN ABOMINATION," SAID NAVAID.
"What do you mean by a Dervish?" I asked.
"Dervish? Don't you know? It's a very old concept.
Fakir? Pir-Baba? Sufi? Silsilah Malang—that beggar
doing magic tricks...?" Navaid was staring at a man
who was sitting cross-legged in the street with a ten-foot
black python wrapped round his neck. "That beggar—
medieval mystics like Shahbaz Qalander—the people
who live and dance at his tomb. They are all Dervish."

When I first met Navaid at the tomb of Datta Ganj
Baksh a week earlier, he had been examining the same
snake man. Now Navaid was standing very still, stroking his white beard. The python was asleep and so was

its owner and no one except Navaid seemed to notice them. For the last ten years he had spent his days at the mosques of the old city of Lahore. He had neither a family nor a job. His voice was quick, anxious, slightly high-pitched, as though he were worried I would leave before he had finished his sentence.

"You foreigners love the idea of Dervish—whirling Dervish, wandering Dervish, howling Dervish—exotic—like belly dancers and dancing camels," he insisted. "Surely you understand what I mean?"

"But what's that beggar there got in common with a medieval Sufi poet?"

"One thing anyway—they are both irrelevant," replied Navaid. "They have nothing to do with Islam or Pakistan. They barely exist any more and, if they do, they don't matter. Forget about Dervish."

Two weeks later I was walking alone along a canal in the Southern Punjab. It had been five months since I started walking across Asia but I had only been in the Punjab for a few days. The arid mountains of Iran had been replaced by a flat, fertile land and I was struggling to turn my limited Persian into Urdu. I was also getting used to new clothes. I was trying to dress in a way that did not attract attention. I was, like everyone else, wearing a loose, thin Pakistani *salwar kameez* suit and because of the 120-degree heat, a turban. I had swapped my backpack for a small cheap shoulder bag and I carried a traditional iron-shod staff. In Iran I was frequently accused of being a smuggler, a resistance fighter, or a grave robber. In the Punjab, because of my clothes, black hair, and fair skin I was often mistaken for one of the millions of Afghani refugees now living in Pakistan. Afghanis have a reputation as dangerous men and this may partly have explained why I had not (so far) felt threatened, walking alone along the Punjab canals.

A snake was swimming down the canal, its head held high over its own reflection, shedding bars of water thick with sunlight in its wake. In a hollow between the towpath and the wheat field was a stunted peepul tree draped with green cloth and beneath it the earth grave of a "Dervish." A thin bare-chested man dragged a bucket through the canal, staggered to the edge of the path and threw water on the dry track. I watched him weaving up and down the grass bank towards me. The history of his labor was laid across the path in thick bars of color. In front of him, where I was walking, was pale sand; at his feet was a band of black mud. Behind him stripe after stripe, each slightly paler than its successor, faded through orange clay until, where he had worked an hour before, nothing remained but pale sand. This was his job in the Canal Department.

"*Salaam alaikum.*"

"*Wa alaikum as-salaam,*" he replied. "Where are you going?"

"To the canal rest-house."

"Respected one," he smiled and his voice was nervous, "most kind one. Give me a sacred charm."

"I'm sorry, I don't have one."

"Look at me. This work. This sun." He was still smiling.

"I'm very sorry. *Hoda Hafez*, God be with you."

I turned away and he grabbed me by the arm. I hit him with my stick. He backed off and we looked at each other. I hadn't hurt him but I was embarrassed.

Navaid had warned me I would be attacked walking across Pakistan. "Violent? Pakistan is a very violent country—the Baluch caught a young Frenchman who was trying to walk here last year and killed him. Or look at today's newspaper—you can be killed by your father for sleeping around, you can be killed by other Muslims for being a Shi'a, you can be killed for being a police-man, you can be killed for being a tourist."

But I could see that the man I'd hit wasn't danger-ous.

He was now smiling apologetically, "Please, sir, at least let me have some of your water."

I poured some water from my bottle into his hands. He bowed to me, passed it in front of his lips and then brushed it through his hair.

"And now a charm: a short one will be enough..."

"No, I'm sorry. I can't."

I couldn't. I wouldn't play the role of a holy man. "*Hoda hafez.*" A hundred yards further on I looked back through the midday glare and saw him still staring at me. He had, it seemed, perhaps because I was walking in Pakistani clothes, mistaken me for what Navaid would call a wandering Dervish.

An hour later, I turned off the tow-path down a tree-lined avenue. There was a peepul, with its pointed leaves, trembling forty feet above. This one had out-grown its pink bark but its trunk was thin, its canopy small. It looked as though it had been planted when the canal was completed in 1913, and it would probably out-last the canal, since part of the peepul under which the Buddha achieved enlightenment, 2,500 years ago, is still alive in Sri Lanka. Farther on, among the banyans, the ruby flowers of the *dak* trees, and the yellow of the labur-num, was the electric blue spray of a Brazilian jacaranda imported I assumed by some extravagant engineer. Two men and two boys were sitting on the lawn.

"*Salaam alaikum.*"

"*Wa alaikum as-salaam*. We had been told to expect someone. Please sit down."

I sat on the charpoy string bed and we looked at each other. They knew nothing about me and I knew nothing about them. They were looking at a twenty-eight-year-old Briton, seated on a colonial lawn, in a turban and a sweat-soaked *salwar kameez* shirt. I was looking at a man, also in *salwar kameez*, but with a ballpoint pen in his breast pocket—an important symbol in an area where less than half the men can write their own name. The other man, standing on the balls of his bare feet, staring at me with his hands forward like a wrestler, looked about sixty. He had shoulder length gray, curly hair and a short beard. He was wearing an emerald-green *kemis* shirt and a dark-green sarong, a silver ankle ring, four long bead necklaces and an earring in his left ear. I asked if I could boil some water.

"*Acha, acha*, boil water," said the old man with the earring and immediately loped off in a half-run, with his hands still held in front of him, to the peepul tree. I watched him build a fire and shout to a boy to bring a bucket of water from the canal. He and the column of smoke seemed small beneath the Buddha's tree. The man in green returned with the handleless pot of boiling water in his hands. When I took it from him, I burned my fingers and nearly dropped the pot. He asked if I'd like some honey and I said I would very much.

Ten minutes later, he returned breathless and sweating with part of a cone of dark wild honey in his hands.

"Where did you get it from?"

"From there," he pointed to the peepul, "I just climbed up there to get it." I thought I could see where the cone must be—it was on a branch, some way out, about forty feet above the ground. It was a difficult climb for a sixty-year-old, even without the bees.

"What do you do?"

"Me?" He laughed and looked at the others, who laughed also. "Why, I'm a Malang—a Dervish, a follower of Shahbaz Qalander of Sewhan Sharif."

"And what does it mean to be a Dervish follower of Shahbaz Qalander of Sewhan Sharif?"

"Why, to dance and sing." And he began to hop from foot to foot, clicking his fingers in the air, and singing in a high-pitched voice:

"*Shudam Badnam Dar Ishq/Biya Paarsa Ikanoon/The Tarsam Za Ruswaee/Bi Har Bazaar Me Raqsam.*" Come, behold how I am slandered for my love of God/But slander means nothing to me/That's why I'll dance in the crowd, my friend/And prance throughout the bazaar.

"Who wrote that?"

"My sheikh, my master, Shahbaz Qalander, when he lived in the street of the whores."

"And where are you from?"

"Me? Well my family is originally from Iran not Pakistan—we came like Shahbaz Qalander."

Laal Shahbaz Qalander was a twelfth-century mystic, what Navaid would call a Dervish. He belonged to a monastic order, wandered from Iran to Pakistan preaching Islam, performed miracles, wrote poems like the one above, and was buried in a magnificent medieval tomb in Sewhan Sharif, a city founded by Alexander the Great. His name, Laal Shahbaz, they say records his brilliant red clothes and his spirit, free as the Shahbaz falcon. He is one of the most famous of a group of mystics who arrived in Pakistan between the eleventh and fourteenth centuries. Their poetry and teachings often celebrate an intoxication with and almost erotic love of God that appears at times to transcend all details of religious doctrine. Their mystical ideas seem to have passed, like the use of rosary beads and the repetition of a single phrase for meditation, from the subcontinent through the Islamic world, and from the Crusaders into Christianity. It is they, not the Arab conquerors of the earlier centuries who are credited with peacefully converting the Hindus of Pakistan to Islam. Indeed, if the shirt of the man in front of me was like Shahbaz's red, not green, he would look, with his long hair and jewelry, exactly like a Hindu sadhu. And he is one of half a million Pakistanis who gather at Shahbaz's tomb once a year to celebrate with dancing and singing.

"Do you not have land?" I asked, "Work as a farmer?"

"I used to but I gave it all away—I have nothing now."

"Nothing?"

"I need nothing else. As the prophet says, 'Poverty is my pride,'" he replied, smiling so broadly that I wasn't sure whether I believed him.

When it was time to go, the Dervish accompanied me to the gate hobbling slightly on his bare feet.

"Have you always been a Dervish?" I asked.

"No, I was a civil servant in the Customs Department. I worked in the baggage inspection hall of Lahore airport for fifteen years."

At the canal bank, I took out some money to thank him for the cooking and the honey. But he was horrified.

"Please," I said, employing a Persian euphemism, "take it for the children."

"There are no children here," the Dervish said firmly. "Good luck and goodbye." He shook my hand and, bringing his palm up to his chest, added in a friendlier voice, "God be with you—walking is a kind of dancing, too."

When I walked back into Lahore, I met a very different kind of Muslim civil servant. "Umar is a most influential person," said Navaid. "He knows everyone in Lahore, parties all night—meets Imran Khan all the time. And you must see his library. He will explain to you about Islam."

I was invited to Umar's house at ten at night because he had had three parties to attend earlier in the evening. As I arrived, I saw a heavily built, bearded man in his mid-thirties stepping down from a battered transit van. He was talking on his mobile and holding up his arms so his driver could wrap a baggy, brown pinstriped jacket round him but he managed to hold out a hand to greet me. Still clutching my hand, he led me into a government bungalow of a very similar age and style to the canal rest-house. We removed our shoes and entered a small room, with shelves of English-language books covering all the walls and no chairs. Umar put down the phone, sat on the floor and invited me to sit beside him.

"*Salaam alaikum*, good evening. Please make yourself comfortable. I will tell the servant to get a blanket for you. This is my son, Salman," he added. The eight-year-old was playing a video game. He waved vaguely but his focus was on trying to persuade a miniature David Beckham to kick with his left foot.

Umar's eyes were bloodshot and he looked tired and anxious. He never smiled, but instead produced rhetorical questions and suggestions at a speed that was difficult to follow.

"Multan, but of course," he said, "you must meet the Gilanis, the Qureshis, the Gardezis—perhaps as you move up the Punjab—Shah Jeevna. I know them all. I can do it for you." All these people were descendants of the famous medieval saints who had converted Pakistan—Navaid's Dervish or Pirs. It was said that they had inherited a great deal of their ancestors' spiritual charisma—villagers still touched them to be cured of illnesses or drank water they blessed to ensure the birth of a male son. They had certainly inherited a great deal of land and wealth from donations to their ancestors' shrines. But Umar, it seemed, was not interested in their Dervish connections. He was concerned with the fact that they were currently leading politicians. Thus the female descendant of a medieval mystic, who once stood in a Punjabi river for twelve years reciting the Qur'an, had just served as Pakistan's ambassador to Washington. Another Dervish, who it is said entered Multan riding on a lion and whipping it with live snakes, and 600 years later is still supposed to stick his hand out of the tomb to greet pious pilgrims, has descendants who have served as ministers in both the federal and provincial governments. Umar knew them all and perhaps because he was rising fast in the interior ministry he was able to help them occasionally.

Umar's mobile rang again. He applauded one of his son's virtual goals, dragged off his shiny silver tie, dark brown shirt, and brown pinstriped trousers for a servant to take away, pulled a copy of V.S. Naipaul's *Beyond Belief* off the shelves and pointed me to a chapter, which

I slowly realized was about himself—all the while still talking on the phone.

I had seen Umar earlier in the evening at the large marble-floored house of a wealthy landowner and Dervish descendant. A group of clean-shaven young Pakistani men in casual Gucci shirts had been standing beside Umar drinking illegal whisky, smoking joints, and talking about Manhattan. And there he had been, in his brown suit and brown shirt, bearded and with a glass of fruit juice in his hand, not only because he was not educated abroad but also, it seemed, because he had very different views about religion.

"My son," said Umar proudly, putting down the phone, "is studying at an Islamic school—his basic syllabus is that he must memorize the whole book of the Qur'an—more than 150,000 words by heart—I chose this school for him." The boy concerned was trying to decide which members of the Swedish squad to include in his dream team. "You know our relationship with our families is one of the strengths of Islamic culture. I am sorry it will not be possible for you to meet my wife—but she and my parents and children form such a close unit. When you think of the collapse of families in the West, the fact that there is (I am sorry to say it but I know because I have been to the West) no respect for parents—almost everyone is getting divorced, there is rape on the streets—suicide—you put your people in 'Old People Homes' while we look after them in the family—in America and perhaps Britain as well I think, there is rape and free sex, divorce and drugs. Have you had a girlfriend? Are you a virgin?"

"No, I'm not."

"My friend," he said, leaning forward, "I was in a car with a friend the other day, we stopped at the traffic lights and there was a beautiful girl in the car next to us. We wanted to gaze at her but I said, and my friend agreed—do not glance at her—for if you do not stare now you will be able to have that woman in heaven." He paused for effect. "That is what religion gives to me. It is very late, my friend, I suggest you sleep here tonight and I will drive you back in the morning."

"Thank you very much."

"No problem." He shouted something. The servant entered, laid two mattresses and some sheets on the floor and led Umar's son out. Umar lay on his mattress, propping himself on one arm, looked at me with half-closed eyes and asked, yawning, "What do you think of American policy in Iraq?"

His phone rang again and he switched on the TV.

I reopened Naipaul's *Beyond Belief*. Naipaul portrays Umar as a junior civil servant from a rural background with naïve and narrow views about religion, living in a squalid house. He does not mention Umar's social ambitions, his library, his political connections, his "close friends" in the Lahore elite. He implies that Umar's father had tracked down and murdered a female in his family for eloping without consent.

When Umar had finished on the phone I asked whether he was happy with this portrait.

"Yes, of course I am—I have great respect for Naipaul—he is a true gentleman—did so much research into my family. You know most people's perspectives are so limited on Pakistan. But I try to help many journalists. All of them say the same things about Pakistan. They only write about terrorism, about extremism, the Taliban, about feudalism, illiteracy, about Bin Laden, corruption and bear-baiting, and about our military dictatorship. They have nothing positive to say about our future or our culture. Why, I want to know?"

He pointed to the television news which showed a Palestinian body being carried by an angry crowd. "Three killed today by Israel—why is America supporting that? Why did they intervene so late in Bosnia and not in Chechnya? Can you defend the British giving Kashmir to the Hindus when the majority of the population is Muslim? Is it a coincidence that all these problems concern Muslims?"

I tried to say that the West had supported Muslims in Kosovo but he interrupted again.

"Let me tell you what it means to be a Muslim," he said, lying on his back and looking at the ceiling. "Look at me, I am a normal man, I have all your tastes, I like to go to parties. Two months ago, a friend of mine said to me, 'Umar, you are a man who likes designer clothes, Ralph Lauren suits, Pierre Cardin ties, Italian shoes, Burberry socks—why don't you do something for Allah—he has done everything for you—why don't you do something for him—just one symbol—grow a beard.'" He fingered his beard. "This is why it is here—just a little something for Allah."

He was now lying on his mattress in a white vest and Y-fronts. I didn't really remember his designer clothes. Perhaps he had been wearing Burberry socks. The new facial hair was, however, clearly an issue for him. I wondered whether as an ambitious civil servant he thought a beard might be useful in a more Islamic Pakistan. But I asked him instead about Dervish tombs. He immediately recommended five which I had not seen.

"What do you think of the Dervish tradition in Pakistan?" I asked.

"What do you mean?"

I repeated Navaid's definition.

"Oh I see—this kind of thing does not exist so much any more except in illiterate areas. But I could introduce you to a historian who could tell you more about it."

"But what about their kind of Islam?"

"What do you mean? Islam is one faith with one God. There are no different types. You must have seen the common themes that bind Muslims together when you walked from Iran to Pakistan. For example the generosity of Muslims—our attitude to guests."

"But my experience hasn't been the same everywhere. Iranians, for example, are happy to let me sleep in their mosques but I am never allowed to sleep in a mosque in Pakistan."

"They let you sleep in mosques in Iran? That is very strange. The mosque is a very clean place and if you sleep in a mosque you might have impure thoughts during the night..."

"Anyway, basically," I continued, "villagers have been very relaxed and hospitable in Pakistan. Every night they take me in without question, give me food and a bed and never ask for payment. It's much easier walking here than in Iran. Iranians could be very suspicious and hostile, partly because they are all afraid of the government there. In some Iranian villages they even refused to sell me bread and water."

"Really, I don't believe this—this is propaganda. I think the Iranian people are very happy with their government and are very generous people. I cannot believe they would refuse you bread and water."

"Listen to me—they did."

"Well, this may be because of the Iran-Iraq war which

you and the Americans started and financed. Do you know how many were killed in that war? That is why Iranians are a little wary of foreigners. But look how the Iranians behaved..."

The phone rang again and he talked for perhaps ten minutes this time. I examined the bookcase while I waited. Many of the books were parts of boxed sets with new leather bindings and had names like *Masterpieces of the West*, volumes 1-11.

When he turned back to me again, Umar seemed much more animated. He sat cross-legged on the mattress and leaned towards me. "My friend," he said. "There is one thing you will never understand. We Muslims, all of us—including me—are prepared to die for our faith—we know we will go immediately to heaven. That is why we are not afraid of you. We want to be martyrs. In Iran, twelve-year-old boys cleared minefields by stepping on the mines in front of the troops—tens of thousands died in this way. Such faith and courage does not exist in Britain. That is why you must pray there will never be a 'Clash of Civilizations' because you cannot defeat a Muslim: one of us can defeat ten of your soldiers."

"This is nonsense," I interrupted uselessly. What was this overweight man in his Y-fronts, who boasted of his social life and foreign friends, doing presenting Islam in this way and posing as a holy warrior? It sounded as though he was reciting from some boxed set of leather books called *Diatribes against Your Foreign Guest*. And I think he sensed this too because his tone changed.

"We are educated, loving people," he concluded. "I am very active with a charity here, we educate the poor, help them, teach them about religion. If only we can both work together to destroy prejudice—that is why people like you and me are so important. All I ask is that the West recognize that it too has its faults—that it lectures us on religious freedom and then the French prohibit Muslim girls from wearing headscarves in school."

"Do you think Pakistan will become an Islamic state on the Iranian model?" I asked.

"My friend, things must change. There is so much corruption here. The state has almost collapsed. This is partly the fault of what you British did here. But it is also because of our politicians. That is why people like me want more Islam in our state. Islam is our only chance to root out corruption so we can finally have a chance to develop."

I fell asleep wondering whether this is what he really believed and whether he said such things to his wealthy political friends.

When he dropped me off the next morning, Umar's phone rang again and as I walked away I heard him saying in English: "Two months ago, a friend of mine said to me, 'Umar, you are a man who likes designer clothes, Ralph Lauren suits, Pierre Cardin ties, Italian shoes, Burberry socks—why don't you do something for Allah...'"

"A beard?" said Navaid, stroking his own, when I went to meet him again that afternoon at the tomb of Datta Ganj Baksh. "When people like Umar start growing beards, something is changing. But he must have enjoyed meeting you. His closest friends are foreigners."

I told Navaid what Umar had said about a clash of civilizations and Navaid shook his head. "Forget it— don't pay any attention. He was only trying to impress you. He doesn't mean it. People should spend less time worrying about non-Muslims and more time making

Muslims into real Muslims. Look at this tomb for example. It is a scandal. They should dynamite this tomb.
That would be more useful than fighting Americans."

Behind us were the tomb gates which Navaid swore
were solid gold and which had been erected in the saint's
honor by the secular leftist prime minister Zulfiqar Ali
Bhutto, Benazir's father. He gave gold gates to the tomb
of Shahbaz Qalander in Sewhan Sharif as well. "That
beautiful glass and marble mosque in front of us," continued Navaid, "was built by General Zia after he executed
Bhutto and took power. Then the CIA killed Zia by
making his airplane crash. So the marble courtyard we
are standing on was built by our last elected prime minister Nawaz Sharif. It hasn't been finished because of the
military coup."

"But," he reflected, "this Dervish of Shahbaz Qalander
is all nonsense. This tomb of Datta Ganj Baksh is nonsense. It has nothing to do with Islam, nothing at all.
There is nothing in Islam about it. Islam is a very simple
religion, the simplest in the world."

Beside us a man was forcing his goat to perform a full
prostration to the tomb of the saint, before dragging it
off to be sacrificed.

"But what do people want from these saints' tombs?"
I asked.

"Babies, money—but the Prophet, peace be upon him,
teaches that we should not build tombs. They tempt us
to worship men not God."

"And the Dervish?"

"They are cheaters, beggars, and tricksters, who sit at
the tombs becoming rich by selling stupid medicines."
He led me to the balustrade. "Look at him, for example." There was a half-naked man in the dust below

the courtyard, where the snake-charmer usually sat. His upper body was tattooed with the ninety-nine names of Allah. "He's probably got a snake in that box, and," Navaid dropped his voice prudishly, "has intercourse with his clients."

"And the history of these saints, their local traditions?"

"I think looking too much at history is like worshipping a man's tomb. Allah exists outside time. And we should not look at local things too much because Allah does not have a nationality."

"People say there are seventy-four forms of Islam in Pakistan, what do they mean?"

"Nonsense." Navaid was being very patient with me. "Islam is one—one God—one book—one faith."

"But what do they mean? Are they referring to Qadianis?"

"Of course not...Qadianis are heretics, they are not Muslims. General Zia has confirmed this in law."

"Or are they talking about differences between Naqshbandiyah, Wahhibis, Shi'as...?"

"Pakistani Shi'as are not true Muslims—they are terrorists and extremists—worshipping tombs—they are responsible for these Dervish. But in fact there is only one Islam. We are all the same." He turned away from the beggar. "There are no real differences because our God is one."

The politicians had spent millions on this tomb to win the support of the saint or his followers. But it was only superficially a tribute to the older Pakistan of wandering holy men. Ten years ago, the courtyard of this tomb was the meeting place for all the diverse groups which Navaid calls Dervish. There was Datta Ganj Baksh, the medieval Sufi himself in his grave, and around him were pilgrims, beggars, mystics, sellers of pious artifacts, drummers, tattooists, dancers, snake charmers, fortune-tellers, men in trances. But most of these figures were now hidden in the narrow streets below the marble balustrade. The politician's gift both asserted the significance of the saint's tomb and obliterated the cultural environment which surrounded it. Their new architecture seemed to be echoing Navaid's vision of a single simple global Islam—a plain white empty courtyard and a marble and glass mosque, bland, clean, expensive—the "Islamic" architecture of a Middle Eastern airport.

But I still could not understand why Navaid wanted to link these modern dervishes, one of whom was now shouting drunkenly at us from the street, to the medieval saints. "Navaid, what do you mean by a Dervish? Are you complaining only about mystics, who belong to a monastic order?"

"Of course not." Navaid gestured at the man who was now cursing our descendants. "You think he is a mystic in a monastic order?"

"Then what's he got in common with a Sufi poet or a medieval saint?" I was confused by the way he put medieval intellectuals, mystics, and poets in the same group as magicians on the fringes of modern society.

"They're all Dervish—you know where that word comes from—from the Old Persian word *derew*, to beg? What they have in common is that they are all rich idle beggars."

I presumed that explained why he didn't call them "Fakir," which means "poor," or "Sufi" which refers to their clothes.

"But why have you got such a problem with them?" I asked.

"What do you think? Those people down there," he said pointing at the varied activities in the street, "wear jewelry, take drugs, believe in miracles, con pilgrims, worship tombs—they are illiterate blasphemers."

"All right. But why do you reduce the Sufi saints to the same level?"

"Partly because people like you like them so much. Western hippies love Sufis. You think they are beautiful little bits of a medieval culture. You're much happier with them than with modern Islam. And you like the kind of things they say. What is it the Delhi Dervish Amir Khosrow says?" Navaid recites: "'I am a pagan worshipper of love / Islam I do not need / My every vein is taut as a wire / And I reject the pagan's girdle.' That's why I don't like them. Medieval Islamic mystics have no relevance to Islam in Pakistan."

"Then why do you keep attacking them? Or comparing them to these men in the street?"

Navaid just smiled and wandered off down the court-yard.

Medieval mystics were, I was convinced, not irrelevant. It was they (not Arab invaders) who had converted the bulk of the Hindus to Islam in the first place, while their clothes, practices, poetry, and prayers showed strong Indian influences. They were thus both the cause of Pakistani Islam and a reminder of its Hindu past. Furthermore, by drawing the link to the present, Navaid was conceding that the medieval "Dervish" remained a live tradition in rural Pakistan.

Umar, by contrast, had not felt the need to recognize this. His modern Islam flourished among migrants into Pakistan's cities. He could thus ignore the half a million people who still danced at the tomb of Shahbaz

Qalander, and the fact that his friends the politicians were credited with inheriting miraculous spiritual powers from men six centuries dead. His Islam, he felt, was the future. He could safely leave the Dervish behind in a marginalized, illiterate, impoverished world—leave them, in other words, in the rural communities where 70 percent of Pakistanis still lived.

At last Navaid turned back towards me. "When I said that Dervish were irrelevant, I meant that Islam is simple, anyone can understand it, it is public, it helps in politics, it does practical things for people. But for a Dervish, religion is all about some direct mystical experience of God—very personal, difficult to explain. Islam is not like that at all—it's there to be found easily in the Qur'an—we don't need some special path, some spiritual master, complicated fasting, dancing, whirling, and meditating to see God."

I could not imagine Navaid dancing. He was a reserved man, basically a puritan by temperament. When he admitted to being anything other than "a Muslim pure and simple," he said he was a Wahhibi. His Islam, like Umar's, was in a modern Saudi tradition, the tradition of the plain white mosque. It rested on a close attention to the words of the Qur'an, it refused to be tied to any particular place or historical period, it was concerned with "family life," the creation of Islamic states—an approach that was underwritten by extensive global funding networks. I could guess, therefore, why Navaid was troubled by an other-worldly medieval tradition with strong local roots, personal and apolitical, celebrating poverty, mystical joy, tolerance, and a direct experience of God. I could also guess why he wanted to reduce this tradition to a roadside magic trick.

But I might have been wrong. Although Navaid was fifty, he was, unusually for a Pakistani man, not married. He claimed never to have had a girlfriend. He was very poor but he did not get a job. Instead he spent his days discussing religion in the courtyards of the ancient mosques in the old city. He could recite a great deal of Persian poetry as well as most of the Qur'an. He was a wanderer and had lived for eleven years in Iran, arriving just after the revolution. He was a very calm and peaceful man, he had few criticisms of the West and he rejected most of the religious leaders in Pakistan. Although he attacked Dervishes, he knew the name of every obscure Dervish grave in Lahore. I left him by the outdoor mosque of Shah Jehan. He had seated himself under a large peepul tree, to recite a *dhikr*, a repetitive mantra for meditation favored by the Sufis. As I walked off, I heard him repeating, "There is no God but God..." with a half-smile on his face, entirely absorbed in the words and I was no longer certain who was the Dervish.

～ ～ ～

Rory Stewart served briefly in the British Army and then as a diplomat in Jakarta and Montenegro. From 2000 to 2002 he walked 6,000 miles across Iran, Afghanistan, Pakistan, India, and Nepal. His book, The Places In Between, *tells the story of his walk across Afghanistan. He is also the author of* The Prince of the Marshes, *an account of his year as appointed governor general of two provinces in southern Iraq shortly after the 2003 invasion.*

❧ ❧ ❧

At the Foot of Mount Yasur

*An active volcano in "paradise" drives
home lessons about life.*

I AM 600 MILES EAST OF THE GREAT BARRIER REEF IN the archipelago of Vanuatu—or, as they say in Vanuatu, the "*ni*-Vanuatu" archipelago—home to nine active volcanoes. One of these, Mount Yasur on the southern island of Tanna, is said to be the most easily accessible live volcano in the world. Anyone can walk right up and peer down into its fiery belly. A real volcano: fire and brimstone and flying ash.

It is late in the dry season when I get to Tanna with my friend, Michael. The days are crisp and warm, the nights cool enough to require long pants and a sweatshirt—a departure from the perpetual warmth of Ambae, more famously known as Michener's *Bali Hai*, which is the more northerly island, just shy of the equator, where I have lived and worked for eight months as a Peace Corps science teacher. We plan to spend three days at Port Resolution, and then head up to Ienemaha, the village closest to the crater, where Michael's tenth-grade student, David, lives. David adores Michael as his teacher and a living soccer maestro, so his family graciously asked us to be their guests for a couple of days.

We climb onto a flatbed truck near Lenakal, the tiny capital of Tanna, alongside about a half-dozen Tannese, and jostle and bounce the dirt road distance across the island to Port Resolution. As teachers and foreigners, it always feels we are the objects of special attention, especially from the children. In animated Bislama, the local lingua franca, they ask about us and are eager to tell stories along the drive. Mostly, they recite meandering folk tales, busting into giggles at the anthropomorphized exploits of familiar animals and magical beings.

When we drive across the ash flats that flank Mount Yasur, its black cone smoking above us, our fellow passengers provide details about the mountain's random acts of carnage: Three years ago, a tourist and her *ni*-Vanuatu guide were both burned alive near the crater's lip when gobs of molten lava rained down on them. After that, the *ni*-Vanuatu government shut down tourist access to the volcano for two years. With animated gestures and vivid language, the children describe further particulars: how half of the guide's body was found, the right side of it burned away; how the woman, well…had lost her head; how, more recently, a local village boy felled by a blob of brimstone lived long enough to be carried back to his village, his one leg burned away below the knee. He did not last much longer, lacking access to more advanced medicine than his village could provide.

I look at Michael with fresh trepidation, and I can see he shares my thoughts.

Oblivious to our fears, a fine-faced boy brightens up and asks me, "Have you heard the good news?" I have heard this before from *ni*-Vanuatu children; the first time, it stumped me, but I learned that it is always followed by, "Do you know about Jesus?"

I evade the question. "Yes," I reply with a smile, "I've heard it."

Until the latter years of the nineteenth century, the islanders, themselves, had never heard the Good News. But when missionaries arrived to help colonize the islands in the nineteenth century, a veneer of Christianity spread rapidly over the indigenous animism. And, for the most part, the *ni*-Vanuatu still practice a Christianity that seems to have changed little in a century. To sit on decaying benches in an unlit, unadorned, square wooden church, surrounded by the steamy breath of vivid green forest, to hear old Anglican hymns sung in the spontaneous, nasalized harmonies that characterize the traditional vocal style, one imagines a fervent, sweating missionary might any moment swagger to the front of the assembly. But things have changed; bibles are now printed in Bislama, and the islanders have made this religion their own.

Still, alongside this ardent devotion to Jesus, the indigenous ideas persist, still regulating life and social power in communities: In times of social crisis, people commune with the spirits of the dead; misfortune and anti-social behavior are attributed to supernatural forces. Nor is such belief in *tabu*, magic, and all manner of spirits seen as being at odds with Christian practice. And while Jesus's presence is abstract, spirits and demons are manifest around us, giving context and sense to everyday life, providing limits and contrast to our humanity.

At Port Resolution Guest House we are shown to our bungalow. Spacious, with latticed strips of wood for walls under a thatched roof, it contains only two beds and a small table. Accustomed as we are to the lack of electricity and heated water, the bungalow feels luxurious for the mosquito netting covering the beds. Out front lean two wooden lounge chairs overlooking Port Resolution bay, a circular body of placid, azure seawater, ringed by a mango colored ridge that once demarked a volcanic crater.

Had I just arrived to this place from the United States, I might have imagined it the most picturesque and serene spot on earth. *Paradise*. But I came from Ambae—likewise a "paradise," surrounded by the clearest water in the world, water warm as a baby's bath, swarming with vibrantly colored creatures that harbor and hunt in its offshore reefs—and I already know the limits of this metaphor. Already, I had learned to watch out for cone shells and sea snakes near the beaches, to guard vigilantly against malaria, and to lock my door at night.

Lounging in the sun, we hear the faraway booming of Mount Yasur. But for the present, we focus on the tranquil beauty of the bay, and wonder about the resident dugong—a large, marine mammal, cousin to the manatee—who is said to enjoy playing with swimmers. "You notice, the local people don't get in there to swim," Michael observes one afternoon. "It's only the tourists who talk about it."

It is true. We have met a dozen tourists at the guesthouse—French, Australian, Kiwi, American—who speak excitedly about their attempts to flush out the dugong. We watch them swim around the bay in large circles, in search of the elusive creature. We hear them clap and slap the water, following the example of their *ni*-Vanuatu guides, to rouse the old guy. Still, though the guides happily demonstrate how to "call" the dugong, they never venture into the water themselves. Children never wander in above their waistlines. Fishermen stay in their canoes. Only the tourists swim here, to whose chagrin, the dugong does not appear.

In the guesthouse book, we read of past encounters with the dugong and the wistful regrets of tourists who missed him. Some have seen him from a distance or even turned a few delighted circles with him. Others give warnings explicitly or implicitly in their tales: keep your distance; do not attempt to touch him; get out of the water if he swims straight toward you. One marine biologist emphasized his point with capitals: REMEMBER THAT THIS IS A LARGE, WILD ANIMAL. HE IS NOT TAME. HE IS NOT PLAYING WITH YOU.

I am increasingly convinced that an encounter with the dugong is not to be taken lightly, any more so than an encounter with a wild elephant. Listening to more tourists eager to jump in, I am struck by how blithely we pass through here, as though this really is a Paradise: a benign and thrilling place, here to serve our wishes. But the Western dream of a clean, safe, ordered world is not more well met in Vanuatu than it is in most of the world.

In the guesthouse we also hear stories from those who have climbed the volcano. They went up by jeep at night, when the fiery glow is most stunning. They hiked the last ten minutes to the top and stood around for a few minutes, waiting for something to happen. But Mount Yasur has been quiet lately, so there are few tales of spewing lava. One couple says they laid out their bags and slept overnight a few feet from the crater. When I ask if they had been scared, imagining clumps of molten rock raining down on them in their sleep, singeing holes through their bags then their flesh, as the high-tech, synthetic materials ignite, they laugh dismissively as though I am naïve: Bad things will not happen to them; they are Westerners on holiday.

It is our last morning at Port Resolution when a young couple arrives with a bevy of local men who had promised to show them the dugong. They clap and slap and out of nowhere a fat, gray body slides into view under the perfectly transparent skin of the water. It looks about the size of a rhinoceros. Clearly, the young man considers this opportunity a highlight of his life, given the gusto with which he dives in behind the creature.

At first the dugong shows little interest in him, so the young man—an athletic swimmer—draws up behind him. But the dugong, at home in his element, casually evades the swimmer, who laughs and keeps up the chase. Within minutes, however, the game has changed, and it is the dugong chasing the swimmer. He laughs until the dugong makes contact, ramming him in the gut and rushing him backwards through the water. When the dugong moves off, the swimmer appears stunned at his unexpected loss of control, at the unexpected aggression of the dugong, and he moves back towards the shore. Before he reaches it, the dugong is upon him again, having circled round to his front, shoving him forcefully and speedily backwards. The girlfriend on shore looks frightened. And when the dugong releases him and he recovers his breath, the boyfriend swims as fast as he can for the rocks. The dugong comes at him a third time, and the man flails awkwardly, yelling wildly for help. His girlfriend is at a loss, dropping to her knees at the water's edge, and his *ni*-Vanuatu guides, till now clustered on shore, talking amongst themselves, take notice of their man's situation and chuckle nervously. No one, though, is ready to jump in, not even his girlfriend.

I expect the dugong has never killed or seriously injured anyone. He is, after all, a vegetarian. But he makes a clear point that he is nobody's pet and no human is in control here. This place is not paradise, for paradise is a human creation, and this place yet exceeds our human imagination.

A fisherman glides by in his outrigger canoe, and the men on shore coax him to pick up the panicked swimmer. The fisherman complies without speaking, his eyelids fluttering with annoyance. As soon as it comes within range, the swimmer grabs the narrow front of the canoe and desperately tries to pull himself aboard. This capsizes the small craft, and swimmer, fisherman, morning's catch, and fishing gear are plunged into the clear brine. The fisherman sighs as the swimmer still scrabbles with mad futility to mount the upturned hull. By now the dugong has swum off, and the men ashore are roaring with laughter. I am relieved the man is not hurt, but I wonder what stories this couple will tell their friends back home.

Later this same morning, David arrives with his father, sisters, and some friends. We head on foot across the island to Ienemaha. For two hours we hike up and down narrow, forested ridges, between stands of ferns thick and tall as trees. And as we move toward the volcano, we hear more of its clamor. By the time we reach Ienemaha, we smell sulfur lightly on the breeze. The muted rumbling of the volcano blends with the rustle of leaves, the call of birds, and the voices of playing children, occasionally giving way to a fierce, guttural blast.

As soon as we arrive, the village boys are eager to play soccer with Michael and they lead us down to the beach. Michael has carried his surfboard the entire way, an unshakable habit of his San Diego heritage; he is on a quest for the right wave in Vanuatu. So far, no luck: at Lamen Bay on Epi, where he lives, the waters are calm and he had taken to using his surfboard as a fishing canoe. He ended this practice and purchased a tiny outrigger when once, his feet dangling over the edge of his surfboard, he struggled with the monster on the end of his fishing line and realized he had snagged a small shark. Now he looks at the rolling surf with relish, though it still is not as high as he prefers.

I converse with the children in Bislama until they became incoherent with giggles. Then they whisper to each other in their local language, which is completely opaque to me. Before the missionaries and blackbirders and colonists came here, before the populations were decimated, these islands were populated with nearly a million people speaking over a thousand different languages. The fractionization of languages is attributed to the rugged terrain and the surprising fact that, in this land of natural abundance, the traditional cultures were extremely warlike. Apparently, the combined onslaught of Christianity, blackbirding—kidnapping youngsters for the slave trade—colonization, and population decline subdued this aspect of their culture, but most of the original languages have died out. Yet even today, the *ni*-Vanuatu archipelago is home to one of the highest ratios of languages to people in the world. Some 170,000 people speak over a hundred surviving languages.

I learn that David's father is a baker. This means that most days he rises early and mixes up a huge batch of plain, basic bread dough (the only kind of bread one can get on the islands). He cuts and divides it among his couple of dozen aluminum bread pans, then bakes it in his homemade oven. As the sun rises, the bread is done, and he stacks some of it in the back of a hired truck for delivery to a small market; the rest he sells to his neighbors. In this way, David's family has some cash flow, which is used to send David to school on faraway Epi, and to buy the few foreign goods that have become staples of life here, like the cheap Western clothing—produced in China—that is now worn almost everywhere on the islands. The rest of the time, David's father does what village men do: visit with neighbors and take care of whatever needs doing in the home and community.

Like nearly all *ni*-Vanuatu, David's family subsists primarily on traditional horticulture. The garden plots take a fair amount of tending, which is women's work, but the gardens are probably smaller than they traditionally were, since now the table is supplemented with foreign foods such as rice, tinned beef, and Top Ramen, more cosmopolitan cuisine than the staples of taro, manioc, yams, plantains, and the enormous variety of local fruits, vegetables, greens, and seafood. But the most prized food is the occasional pig or cow that gets slaughtered for special occasions.

In preparation for our morning walk to the foot of the volcano, I steal a moment to dash fifty meters down the path to the local store for film. Like most island stores in Vanuatu, this is a square wooden shack with mostly empty shelves built onto the walls. Luckily, this one has a few boxes of film for the volcano tourists, like me.

After dinner, David's father takes Michael away to drink kava. Michael does not relish it, but, being a man, it is expected that he should go. As I settle down with a book and a hurricane lamp, David's mother knocks and steps in for a chat. She entreats me not to run off by myself again. "I have two daughters, and there is a whole village full of girls. Just ask one of them to come with you if you want to go somewhere." She stresses that they do not want me to get hurt, not to fall, for instance. And then she reminds me of the devils in the forest.

I have heard this before. On Ambae I am warned often that I should not leave the village alone, that I should be cautious of *ol devil* who inhabit the surrounds. But this is an injunction I routinely ignore; I walk by myself nearly every day. Still, I have become more hesitant about it, experiencing that, in this culture, a lone woman is fair prey to any group of young men who might wish to exert their will over her. Already I have been chased and grabbed a number of times in various situations, fortunately, never when I was alone in the forest. Listening to David's mother's sincere concern, it occurs to me that groups of roguish boys might be the very "devils" that the women are trying to warn me about.

David's mother also talks about the ancestors who live in the volcano. They sleep in there most of the time, she says. Sometimes they wake up, and that is when the real pyrotechnics begin. She cautions me to be quiet when we ascend the volcano, so as not to disturb *ol bubu*.

I cannot sleep in the cool night air; after months on Ambae, Tannese nights are too cold. When Michael returns, we lie awake in the darkness, listening to the rumbling of the island below and around us. "Are you sure you want to go up there?" he asks. "It's kind of crazy. We don't have to go." I am scared, I tell him, but also certain. At his suggestion, we make a pact: If either one of us gets too scared to go all the way up, for any reason, at any point, we will both turn around and come back down together.

The next day the children take us to the ash flats, a wide, treeless space, a surreal landscape of orange, red, black, and gray, rolling here and jagged there around the edges. The ash cone called Mount Yasur peaks sharply above the plain, and to one side a large pond reflects the bare branches of long dead trees that reach up from its stillness in supplicant poses. Above us, a steady cloud of light gray smoke issues from the crater. As the children play soccer with Michael, I take in what I can, knowing that when we return in the immaculate darkness of the *ni*-Vanuatu night, I will see none of this.

Beneath the stark landscape, the earth rumbles; the volcano's power is inescapable. It is impossible not to feel small. I watch the children chasing the ball with Michael, laughing and playing; they look up now and then, glance at Yasur's smoldering crown. This is a special place, some-where close to the beginning of the world, a place where creation and destruction feel the same.

Fire is like life, disembodied. And a fascination for volcanoes is ancient and universal among those who live around them. They are touch points with the divine, the dwelling places of gods and spirits. The goddess Péle of the Hawaiian islands, the Roman god Vulcanus of Vulcano, and *ol bubu* of Mount Yasur are only a few among them.

After soccer, the children run into the stagnant pool and swim before the bone-white branches of the trees. Perhaps these children already understand something of death. I sense it is not alien to them, not separate. These girls and boys will not be blindsided by the apprehension of their mortality one fine day in mid-life, as we are in the West, witnessing the death of a parent or friend, feeling our bodies dry up. Here, life and death surround them; their lives, the life of their whole community, is poised in between, at the mercy of spirits, magic, and other mysterious powers. Neither will these children grow up to share our illusions of safety, of dominion, of control. Every day tells them that they are only human, small compared to what lies around them, and strength lies in numbers, in community. In the West, we expect the opposite: that strength lies in our individuality; that we are at the top of all things.

It is too soon after dinner that we start back to the volcano that evening. My stomach is overfull with our hosts' generosity. I bring my flashlight, but one of the older children commandeers it for the walk. They grew up in these long, black nights, and can see in it far better than we can. They walk easily in the darkness and flick on the torch only for a micro-second, if something large is in the path.

Emerging from the forest onto the ash plain, no feature of the landscape is visible to me in the moonless night. Only Yasur's luminous, amber halo looms in the sky above us, Venus and Saturn standing as sentinels to each side. It is alive, a breath of fire from blackness.

We make our way across the rough ground. The ascent starts immediately and steeply. The children stop us after a few feet, reminding us to be quiet as we walk; no laughing. And then the way grows steeper, though we follow a path of sharp switchbacks. We are ascending the "backside" of the volcano. This is the way the locals go up, not the trucks carrying tourists. On the other side of the volcano, the truck path goes nearly to the top. But we have a long climb ahead of us.

Maybe it is twenty-five minutes, but it feels like forever, walking blind up a sharp incline, beneath us the ash sliding down from our footsteps into nothingness. The cone is so steep, tipping to one side, I could sit against it; leaning away from it will send me tumbling to oblivion. But we do not rest on the ascent. My rugged sandals are a liability in the deep ash, so I remove them and sink my ankles into its warmth. As we climb higher, more chunks of dried lava litter our invisible path, and the hillside heats up beneath my feet; the crust is thinner near the top.

The slope ends abruptly, and we are standing on the crater's flat lip. A few feet in front of us yawns its cavernous mouth, nearly a perfect circle. The inner walls are illuminated by the glow of lava somewhere deep below. We approach the mouth cautiously until the children tell us to stop. Standing three feet from the edge, I lean over. Anxiously, children grab each of my hands and lean back. I am contained, held by them.

It is magnificent. Some distance below me—I cannot say how far down—a churning sea of iridescent orange. Above it tiny fairies careen, shimmer, and dance, as though in slow motion, whirling drops of radiant lava wheel toward us and then fall back to their source. I am looking back through time, past myself, through the ancestors, and into the eye of god. I have no sense of safety or danger or self-preservation; arched over the mouth of the volcano, I stand outside of time.

Yet it is not long enough. Michael interrupts my meditations. "I have a bad feeling about being here," he says. "Let's go."

For the sake of the promise, I follow him. Our descent is rapid. Following the children, we slide and skid haphazardly through the loose ash, running blindly down the cone, like falling. When we hit the flat, we keep moving without words, swimming through the darkness to the edge of the forest. And there we sit on a craggy stone, looking back at Yasur's halo.

We are not seated more than a few seconds when the volcano lets out a momentous boom. Great, glowing whirls of lava explode from its mouth. We watch them twist skyward, searing light and dark as their surfaces cool and break open again. The largest of the globs leers leftward and thuds finally down on the crater's lip, the very spot where only minutes before we were standing. No one says anything as we watch the lava cool and darken until it is invisible in the night.

Elation comes over me. Awe. Wonder. I am completely alive within the bounds of my pressing mortality. Around me, the children share my secret of life in death. And this binds us, binds all people, I know then.

Michael looks at me somberly.

"Good call," I whisper. He nods.

❧ ❧ ❧

Usha Alexander is a former student of science and anthropology and the author of the novel, Only the Eyes Are Mine. *She divides her time between India and the San Francisco Bay Area. Visit her on the web at www.UshaAlexander.net.*

~~ ~~ ~~

Only Fish

If only life were always so simple.

EACH ITALIAN TRAVEL MORNING AS I HEAD OFF TO see the shinbone of a saint or a (now bloodless) Renaissance anatomy theater, my husband crisscrosses the street in front of me like a hound on a scent. I hold back as he disappears into backdoors of restaurant kitchens or reads menus posted out front. My husband is a chef, and he's in search of what food people call the *vibe*. I wait for the magic words, "That's it. We'll come back here tonight." Those words mean my husband is happy to accompany me the rest of the day.

One rainy week in a small Italian beach town with a single pizzeria, the balance between my husband's hunger for extraordinary dining and my insatiable appetite for the bizarre tipped precariously to my side.

Jeff would have protested a visit to the church

I spotted at the summit above the beach but any destination was an excuse to be in the heated car. We found the narrow lane leading into the backcountry and climbed up away from the sea. Halfway to the top, Jeff suddenly stopped.

"Go in and make a reservation," he said. No kitchen check, no menu review, only a faded sign with a ship's wheel.

I hopped out and went into the restaurant—I'd learned to trust his instincts. "*Buon giorno, buon giorno*," I called out into the silence. A young man appeared and I asked if dinner was being served that evening.

"Yes, yes, but it is a meal of only fish."

"Great, fish," I assured him, wondering why he was warning me about fish, the Mediterranean being directly in front of me. I watched over his shoulder as he wrote our reservation in his book. *Due stranieri*, we were the two foreigners, no names required.

We never found the church that afternoon but at 7:30, pressed and dressed, we returned to the restaurant. The entrance was dark, but the little dining room glowed. Six tables were dressed in crisp white linen and lit from above by globes of hand-blown glass. The young man who had taken my reservation introduced himself as the chef's son. "Come in, come in. *Prego, prego*."

A local couple dressed for a special occasion joined us; a German couple who'd hiked up from the train station completed our party. The dining room sat suspended at the edge of the cliff. Our table had a prime view of the curve of the bay and the rugged outline of the peninsula that hid this spot from an army of tourists nearby. A few lights sparkled in the town below as the sun faded and we turned our attention to dinner.

Edoardo, playing host and sommelier, poured champagne and set out a bowl of pine nuts and white raisins. Polite greetings passed among the three tables and then we began to eat. Our first course was a delicate octopus and tomato salad. Local white wine replaced the champagne, Edoardo attending to each of us as if we were his only guests. Like an orchestra warming up, each couple began to add sounds to the room. "Hmm." "Ohh." "Ahh."

Sautéed squid glazed in an earthy porcini mushroom sauce followed—it slid down silky and smooth. Then came calamari and vegetable tempura, light, fluffy as lace, and topped with crunchy black caviar. We six guests were starting to nod at one another in appreciative accord. We savored each dish and luxuriated in each wine. The grand maestro in the kitchen, as yet unseen, had us in his control. The portions were perfect and I sensed that he was determined to take each of us all the way to the end of the meal.

He slowed our pace with an intermezzo of aioli whitefish and then a clatter from the kitchen announced the end of our pause. Edoardo emerged with inky squid stew. As soon as each table was served, as soon as we were caught in the rapture of the ink, he popped out of the kitchen with his camera and said, "Cheese." We were caught with black teeth and dirty napkins. By now the six of us were laughing and talking the international language of food. Even the older Italian couple, serious about eating and a little reserved, was laughing along with us. The Germans, world travelers, second-time diners here, were eating at full tempo. The noise in the room had peaked and we were having a party.

Without announcement maestro Compiano made his appearance. In chef's hat and apron, a Santa with cherry red cheeks and a smile, he came in carrying his masterpiece: six baby lobsters, steamed bright orange and sporting tomato-red pinchers, climbed the sides of an upright celery stalk. We gasped. Then one tiny lobster at a time, we deliriously ate our way through to the finale. Symbols crashing, violins playing madly, I could hardly hear from the sounds of pleasure in my head. Our eating was done, our *ohs* and *ahs* subsided, and our conversations returned to our individual tables. Only then I remembered Edoardo's warning about fish—fish, fish, only fish—and I smiled.

The chef returned with his crepe cart for an encore. From a pan of flaming banana liquor, crepes were the closing cadence, our sweet goodnight kiss.

Last to leave the party, Jeff went to settle our bill and I went to gather our coats. When Jeff did not return, I knew he had made his way into the chef's kitchen. I heard the sound of two cooks talking the common language of food, and I put our coats back on the hook. The night was about to begin anew—just as it had after meals with gangsters in Rome and farmers in Umbria. This time we would be sharing the ritual glass of grappa with Signor Compiano.

Late afternoon light woke me the next day and I finally asked Jeff, "How did you know last night would be so great?"

"If a place can survive for so long that far from the waterfront, it must be good," he said. Simple. Instinct.

That night in Liguria, Jeff and I had slid from our parallel universes into a new one together—and we didn't want to go home.

❧ ❧ ❧

Bonnie Smetts is a Bay Area writer who spends part of each year in Italy. She shares her adventures on the rough road to fluency in Italian as a guest columnist on italian.about.com. Her essays appear in Travelers' Tales anthologies The Best Women's Travel Writing 2006 *and* 30 Days in Italy.

※ ※ ※

Grandpère

The secret to navigating West Africa is its people.

THE FIRST TIME I SAW GRANDPÈRE HE WAS SITTING on a stoop in the courtyard of a dilapidated hotel in the suburbs of Bamako, the capital of Mali. My first impression was one of surprise, for he looked young, with chiseled features colored in dark chocolate. His sharp, intelligent eyes were nothing like the wizened and compassionate visage usually associated with the term *grandpère*, French for grandfather. He was dressed in Western clothes, blue jeans with an open-necked button-down shirt, hiking boots, and baseball cap. Next to Grandpère sat a more traditional West African man, an overweight moneychanger clad in a sweat-stained parody of a leisure suit. With Grandpère translating between English and French, the moneychanger counted out piles of tattered, filthy notes of Malian currency known as CFA. Grandpère carefully audited the transaction as I offered four crisp hundred-dollar bills to the ersatz banker in return for black-market money. I had never before met Grandpère. I knew nothing of his history or his character. Yet in his presence I somehow felt relieved that my interests were being looked after.

I was traveling with twenty Westerners on an overland journey through the heart of West Africa, from Senegal in the west to Ghana in the south. Nestled between these two coastal countries lies the subSaharan nation of Mali. For many travelers Mali is the focus of a West African visit. Famed for music and art, Mali is home to a variety of unique indigenous tribes and cultures, contemporary remnants of a thousand-year-old empire. While Europe struggled through its Dark Ages, Mali's most famous city, Timbuktu, lured North Africans to a cosmopolitan metropolis known for its wealth and respected as a center of learning and sophistication. Today, Timbuktu is an isolated and forlorn fossil, inhabited by the ghosts of its glorious past and the trickle of tourists who wander into the town from its relatively new international airport. Timbuktu was once a major port on the Niger River. But even that esteemed watercourse abandoned Timbuktu, leaving the city an orphan, cut off from its umbilical, which now flows fifteen miles south of the town.

In Mali, anything or anyone cut off from the Niger withers and eventually dies. The Niger irrigates the history and culture of Mali as surely as it irrigates its crops. It is the dominant geographic feature of the country, the bringer of life, a ribbon of water that provides transportation and communication for most of the nation. In a very real sense, the Niger is to Mali what the Nile is to Egypt, albeit with a French accent.

For most of our trip through Mali we would be following the immense arcing loop sketched on the West African savannah by the river. Entering Mali in the southwest, the great river meanders to Bamako, continues northeast to Mopti, past the Bandiagara Escarpment of the Dogon people, eventually approaching the Saharan town of Timbuktu. After tasting the Sahara there, the river makes a great turn to the southeast, eventually flowing into the Atlantic Ocean in southern Nigeria. As with most things in Mali, my group of travelers would be dependent on the Niger. It would be our nurturer, our mother. Unknown to me at the time, we would also have a father. The father was Grandpère.

Grandpère was a quiet man, invariably courteous, happy to answer questions about Mali or details of our trip, but he rarely initiated a conversation. Despite having an easy laugh, he was not the kind of person who invited inane discussion or idle chat. Although he appeared young, perhaps still in his thirties, Grandpère was able to assert his authority effortlessly, with the easy grace of one who has no doubt in his ability. He was a serious man, but he wore the mantle of responsibility lightly, as if the possibility of things going seriously wrong were so remote as to not warrant undo anxiety. His attitude was exceptional, as Mali is a country where things going seriously wrong are the norm, not the exception.

We drove north, by truck, from Bamako to the port city of Mopti on a tributary of the Niger. Ancient wooden boats, painted in an explosion of brilliant reds, greens, and yellows were moored on the river. Handmade signs advertising Djenne, Gao, or Timbuktu as destinations provided hints to where the boats might be headed. Hawkers ambled along the docks selling hats or shirts, food and cigarettes. The quiet bustle created an atmosphere that seemed to mimic the flow and rhythm of the river. This rhythm quickly changed once we climbed down from our truck. Our presence in Mopti distorted the flow of the town the way a rock in a rapidly flowing river creates eddies and turbulence. Pestering locals surrounded me asking for gifts or offering illicit goods. *"Bonjour mon ami,* where are you from?" poured from multiple mouths, each trying to outdo the others. I tried to smooth the cacophony, offering up simple greetings with a smile and disarming gestures. I tried to explain that I didn't need friends, I merely needed to do a bit of shopping. I spoke in English and in French. My efforts were futile. Visitors were rare in Mopti and were often viewed either as potential marks for absurd scams or benevolent missionaries from a rich idyllic country.

In a fit of exasperation I finally growled *"Je suis avec Grandpère,"* I am with Grandpère. The world changed instantly. Aggressive young punks became solicitous. The pleading eyes of the women hawkers, eyes used to squeeze a sale, were transformed into soft orbs that communicated kindness. A young tough grabbed my hand and led me across the street saying that he would accompany me to the store to make sure the owner did not rip me off. The incantation of the phrase, "Grandpère," had been powerful and immediate, and to me, the results were extraordinary.

We were in Mopti to begin a three-day trip on the Niger. We would motor upstream by day and camp on the shore at night. In the late afternoon of the third day, if all went well, we would arrive in Timbuktu. Grandpère owned the boat. It was a pirogue, perhaps forty feet long and six wide. Helpers loaded up the boat with coolers of food provided by Grandpère, and we climbed aboard. This day Grandpère was dressed West African style in a grand *boubou*, a riotously colored robe-like shift. As we poled away from the wharf, he sat cross-legged on the roof towards the stern of the boat waving his arms and shouting directions to his staff in a mix of English, French, and Bambara, the local language.

I got to know Grandpère a little better during our voyage. He told me how he grew up in Timbuktu. He described a life with no future, only a past. The past was shadowed by the lives of his parents, and his parents' parents. The future was something no one had any control over. One merely endured. We discussed the world of the *marabouts*, the Islamic rulers of the many clans of Mali, the true men of power in the country. I learned how he came to see the tourists of Timbuktu as a potential way out of the fatalistic and overbearing world of West Africa. In his quiet undulating voice he told me how he had approached tour groups as a teenager and offered to carry luggage for less than a dollar a day. He became a guide and led tours through the old Islamic universities of Timbuktu. His keen mind quickly understood the need to move to the next level of the tour business, and so he started making agreements directly with tour companies and travel agencies. He gradually became known in central Mali as the "go to" guy. Local businesses tried to solicit his business, and more importantly, the business of the tourists who were under his guidance and protection. Wielding his newfound power like a stiletto he created alliances among community business and clan leaders. He became a man to be respected. He became Grandpère.

As we slowly chugged down the Niger it became clear
that our group lived within a world of West African pa-
tronage. Grandpère created a corona of security that af-
forded us a view of West African life while insulating us
from the realities of the land. A couple of times a day we
would pull into a village on the banks of the Niger. We
would spend a few hours exploring, talking, and trad-
ing stories with the locals. The villages were invariably
attractive, the people friendly. We took pictures and left.
There were no arguments, no altercations. Grandpère
was everywhere, explaining village life, translating,
overseeing his minions, making sure that nothing unpleasant took place. When pressed, Grandpère would
explain that the Niger was in flood and that most of the
villages we visited were economically devastated. If not
questioned, he left us on our own, offering little in the
way of political or economic commentary.

Only once did he falter. That was when we inadvertently left the Canadian, Tino, behind after one of our
village visits. An hour after leaving the village we put
in for the night on a deserted stretch of beach. Tino
was missing. How had we forgotten him? He had no
money or passport. There were no roads to the village. The river was the only connection between the
village and the rest of the planet. We immediately ran
to Grandpère. Startled, he quickly turned and spoke
in Bambara to one of his helpers. After a brief conversation with his aide, his smile quickly returned. "No
problem," he said in English. "He will be here soon."
Twenty minutes later Tino turned up in an outrigger
paddled by two villagers.

Timbuktu was our final stop on the Niger. Although
the town will be forever linked with mystery and

isolation, Timbuktu is in reality an ugly village perched on the southern rim of the Sahara. Its streets are unpaved, covered with four or five inches of fine powdered dust. The dust seeped into my shoes. When the wind blew, swirls of dust enveloped me, coating my face in a patina of gray. It got into my eyes and into my mouth. When I sipped water to try to wash away the grit, the only effect was to transform the dust into mud, mud that slowly dripped down my throat. My fondest wish was to take a shower and wash my clothes. Late on the last day, I bundled up my river garb and gave them to a local to launder before diving into a luxurious shower in preparation for a farewell banquet organized by Grandpère.

Dinner was a magnificent outdoor affair. Grandpère was dressed in casual Western business clothes. A Malian feast, augmented with local beer, enlivened the retelling of our trip to Timbuktu. For a few hours the gritty realities of West Africa drifted away in the smoky evening air of the Sahel. For the first time in weeks I felt I could completely relax. As I went to pay for the meal, I reached into my pocket to extract the grimy CFA I had purchased from Grandpère and the black marketer so many days before. Instead I found nothing. There was no bundle of notes. Nearly two hundred dollars worth of CFA was missing. In a panic I realized that when I handed my clothes to the cleaner, I had forgotten to remove my money. The amount of cash I had lost was the equivalent to a year's salary for the average Timbuktuan.

I ran over to my guardian, Grandpère, and explained the situation. He listened carefully and said, "Do not worry. The man found the money and took it home for safekeeping. He will bring it to town tomorrow with the rest of your clothes." Problem solved. It never occurred to me that Grandpère might have been lying, or that the man might not return. I was in Timbuktu, one of the most isolated towns on earth, on the edge of the Sahara desert. It was an area noted for its lawlessness and banditry. A stranger had walked away with all of my cash. His home was nearly an hour's walk from town. Yet when Grandpère almost casually assured me there was not a problem, I believed him. Such was his power.

The laundry man returned with both my clothes and my money. As I thanked Grandpère, and wished him well, I reflected on the journey from Bamako to Timbuktu. The story was now complete. Our relationship began when I changed money, chaperoned by his trusting nature. Our relationship ended when the same money was lost, then found, under his watchful eyes. We both promised we would keep in touch, but both of us knew this was a fiction. Grandpère would begin his next cycle with a new group of tourists. I would continue my travels to Ghana. Our paths were now separate. Yet I did not forget him. The image of Grandpère and the mysteries of West Africa remain intertwined. Embodied in his dancing eyes and quick wit is the personification of the continent. Although he grew up in a land of ossified custom and stupefying fatalism he took control of his life and was able to bend the fates to his will.

Whenever I reflect on West Africa now, the smiling face of Grandpère invariably emerges from the mists of my mind. And when it does, a little smile creeps across my own face, a tacit and silent greeting.

❦ ❦ ❦

Ken Matusow is a Silicon Valley entrepreneur. Between technology startups and consulting contracts he usually takes off to explore the developing world, often for months or years at a time. He also works as a volunteer to assist technology companies in remote parts of the globe. Working with groups such as Geek Corps and the International Executive Service Corp, he has assisted and advised technology companies in Bulgaria, Mongolia, South Africa, and West Africa. He lives in Northern California with his wife, Barbara.

≈ ≈ ≈

Smackdown in Tijuana

It was just another night on the town.

It's Friday night in a small Tijuana arena, the kind of rickety Mexican structure that can make you misty for American building-and-safety codes, and in the ring before me, masked wrestlers are smacking and flipping and generally abusing one another for my viewing pleasure.

Whap! The great Hijo del Santo goes down. That's gotta hurt.

The crowd breaks into a sympathetic chant: "San-to! San-to!" I take a gulp of ice-cold Tecate, lean back in my wobbly folding chair (not unlike the ones occasionally slammed onto these wrestlers' substantial heads) and smile.

While many of my fellow Americans are watching Jack Black play an aspiring Mexican wrestler in *Nacho*

Libre, I've come south on this balmy summer evening for the real deal: authentic *lucha libre*—roughly translated, "freestyle wrestling"—the kind practiced by beefy men with such names as El Dyablo who sport menacing masks and, it should also be noted, demonstrate no fear of wearing tights.

It's an easy trip. My wife, Leslie, and I drive twenty minutes from our home in San Diego until we spot a freeway sign that never fails to stoke my wanderlust: "Last USA Exit." Veering off, we park in a lot abutting the Mexican border and walk through a creaking turnstile into the other world that is Tijuana.

I know, I know, Tijuana has a bad reputation. The worst. Poverty. Drugs. Crime. Violence. You name it. It's all true. Just days before my visit, in fact, the heads—and only the heads—of three local police officers turned up in the Tijuana River. It's enough to make even the most intrepid traveler think twice.

But there's more to Tijuana than bad news. As I've discovered since moving to San Diego two years ago, the city offers plenty beyond the one street that most visitors see, Avenida Revolucion, with its bars, strip clubs, and curio shops hawking knockoff *Finding Nemo* beach towels. The scene there, replete with drunken Americans posing for photos atop dejected donkeys painted to look like zebras, calls to mind the famous line attributed to former Mexican president Porfirio Díaz: "Poor Mexico, so far from God and so close to the United States."

Tonight, we take a cab ten minutes to Palenque arena at the city's Hippodrome, where the wrestling extravaganza is scheduled to begin at 8:30.

Out front, in a sprawling dirt lot, a vendor sells corn on the cob from a steaming pot. A man stands before hundreds of colorful wrestling masks for sale, calling out, "*Máscaras, máscaras.*" We buy our tickets at a small window—$18 for two bleacher seats, with tonight's proceeds going to charity—and head inside, savoring the scent of grilling, bacon-wrapped hot dogs. The dimly lit building, with its metal roof and sides, feels more like a tin barn than an arena. We climb a dozen steps and plop down on a long, narrow metal bench.

Radio placards line the ring; beer and brandy ads are plastered across the arena's walls. The wrestlers are nowhere to be seen, but the party is well underway. Around us, early arrivals are devouring mango slices doused with chili sauce. A boy in a gold wrestling mask nibbles awkwardly on cotton candy through a small mouth slit.

I don't see many fellow gringos. The crowd appears to be made up of hundreds of locals—husbands and wives, groups of teenagers, fathers carrying masked toddlers. Down below, in a scene that would give an American property manager liability nightmares, two dozen kids have broken away from their parents and commandeered the wrestling ring, flopping on top of one another, swan-diving off the corner ropes, shouting and giggling. I love it.

Around 9 P.M., a bell rings, the kids take their seats, and a man in a dark suit announces the first match. Four masked wrestlers (two tag teams) take the ring. As the crowd roars, the men take turns beating, bouncing, and flipping one another. One guy pulls a classic Three Stooges stunt and shoots two outstretched fingers at his opponent's eyeballs. It's a bold move. The crowd approves.

The men are facing off in a tradition that dates back to 1930s Mexico. Like World Wrestling Entertainment in the States, the emphasis is not on serious fighting but on fun, family entertainment, and nothing less than the triumph of good over evil.

Tonight's bill features four half-hour matchups, each comprising three rounds. After the second fight, those of us in the bleachers are invited down by the ringmaster to fill the more expensive empty seats below. Hundreds of us file down.

By 11 or so, as the final match draws near, I find myself chatting in Spanish with José, a soft-spoken man sitting nearby with his two boys.

José tells me that when he was a kid growing up in Mexico City, he attended wrestling matches with his father. Now, living in Tijuana, he often brings his sons.

"It's part of our culture," he says. "And we're aficionados." Observing the spectators during the evening, I notice that boisterous fathers tend to have loud, screaming sons and daughters. But the opposite is also true. José is quiet throughout the matches, and so are his boys.

Twelve-year-old Iván and ten-year-old Adrián watch intently, even respectfully, rarely making a sound. Iván clutches photos of his favorite wrestlers, including El Hijo del Santo.

"El Hijo del Santo is a great wrestler," José explains. "He has charisma." The charisma is evident as soon as El Hijo del Santo takes the ring. The son of the great wrestler Santo, who decades ago also made wildly popular Mexican movies, El Hijo del Santo enters the arena wearing a shiny silver mask, silver briefs over white tights, and a long silver cape. His bare, waxed chest shines wth nearly mirrorlike reflective qualities.

This final matchup features some of Mexico's great wrestlers—including El Hijo del Santo, Blue Demon Jr., and Rey Misterio. Tension mounts. "We have some stars here tonight!" the announcer hollers in Spanish.

As the fight gets underway, Rey Misterio bounces off the ropes and slaps Blue Demon's chest. Board-pounding flips ensue. Angel Blanco pins El Hijo del Solitario. The crowd cheers.

Several minutes into Round 2, the action really heats up. Angel Blanco lunges out of the ring and into the crowd, chasing El Hijo del Santo and sending spectators scattering. A cry goes up. Angel Blanco orders several women from their seats, then slams Santo into the chairs and splatters him onto the floor.

A low-level "Oooooohhhh" rumbles through the arena. Leslie winces and chuckles.

I glance over to see José's son, Adrián, rise to his feet and quietly assess the situation. The referee, it seems, is not pleased. He stops the fight and threatens to end it entirely before the final round.

"There are women and children here," an official admonishes the wrestlers. Several wrestlers take the microphone and apologize, requesting that the match be allowed to continue for the sake of the blameless fans.

It's a gallant move, and the audience fills with hope.

"*O-tra! O-tra!*" we chant. Another round! Another round!

The official, in his benevolence, gives the men the O.K., and moments later, to our collective relief, Angel Blanco is pummeling El Hijo del Santo, slapping his head with a ferocity that is rare these days. Then Santo makes a stunning comeback, knocking down Angel Blanco. After several minutes of bodies smacking and limbs whirling, El Hijo del Santo, Rey Misterio, and Rayo de Jalisco raise their arms in victory. We all cheer.

Leslie and I walk out into the Tijuana night, and we are pleased. In this teeming border city with such a bad reputation, the forces of good can still triumph over the forces of evil. And a masked man can be tough even when he is wearing tights.

☙ ☙ ☙

Jim Benning is a Southern California-based writer and the coeditor of World Hum (www.worldhum.com).

GREGORY KENNEDY

~ ~ ~

The Howrah-Puri Express

Life on the rails in India is never, ever boring.

THE HOWRAH-PURI EXPRESS LURCHES FORWARD AND pulls slowly out of the station. My clothes drip with sweat; my mouth tastes of diesel fumes; and my pulse races with adrenaline produced by that glorious combination of beginning-of-the-journey excitement and fear of the unknown. Standing in the open door and watching shrouded figures lurk along the lantern-lit alleyways of Calcutta, I savor the first kilometer of what—assuming all goes according to plan—will be a 10,000 kilometer circumambulation of India by train.

Five of the six berths in my second-class sleeper compartment are already occupied, and I inadvertently use the face of the man lying in the bottom bunk as a springboard towards the empty top bunk. He growls like a bear rousted from hibernation, sending me scrambling into the upper berth where I bang my head solidly on the slanted ceiling. A lump the size of a halved tomato instantly emerges on my crown, and I let loose a stream of internationally recognized foul language that draws derisive laughter from below: the Bear sounds supremely satisfied with this instant karmic retribution, which I begrudgingly acknowledge is his due.

After wrapping a shawl in a sarong to fashion a makeshift pillow, I toss my daypack—which contains everything valuable that I've brought along—in the far corner of the berth, and then wedge myself into the remainder of the cavity. Straining to turn on my side, I see two incandescent brown eyes peer from beneath a shawl draped over the body of a little girl lying on the opposite bunk. Fully extended, she covers not even half the bed, and looks like a Lilliputian compared to my six-foot-tall Gulliver. I smile and wave; she gasps and squeaks and pulls the shawl completely over her head. A moment later she peeks out again and furtively inspects the strange foreigner—me—struggling to make himself comfortable in the opposite berth. But exhaustion eventually sets in: her eyelids droop, her tiny mouth begins to open and close like a goldfish, and soon she is asleep.

Several hours later, still feeling the adrenaline rush, I lie awake listening to the *clack-clack, clack-clack...clack-clack, clack-clack* of wheels on track, and rolling with the sway of the slow moving train as it trundles across the Bengali countryside. The horn blows into the black night and the train picks up speed like a Zakir Hussain tabla, turning to a *clacka-clacka, clacka-clacka* and then a *tshu-tshu-tshu-tshu, tshu-tshu-tshu-tshu,* and from swaying to rocking and rolling.

The woman in the middle bunk below me shrieks!

I sit up and see a scrawny, ragged man clutching a pair of women's flats and standing frozen in the aisle like a deer on the verge of becoming road kill. She screams again, this time letting lose a high-pitched, thirty-second long, verbal barrage. The Bear springs to his feet and head slaps the Thief with the palm of his hand. Another passenger jumps up and punches the perpetrator in the shoulder, and soon a half-dozen men are pummeling the hapless miscreant down the corridor.

One of the vigilantes opens the vestibule door and another unbolts and heaves open the heavy train door. The Bear grabs the Thief by the arm and threatens to toss him off the train. The victim, apparently the Bear's wife, scrambles down to retrieve her shoes, which now lie in the middle of the aisle. She screams something down the corridor, which by intonation I guess to be, "Make the bloody scoundrel walk the plank."

The bug-eyed Thief flops on the floor like a fish and presses his hands together, pleading for mercy like... well, like a man about to be tossed off a moving train. Then the Bear grabs the Thief by the collar, hoists him up, turns to his cohorts, and displays his prized catch. They all yelp in unison. The Bear snarls, head slaps the Thief once more, looks back at his wife, and throws the captured criminal in a heap to the metal floor of the vestibule, where the Thief bows and begs and grovels for several more minutes.

Now the moment of truth has arrived—where macho testosterone meets reality. Will the posse follow through with their hang 'em high threats? No. The Bear and his deputies give the wannabe culprit a few more smacks and then let him go, congratulating themselves as they march back to their berths, apparently satisfied that the induction of sheer terror and humiliation constitute sufficient punishment for an unsuccessful petty pilferage.

Within seconds all is quiet in the carriage. Feeling it is better to be safe than barefoot, I decide to collect my sandals, but just as I start to jump down, the Thief rights himself and runs down the aisle, colliding with me as I hit the floor. The Bear growls. The Thief pushes me away and rushes out the opposite door. I crawl back to my bunk and listen to the Bear's wife berate him, presumably for failing to finish off her assailant when he had the chance.

Once the woman has exhausted her shrill abuse, I look across the compartment and check in on the little girl: like a kitten in a closet, she has slept through it all.

When I wake in the morning, the Bear and his wife are gone. Taking their place is a young, fair-skinned man with a smudge of sandalwood paste on his forehead whom, during the night, I'd seen sleeping on the vestibule floor. He has folded the middle bunk down against the wall, converting the bottom and middle bunks into a single bench, and sits staring blankly out the window.

"*Chaieee...Chaieee...Chaieee...*"

The vendor's deep baritone echoes throughout the carriage. I leap down and order up two cups, then hand one to my new bunkmate and offer him some cashew *barfi*. He smiles politely but half-heartedly, revealing a gap tooth that gives him a boyish look, and introduces himself as Deepesh. When he finishes his chai, Deepesh slumps down in the seat and stares out the window once more. "We have entered Orissa," he says forlornly, without turning his head.

Monsoon rains pelt the half-shut window. Drops slither down the fogged-up glass. Deepesh rubs the window with his shirtsleeve, and through the portal I view a continuous reel of rice fields interrupted only by an occasional hill burping out of the plain. The paddies and coconut palms are vibrant green, complemented by sporadic clumps of red brick houses and strips of red dirt roads, and decorated by dozens of white egrets in every field and hundreds of white lotuses in every pond. Everything uncovered is as saturated as a towel dropped in a drawn bathtub. The train crosses a bridge over a swollen, silt-brown river, slows near a village, and then stops for no apparent reason (as trains in India often do).

The ragged collection of thatched roof houses forms an island in a sea of flooded rice fields. At the edge of the hamlet, a man nestles among fronds in the top of a tall, slender palm tree, cutting coconuts and tossing them to a young boy below. The scene reminds me of a Bengali village I once visited, the home of a schoolteacher I met in western Bangladesh. I tell Deepesh the story of how the schoolteacher and I walked three kilometers along dirt berms separating the ubiquitous rice paddies, were ferried by canoe across a river, walked three more kilometers, and were finally ferried across another river to reach the village. When we arrived, the headman promptly sent a young boy scurrying up a palm tree to fetch several coconuts, and upon return the youth used a razor-sharp machete to hack open each coconut while holding the green shell in his bare hand. The schoolteacher and I slurped the clear, sweet juice directly from the shell and then devoured the tender, white meat. That was the beginning of my love affair with, as the Bengali schoolteacher called them, "fresh young coconuts."

Deepesh does not seem impressed by my story: the scenario is probably as familiar to him as having a burger at Murphy's Bleachers across from Wrigley Field would be to me. But *my* mouth salivates with the remembrance of my first time with a fresh young coconut. And now I crave coconut juice.

As if summoned by my desires, two women from the village run towards the train, one with a basket of bananas on her head, the other with a basket of fresh young coconuts. I wave the women over and buy a small bunch of tiny bananas ("banana poppers" I call them, because their size and shape remind me of a jalapeno popper) and two coconuts. Deepesh smiles again, this time a little wider, when I hand him a coconut and three bananas. Nobody, not even a jaded young man, can resist a fresh young coconut.

"Are you coming from Calcutta?" I ask.

"Yes," Deepesh replies, without elaboration.

"You live there?"

"No."

"Visiting family?"

"I was looking for a job."

"Any luck?"

"No. I have no connection."

Deepesh's taciturn demeanor signals, I assume, that he doesn't want to talk, so I pull out *Gitanjali* and begin to read. But then he taps me on the shoulder, points to the village, and fires off a series of staccato bursts from a machine gun of loquacity he'd kept hidden beneath his overcoat of reticence.

"My village is the same. Many people are growing coconut for oil and juice. Everybody is growing rice. People in my village have cow and goat, for making milk and *ghee.* It is a very, very nice village. Life is simple...very, very simple. Most houses are building from the grass. But my family have a very, very nice house. A brick house. I want to take you to visit my house, like your friend in Bangladesh is taking you. But I do not stay there now."

He stops to reload his lungs; I take the opportunity to interject.

"Does your father grow coconut palms?" I ask.

"No, my father was a priest. But my uncles grow."

"So you're Brahmin?"

"Yes."

"Is everyone in your village Brahmin?"

"No, obviously no. There are one thousand people in my village, but only eighty are Brahmin. Most of my friends are Sudra."

"Can Brahmins mix with other castes in your village?"

"Yes, of course."

"And no restrictions? You can eat with them?"

"Before my father would not allow, he is asking that I do everything correct. But now I do what I like, even eat with my friends in their home. My friends worry me. They say the *panchayat* will drop me in caste. But they are my friends. I will go to their house and eat anytime."

"But what does your father say?"

"My father expired. And my mother expired. If they are alive I will be taking you to my village. But they are not alive."

"Do you have other family?"

"My sisters marry and go to their husband's family. One sister is living in Bhubaneswar, the same like me... my other sister is living in Puri. My uncles and cousins are staying in my village, in my family home, but I do not speak to them."

"Why's that?"

"Because they kick me."

"Kick you? Like beat you?"

"No, no. Kick me. They send me from my house."

I laugh inadvertently at the miscommunication. Understandably, Deepesh does not seem to think anything is funny. I apologize and ask what happened with his uncles.

"My mother expired first. When my father expired, Indian law says I get my father's property, but my oldest uncle says I must give to him. I say no and he kick me."

"Kick you out of the house, right?"

"Yes," says Deepesh. "My sisters get the property also, but they give to my uncle so he don't kick."

"Why do you have to give your property to your uncle?"

"It is the custom—to keep property in the family. But I don't like this custom. It is my land. Why should I give?"

"So you still own land in the village but never go back?"

"Sometimes I go to look my property and see my friends, but I never see my house or speak with my uncles."

"How much property are we talking about?"

"Now I have only ten acres. Before I have twenty, but I give property to my sisters for dowry when they marry, and I sell property to pay for university. Only five students from my village go to university, I am one." Deepesh smiles again, briefly, but his fleeting moment of happy disposition quickly disappears. "When I am going to university I am thinking that I do not need my uncles any more. But I am art stream and after I cannot find good job."

Deepesh explains that in India you are science stream, commerce stream, or art stream. These days everyone wants science stream in order to have opportunities in the booming information technology field, and if they can't get science stream they want commerce stream. The last choice, for most students, is art stream, because it is the least lucrative.

Deepesh shakes his head slowly. "Orissa is very, very bad for jobs," he says. "Art stream is very, very bad for jobs. That is why I learn myself computers and English."

"So what do you do now?" I ask.

"Now I work at the internet shop, but I have no future there."

At the internet cafe, they pay Deepesh "not enough for the living" and he sleeps on the floor. His dream is to own his own shop. "I have many ideas, but no money," he says. "The bank will not give money for little property. I also want to marry, but a man cannot marry with no good economic. No one will marry a man whose family kick and who have no good economic. It is not possible. I thought with a degree I would find good job and can marry. But in India you must have money and power and relation. I have nothing."

"So why don't you give the property to your uncle?" I suggest. "Maybe then he'll support you and you can have your own shop."

"Never! I have my freedom. I can go anywhere and do anything. No one can order me." He pauses. "But no one takes me. No one gives me a chance. I try to join the Air Force...many times...but always they say I'm too short."

Deepesh looks as dejected and deflated as possible for a twenty-one-year-old man, so I resist pointing out that his freedom has only landed him on the floor of an internet cafe, or telling him what I think about a man who wants freedom joining the military. But of all people, who am I to advise Deepesh not to have the courage of his convictions, even if he has to sleep on the floor?

"You know, Deepesh, sometimes you just have to work hard and wait for the right opportunity," I say, attempting to strike a reassuring tone. "You're young and smart; somebody will recognize that and give you a shot."

"This is what my sister says," Deepesh spits back. "She tell me I must work hard and be patient. I work hard, but I cannot be patient. I must have my own shop. Then my uncles will not laugh so loud. Then I will return to my village and build my own house on my own property. A brick house bigger than theirs!"

The rain does not stop, but it slows. Men jump off the carriage to grab a smoke, and I walk to the open door to grab some fresh air. Holding the handle and leaning out over the tracks, I see a young boy in the distance, frantically pedaling a black Hero bicycle that is twice his size, racing towards the train along a muddy dirt road. As he rides closer, his wide eyes narrow and his broad grin turns to pursed lip determination.

The horn sounds. He pedals faster. His foot slips. He almost falls.

I root for the boy, wanting him to make it. Surprising myself with how desperately I want him to make it. The train jumps forward and begins to pull away. I brace myself, and imagine extending a hand and lifting the boy up and into the moving car, but the train picks up speed and bursts through the screen of my Bollywood fantasy.

The boy on the black Hero bicycle stops pedaling just short of the tracks. The disappointment on his face is as palpable as his excitement had been only seconds earlier. But then he sees me in the doorway, and the smile suddenly returns. He waves and shouts "hello, hello" in between out-of-breath gasps and pants. His eyes are once again wide with imagination. This boy is a real life Apu.

The previous day in Calcutta, with an afternoon to kill before heading to Howrah Station, I escaped to a screening of Satyajit Ray's famous film trilogy about a boy named Apu. Apu was born in a village in Bengal: a village just like the schoolteacher's village in Bangladesh; just like Deepesh's village in Orissa; just like the boy on the black Hero bicycle's village in front of me; and just like a million other villages in India. As a child, Apu often heard the distant whistle of a passing steam train.

"Father, where does the sound come from?" Apu asked.

"Over the big meadow, beyond the rice fields," his father replied.

"Let's go there some day," Apu said.

"We will…some day," his father assured.

Apu's father was a Brahmin priest, the same as Deepesh's father, and he left to find work in Varanasi before ever taking Apu to the see the train. But one day, while playing with his sister, Apu once again heard the shrill whistle blow. They dashed across the big meadow and arrived just in time to catch a glimpse of the train as it rolled across the rice fields and vanished into the distance, leaving behind a cloud of smoke that lingered like incense in the air.

Apu's young life was filled with tragedy—he lost both his sister and father to illness—and when he was ten years old his mother took him to live in the home of his grand uncle, where Apu was to be educated as a priest. "Mom, a train!" Apu exclaimed upon arrival at his grand uncle's mud house, pointing at a locomotive plowing through a field on the far side of the family pond. For Apu, sighting the train was like making *darshan* of a god, touching something inside his young soul and setting off a cascade of adventure fantasies. His mother, however, did not share his excitement: she knew well what it meant.

I look back at the boy on the black Hero bicycle, who is still waving, and can't help but think that I was once that boy, and I was once Apu. On the surface, this sounds absurd. The town I grew up in was a cultural galaxy away from their tiny villages. But Naperville, Illinois had one thing in common with a rural Indian hamlet: the town was a sheltered enclave encircled by farms, where every home and everybody were pretty much the same.

Naperville was not poor, but in the 1960s and 1970s it was—at least by American standards—by no means rich either. The town was Middle American, middle, middle-class all the way. A good, comfortable, insulated life: a life that adults in town were satisfied with; and a life that youth in town aspired to. Most youth, that is. But not me.

Like Apu, I longed for escape and adventure. I read and reread *Huckleberry Finn* and *My Side of the Mountain* and *Robinson Crusoe* and *Treasure Island* so many times the pages frayed. And just like the boy on the black Hero bicycle riding across the Orissan rice paddies to catch a glimpse of the Howrah-Puri Express, I rode my Raleigh ten-speed across the Illinois cornfields to catch a glimpse of the Burlington Northern.

An august oak presided over the railroad tracks near Old Plank Road on the then-outskirts of Naperville. I loved that old oak. Its shade was conducive to afternoon napping and its limbs were sturdy and ideal for climbing. The trunk was as authoritative and wide as a column on a Greek temple, but as coarse and gnarled as a dehydrated apple. Just as Huck Finn would sit on the banks of the Mississippi River waiting for a passing steamboat, I would sit under that oak tree by the tracks, jotting thoughts and crude poetry into a spiral notebook, and wait for a passing train. Eventually a train would travel by, and in my daydream fantasies I'd become a modern day Huck. If it was a commuter train heading east, I would imagine myself sneaking on board at the Naper Depot, car hopping one step ahead of the conductor, and riding the gleaming silver carriage all the way to Union Station in Chicago. If it were a boxcar train heading west, I would imagine myself jumping onto a flatbed and riding it all the way to the Rockies.

As a teenager, I left my bicycle in the garage in favor of four wheels and an engine. Whenever the opportunity arose, I'd grab my spiral notebook, jump into my faded Ford Ventura, and fly east down the Eisenhower Expressway into the Loop; or drive as fast as possible as far west as possible on Route 34, sometimes all the way to the Mississippi River, before turning and dashing back by evening before anyone knew I had gone. Even then I could feel the adrenaline rush, the travel high, and longed to go everywhere and see everything. But a short time later I hung my dreams in the closet, where they stayed mothballed for many years.

Apu had no closet. And he chose to pursue his dreams while still a teenager. He talked his mother into sending him to the local school, and after years of inhaling books by explorers such as Livingstone, Galileo, Archimedes, and Newton, he won a scholarship to study in Calcutta. Apu informed his mother of the scholarship while holding a small globe in his hands, and she wept with the locomotive whistle wailing in the background. Apu clutched that same globe when he finally boarded the train for Calcutta: a train that would carry him towards his dreams and his new life in the city, but also towards constant struggle, harsh encounters, and, once again, tragedy.

Down the aisle, Deepesh continues to gaze despondently into the ether of his own thoughts. Like Apu in his mid-teens, and me in my mid-thirties, Deepesh gave up the stability and comforts of home and family to pursue his aspirations. And like Apu and me, he discovered that once you climb aboard the speeding locomotive of your dreams, it inevitably collides with the rumbling freight train of reality. I stick my head out the door, let the breeze blow over my closely shorn scalp, and watch the boy on the black Hero bicycle fade into the distance. Some day, for better or for worse, he will catch up to the Howrah-Puri Express and hop on board. The question is: What happens then?

Deepesh departs at Bhubaneswar station, where the shouts of the vendors and porters and commotion of the embarking and disembarking passengers awaken the family in the opposite berths. A middle-aged man with curly salt-and-pepper hair and mustache converts the bunks into a seat and then sits with his wife and young son. His name is Gopal, her name is Jaya, and their son's name is Sunil.

Jaya offers to share some *parathas* and oranges and I accept. She raps the upper bunk and shouts out, "Prema." Then raps again. "Prema, come get your breakfast."

First I see a foot...then a flash of green...and then, for a brief second, a tiny girl's face as Prema slides down from the top berth and quickly disappears in back of her father.

"She's very shy at first," Gopal says. "But give her a few minutes and she will talk your ear off. Ask her where she's going."

"Where are you going, Prema?"

Prema leaps out from behind Gopal.

"To the sea!" she proclaims.

"It's her first time," Gopal says. "We live in Assam, very far from the sea."

"That is far," I say. "How long is the train ride?"

"Thirty six hours...each way. We're traveling over the Durga holiday, so we will stay only two days in Puri and then return to Assam. But I work for the railway so we get a discount on the tickets."

Thirty-six hours. I can travel to almost anywhere in the world in thirty-six hours. Which makes the southern tip of Africa as accessible to me as the Bay of Bengal is to Gopal and his family.

"Have you been to Puri before?" I ask.

"My father took me when I was young," Gopal replies. "It was the last time I visited the sea. Now I want my children to have the same experience."

"And he wants to relive his own childhood!" Jaya chimes in.

"All men do," I say.

Gopal smiles an appreciative smile, but then turns serious. "It is *important*," he says. "Very few people in our state have ever been to the sea. My whole life, I could always say that I am a man from Assam who has been to the sea. My father gave me that gift. And today I will pass it along to Sunil and Prema."

Prema quietly moves around and sits on her father's lap. Her face is cherubic and round—the roundness accentuated by her short boyish haircut and her tiny dollop of a nose. She wears a frilly, knee-length party dress made of shiny green satin. Her eyes grow wide and her face lights up the compartment like a sunburst through the towering monsoon storm clouds. "Tell me about the sea, Papa," she demands, and begins bouncing on his lap.

"It's as blue as the sky with waves taller than you. And there are beaches as far as you can see and sea turtles and dolphins and fisherman catching fish of every kind. And you can ride a pony up and down the beach. This is what I remember most, riding the ponies along the beach." Gopal looks and sounds as excited as Prema. "Have you ever been to the sea?" he asks me.

"Yes, many times. I lived near San Francisco for six years, only a short drive from the Pacific Ocean."

One of my favorite places in the world is Pescadero Beach, forty miles south of San Francisco. Bordered by cliffs on one side and the ocean on the other, the beach runs for miles without any interruption save for high tide. Whenever I could wrestle an afternoon away from work, I would put my two golden retrievers—Jake and Lady Brett—in the back of my Ford Explorer, wind my way through the magical, mystical redwoods of

the Santa Cruz Mountains, and emerge at the wind-
swept beach fronting the Portuguese fishing village of
Pescadero. Often on weekdays we would have the entire
stretch to ourselves, and I would sit for hours with notebook on lap, jotting down random thoughts, watching
Jake chase flocks of seagulls along the shore and into the
surf, and watching Lady Brett chase Jake.

I look at Prema, so young and so tiny, and recall the
first time I saw the ocean, also when I was five years
old. My parents took my two younger sisters and me to
Charlotte, South Carolina to visit my great aunt. What
I remember most about Charlotte was the moss on
the trees. What I remember most about the ocean was
the starfish and the sand dollars and the wind and the
waves. I have very few memories from that age, but I
vividly remember the ocean in South Carolina.

Eight years passed before I saw the ocean again. This
time my parents took the family to California. For a
Midwestern teenager, Los Angeles was too cool, and
Venice Beach a total rush. But San Francisco was more
my style, and I swore at the time that I'd live there some
day. Seventeen years later I was, in the words of Otis
Redding, "Sittin' on the dock of the bay..."

Since that time I have traveled to many oceans and
many seas in many countries: the Atlantic, Pacific, and
Indian oceans; the Black, Caspian, North, Tasman,
South China, Mediterranean, and Caribbean seas; the
gulfs of Mexico, California, Thailand, and Tonkin. But
Gopal is defined as much by his one trip to one sea as I
am by my many trips to many seas. "I am a man from
Assam," he said, "who has been to the sea."

Prema presses her nose against the window and vora-
ciously absorbs the new world opening like a storybook

before her. She is different. I can sense it. Travelers and
artists always recognize their kind, young or old. Only
five years of age, Prema already has a traveler's gleam
in her eye: the gleam of unbridled excitement and an-
ticipation at the thought of experiencing the new and
unknown; the gleam of pure joy. The Bay of Bengal will
be her first, but there is no doubt that Prema will visit
many oceans and many seas in many countries in her
lifetime. She will have to.

❧ ❧ ❧

*Gregory Kennedy is a writer who lives in Chiang Mai, Thailand,
where he is working on a book called* Clockwise India, *from
which this story was excerpted. He landed in Chiang Mai in 2002,
following two and a half years of travel throughout Asia and the
Middle East. In a past life, before saying "goodbye to all that," and
pursuing his twin passions of travel and writing, he was a Silicon
Valley corporate attorney and business executive.*

❧ ❧ ❧

Immortality and the Art of Losing It

A dance with death teaches a lesson in humility.

THE WIND OUTSIDE THE HUT THREATENED THE PAPER-thin window panes with each new gust, causing loose paint chips to bounce around on the sills like Lotto balls. A storm had been blowing in from the northwest all night, rolling across the Tasman Sea, and chopping waves onto the coastline of New Zealand. The storm then climbed the western slopes to the front door of this abandoned cabin in the mountains.

The gut of New Zealand's highest range, the Southern Alps, sprawled in every direction outside the hut's crooked entrance. From the soured mattress inside, I could barely make out piles of mountaintops stabbing up through the underbelly of a thick cloudbank. And I noticed that near the upper reaches of the highest peaks, the clouds were beginning to untangle themselves from the sky, bringing in a wash of silver moonlight. The storm was weakening.

At the first glimpse of a star, I kicked one naked leg from the warmth of my sleeping bag and stuffed toes into a stiff climbing boot. Digging them down, the cold leather groaned, as if annoyed by their presence. My other leg followed, and soon I stumbled out the door where I hopped around in predawn dimness, gathering warmth for a pee.

Bracing against the wind, I was relieved to find the scent of foreignness still in the air, the same scent that continually reminded me I was far from home, on a remote island in the Pacific, and was therefore allowed to act out my deepest impulses of adventure. The scent had given me the ability to climb in the mountains of New Zealand as if I were invincible, endowing me with a certain strain of confidence I had never before felt.

It all started the moment I stepped off the plane from Honolulu and waddled past customs with a new country under my heels. Outside, I noticed the sun was sharp and hypnotic, and the land itself seemed to vibrate with the movement of far-off glaciers. A trance-like state gripped me, some outward force latched onto my common sense, and I was kidnapped for nearly six months while the rest of my body scooted off to climb in the Southern Alps. After a dozen peaks were conquered without harm, I was convinced that each successful peak I scaled in New Zealand would allow me to become more and more invincible, and quite possibly, could lead to powers of immortality.

Back inside the hut, I choked down wet granola, filled my backpack with an assortment of vitals: ice axe and crampons, helmet, map, stove, sleeping bag, and bits of food. The sun was still far off to the east, projecting shadows on some other distant land.

I followed a vague trail through the mud-choked valley and noticed the forests beyond seemed to invent new noises: strange chirps, odd whistles, loud insect sirens that hadn't reached the Amazon yet. And the shape of a mountaintop came into view, hovering above the beech trees.

It was Mount Oates, one of the peaks I had come to climb during that particular weekend in late autumn. Angling away from its summit, I saw a high ridge sketching a skyline to the west, past unnamed ripples, to where it eventually rose to meet the mighty haunches of another peak I had come for, Mount Franklin.

My plan was to climb steep portions of snow and rock to the top of Oates, then traverse across the alpine ridge that led toward the incredible hulk of Franklin. It was to be a long and difficult traverse with uncertain obstacles. Steep rock? Obnoxious exposure? A bivouac?

Moving on, I found a snowfield on the eastern side of Mount Oates and hiked toward it, passing through an invisible line where all things green faded into the grayness of old rock, schist, and limestone where the sea once sat. I fit crampons over the soles of my boots and moved onto snow as hard as oak.

After an hour of rhythmic slogging, I found a gully that had been carved into the mountainside by a century or more of rock slides. I hurried up it before the rays of a new day could lick the relative safety of frozenness away from its loose innards, then stumbled onto the summit of Mount Oates.

But there was little time to celebrate. The ridge I had come to explore buckled down and away and into a cloud soup, poking out once in a while on its journey to join Mount Franklin. The ridge looked lengthy, perhaps two miles in its entirety, and had been sharpened by ice age storms and tectonic movements. Glaciers rubbed against it, perhaps a thousand years later, and left it twisted and serrated like a busted bread knife. Below the ridge, I could see ancient snowfields lapping at its edges. And beyond, all things tall blended into the horizon before dipping into the Tasman Sea.

I moved quickly past nasty drop-offs, dodging the occasional tumble of gendarme parts that protruded from the steepled ridgetops. Once again, I enjoyed a feeling of mightiness, one I could smell, almost taste, on the kiwi wind. And it was my hankering to find that gift of immortality that kept reality at bay and calibrated my fear to courage. At the top of a mere bump on the ridge, I discovered that a section of it had broken off during the last millennia of erosion, leaving me nowhere to go. I was forced to downclimb until I could skim its base, thus avoiding the chunk of missing crest. Down there, I found a few goat bones littered across the rubble, reminding me that I, too, was made of such things.

I needed to regain the ridgetop in order to position myself for Mount Franklin, but the only way I could do that was to ascend the continuation of cliff that lay in front of me where hanging boulders and moss parts collected to define the eastern border of the ridge. The cliff was slick and ugly and looked steep enough to fall freely from if climbed improperly.

But there was little time to stall with my conscience. So I began to climb, hand over hand, foot beside foot, upward, in the usual manner. In fact, I paid little attention to the space that slowly separated me from the ground. Instead, I focused on the several hundred feet of exposed climbing I needed to negotiate before I would be able to flop over the ridge and continue on toward the brawny flanks of Mount Franklin.

Everything was going as planned: The ground was becoming increasingly blurry beneath my legs some 50, 100, then 200 feet below; my nerves were staying where they should; and I was speaking to myself in a low, hushed voice about something entirely off the subject of solo mountaineering.

Suddenly, and unpredictably, a tiny piece of moss disagreed with my boot placement, a slight tug of gravity disrupted my composure, and I felt my weight shift.

Before I could prepare myself, I noticed that I was slipping off the rock. And in that surreal moment of astonishment, I felt something muscle in on the false front of confidence that had been built over the past few months of climbing in the Southern Alps. Just when I needed them the most, my thoughts of immortality began to fade.

The slip was small in a relative sense, and lasted only a few seconds, but the message it sent to the rest of my body was in a font every cell understood: If you let go, you die.

There was clarity in the moment I accepted this as truth. Unfortunately, this did little to help my situation. With an unexpected abruptness, my knees began to jiggle and then opted to quake, my fingertips vibrated and threatened mutiny on their grip, and my head wobbled off my neck and hung there like an overripe grapefruit. My mind played a moving image of me peeling off, spinning through the air, and landing in a heap of compound fractures on the rubble where the goats had already pioneered such feats.

I begged to be anywhere else in the world than on that mountain. I begged to be nursing beers with the boys back home on a Monday night during football season. I begged for the feel of ocean currents and swimming pool lounge chairs. And to rediscover just how great ice cream tasted.

Pathetically, I decided to partake in the number one no-no when dealing with height-related problems: I looked down. And when I did, I saw that the forces of death were gathering beneath my feet. I swear I could feel them mulling my fate.

I attempted a downclimb, but it resulted in another slip and an unplanned shriek. There were only two apparent choices here: Hold on until fatigue forced me to let go or continue upward and face death fighting.

The next handhold was six inches above my left shoulder, a funny-looking piece of rock that seemed to be attached to the cliff side with kindergarten paste. I tested its strength, closed my eyes to the point of pain, and cranked on it. Nothing bad happened. So my feet followed and somehow found holds for themselves. Then little edges appeared from nowhere as if summoned by my terror.

I continued, always on the verge of slipping, for what seemed like hours, and in hindsight, it must have been that long. At times I felt like I was about to go, but each time I would hold on just long enough to find another hidden ledge, a teetering bit of rock, or chunk of moss with good roots.

I remember the frantic relief that coursed through me the moment I crawled to safety on top of that ridge. And I remember how my mind searched for an emotion to fit the moment but found that it had not been given the chance to invent one yet. During this time of inde-scribable relief, I noticed that something was glowing in front of me. When I lifted my head, I saw I was standing above the most beautiful sunset I had ever seen.

To the west, the colors of dusk bred with a newly ap-proaching storm, along with glimpses of a turquoise sea off to one side and pink-rimmed mountaintops poking out from behind. To the east, day-old sunshine blended with the gray-backed hills of the distant Craigeburn Range, and farther on, the mutton-field flatness of the Canterbury plains conjured up the hues of a late-sum-mer forest fire.

It dawned on me that I had never stopped to extract what this land was really lending me: the ability to live my dreams and to build an appreciation for the powers locked in mountains. It was apparent that I needed to live through the days of New Zealand and come away with an understanding for the wholeness of this power, not pieces of it. The lap dances with death and missions to conquer peaks were a misinterpretation of this gift, and I felt silly knowing that just a minute before, I had narrowly escaped a disaster that could have wiped away all of this.

The Southern Alps aren't a place one goes to die; they are a place one goes to begin living. To follow their empty paths and travel to their highest holds was only a part of it. The rest lies in trying to incorporate such beauty and adventure into the bonds of real-life living.

I had persuaded myself that the immortal qualities of mountains would somehow rub off on me the more I tested my own mortality against them. Instead, they proved to me that humans are only capable of living and dying while mountains are the ones that keep on going.

It may be said that flirting with death while climbing is often unavoidable, but it should never be used as a tool to discover the true delicacy of living.

The reality of this was staggering, and it forced me to collapse to my knees where I placed elbows on thighs and cradled a heavy head between my palms. The only thing left to do was cry. Which I did, in repentance, until the last veins of orange, gold, and sapphire had disappeared into the western sky.

❧ ❧ ❧

Thaddeus Laird is a freelance writer who specializes in adventure travel and outdoor-related articles. Visit www.thaddeuslaird.com to see a variety of his published articles that chronicle his experiences around the world.

❧ ❧ ❧

Over There

A renowned writer recounts his four days
as a sexual prisoner in Africa

THIS TOOK PLACE FORTY YEARS AGO IN AFRICA, AND
still I ponder it—the opportunity, the self-decep-
tion, the sex, the power, the fear, the confrontation,
the foolishness, all the wrongness. The incident has
informed one of my early novels and several short stories.
It was something like First Contact, the classic encounter between the wanderer and the hidden indigenous
person, the meeting of people who are such utter strangers to each other that one side sees a ghost and the other
side suspects an opportunity. It won't leave my mind.

I had gone from America to Africa and had been
there for almost a year: Nyasaland. Independence came
and with it a new name, Malawi. I was a teacher in a
small school. I spoke the language, Chichewa. I had a

house and even a cook, a Yao Muslim named Jika. My cook had a cook of his own, a young boy, Ismail. We were content in the bush, a corner of the southern highlands, red dust, bad roads, ragged people. Apart from the clammy cold season, June to August, none of this seemed strange. I had been expecting this Africa and I liked it. I used to say: I'll get culture shock when I go back home.

With Christmas approaching I went via a roundabout route to Zambia and on Christmas Eve was sitting in an almost empty and rather dirty bar outside Lusaka, talking to the only other drinkers, a man and woman.

"This is for you," I said, giving the man a bottle of beer. "And this is for your wife. Happy Christmas."

"Happy Christmas to you," the man said. "But she is not my wife. She is my sister. And she likes you very much."

At closing time they invited me to their house. This involved a long taxi ride into the bush. "Happy Christmas. You give him money." I paid. They led me to a hut. I was shown a small room, the woman followed me in. I stepped on a sleeping child—there was a squawk—and the woman woke him and shooed him from his blanket into the next room. Then she sat me down, and she undressed me, and we made love on the warm patch on the blanket where the child had been lying.

That was pleasant. I had had a year of women in Malawi, the casual okay, the smiles, the fooling, Jika's bantering, Ismail's leers. But, in the morning, when I said I had to leave, to go to my hotel in Lusaka, the woman—Nina—said, "No. It is Christmas," and made a fuss.

The brother—George—overhearing, came into the room and said that it was time to go to the bar. It was hardly eight in the morning; yet we went, and drank all day, and whenever beer was ordered, they said, *"Mzungu"*—the white man is paying, and I paid. We were all drunk by mid-afternoon. The woman was taunted for being with a white man. She answered back, drunkenly. The brother stopped several angry men from hitting her. Loud, drunken fights began in the bar.

We went back to the village hut and I lay half-sick in the stinking room. Nina undressed me and sat on me and laughed, and jeered at me.

I was dressing in the morning when she asked me where I was going. Once again, I said I had to leave.

"No. It is Boxing Day." And she summoned her brother.

"We go," George said and tapped my shoulder and smiled. His smile meant: You do what I tell you to do. We spent Boxing Day as we had done Christmas: the bar, beer, fights, abuse, and finally that dizzy nauseating feeling of mid-afternoon drunkenness. Another night, Nina's laughter in her orgasm and in the morning the reminder that I was trapped. "You stay!"

In her refusal to let me go was not just nastiness but a hint of threat. And her brother backed her up, sometimes accusing me of not respecting them. "You don't like us!"

When I protested that of course I did, they smiled and we ate boiled eggs or cold peeled cassava roots or a whitish porridge, and then off we went to the bar, to get drunk again in the filthy place. And as she grew drunker she pawed me and promised me sex—now an almost frightening thought. Another day passed and I realized I did not know these people at all. The food was disgusting. The hut was horrible. The village was

unfriendly, the bar was outright hostile. The beer drinking was making me ill. I was the only *mzungu* in the
place—as far as I knew, the only one for miles around.
The language that I knew—Chichewa—was not their
language, though they spoke it. Their own language—
Bemba, I think—was incomprehensible to me, and I
knew they were plotting against me when they spoke
it—quickly, muttering, so that I wouldn't know what
they were saying. I belonged to them, like a valuable animal they had poached. Whenever they wanted money
for beer, for snacks, for presents, for whatever reason,
they demanded it from me. When I handed it over they
were excessively friendly, the woman kissing me, licking
my face, pretending to be submissive; her brother and
the hangers-on praising me, praising America, saying
Britain was bloody shit and asking me to let them wear
my sunglasses.

That first night I had been wearing a light-colored
suit. The suit was now rumpled and stained; my shirt
was a sweaty mess. They were the only clothes I had.

They said what a great friend I was, but I knew better: I was a captive. They were out of money. My weak-
ness and arrogance had sent me straying into their world
from my own world. And I represented something to
them—money, certainly; prestige, perhaps; style, maybe.
After the first night we never had a sober conversation. I
was a color, a white man, a *mzungu*. I had been captured
and they wanted to keep me: I was useful. When they
said, as they often did, "You no go!" I was afraid, because
they spoke with such irrational loudness and threat. The
boldness in Nina that had attracted me I now feared as
wildness. Drinking deafened her and made her a bully
as cruel as her brother. George peered at me with odd

brown-spotted eyes, as though at an enemy. Sometimes at night I was wakened by the human stinks in the hut.

I think it was the fourth day. My terror was so great and the days so similar I lost track of time. We went to the bar in the morning and at noon they were still drink-ing—I had lost my taste for it, as I had lost my libido; I just stood there and paid with my diminishing wad of *kwacha* notes. I said, "I'm going to the *chimbudzi*."

"Go with him," Nina said to one of the tough boys hovering near. I protested.

"He will not come back," she said, and I realized how shrewd she was. She had read my mind, another sug-gestion of her malevolence. I took off my suit jacket and folded it on the bar.

"Here's my jacket, here's some money. Buy me a beer, get some for yourselves, and hand over the jacket when I get back." The *chimbudzi* was outside the bar, a roofless shed behind the tin-roofed building, upright bamboos and poles. Maggots squirmed in the shallow bog hole. I stood there and was too disgusted even to unzip, and then I stepped outside, looked around, and seeing no one, I ran—at first cautiously, then really hard until I got to the road and flagged down a car. Of course the man stopped. He was African, I was white, it was Christmas, he needed money for petrol. He took me to my hotel: I had not slept even one night there. I asked him to wait, I paid my bill and got in again and when the driver said where, I said, "Just keep going." He drove me twenty miles outside town and dropped me at a roadhouse, where I spent a sleepless night.

What a fool I had been to trespass. The time I spent had not helped me to understand them. Apart from my initial sexual desire, my curiosity, my recklessness, there

was no common ground, other than mutual exploita-
tion. I was reminded of who I really was, a presumptu-
ous American. In spite of my politics and my teaching in
the bush school, I was little more than a tourist, taking
advantage. To me they were desperate Africans, seizing
their chance to possess me. It was Tarzan turned inside
out, and redefining itself. I saw nothing more. I had simply feared them and I wanted to get out of there. Later
the incident kept resonating, telling me who I was. Much
more dangerous things happened to me in Africa—serious fights, deportations, gunplay—was there anything
more upsetting than being held at gunpoint? But this
was my first true experience of captivity and difference,
memorable for being horribly satirical. It had shocked
me and made me feel American.

꧁ ꧁ ꧁

*Paul Theroux is the author of many books, among them the travel
classics* Riding the Iron Rooster, The Old Patagonian Express,
The Great Railway Bazaar, The Happy Isles of Oceania, Dark
Star Safari, *and* The Pillars of Hercules.

❦ ❦ ❦

The Mexican Taco Stand

In the land of *mañana*, behold the engine of now.

FEW PEOPLE ORDINARILY ASSOCIATE MEXICO WITH efficiency or logistical savvy. On the contrary, most tend to either love or hate our southern neighbor for its glaring lack of both. *Mañana* is a concept charming to those in no particular hurry, but maddening to those who want it done *today*. In Mexico, time is not money. It is rare to experience there the mechanized and streamlined flow of goods and services that we have come to demand and expect in the United States. There is one exception though: the ubiquitous Mexican taco stand. The Mexican taco stand is a wonder of compact efficiency and economy of space. Unlike the Mexican government or the Mexican postal service, the Mexican taco stand gets the job done without a shred of pageantry, pretense, or waste.

Every evening around sunset, on street corners and under sidewalk storefronts across Mexico, taco stands appear out of nowhere. Amidst a flurry of activity, a small metal cart with a cooking space, a serving counter, and a gabled cloth or metal awning is quickly transformed from a rattling trailer pulled behind a vehicle— or a drooping wagon pushed by hand—into a hive of industry. Heavy fry pans are brandished. Gas cylinders feeding the burners are rolled into place. Grimy ice chests full of syrupy bottled sodas are filled with opaque, angular chunks of ice. Stacks of three-inch corn tortillas are laid out, ready to be warmed on the griddle. Knives and cleavers are sharpened on a whetstone. And meat is put to the fire. All kinds of meat: blood-red tubular links of *chorizo*, wafer thin sheets of *bistek*, whole pink cow tongues, spongy white sacks of *tripas* covered with little tentacles, and thick bacon-like slabs of *pastor* speared on a steel spit. Electricity is provided by a charitable neighbor or is borrowed from the electric company through a spliced wire dangling inconspicuously from a nearby utility pole. The grease-splashed light bulbs hanging underneath the awning spill light over the cooking area and surrounding sidewalk. With clouds of heavy smoke boiling out from under its colored awning and the alluring aroma of spicy meat gurgling in pans of melted fat, the taco stand is open for business.

The Mexican taco stand is not a restaurant. It has no tables and no waiters. It is not a place to sit and socialize over a leisurely meal. Rather it is a way station, a place to stop for nourishment and society while en route to somewhere else. Its first patrons of the evening are hungry connoisseurs heading home from work or going out for a night on the town. They stand and share gossip and news between mouthfuls of steaming hot tacos and swallows of ice-cold sodas gulped from frosty glass bottles. The men behind the counter tell jokes and swap yarns with customers while they work. Their deft hands fly from the stacks of tortillas to the mountains of chopped and sliced meat keeping warm on the rim of the *comal* before plunging into metal bins of the finely diced onions and cilantro that garnish the tacos. Their hands move with such speed and adroitness that it's difficult to determine what type of taco is being prepared until it's slapped onto a plastic plate wrapped with cellophane and slid across the chest-high countertop towards a hungry customer.

When a patron has finished his tacos, he pulls the cellophane wrapper—now dripping with grease—off the plate, tosses it into the trash can, and hands the clean plate back to the man behind the counter where it is wrapped with fresh cellophane and placed back on the stack to await a new customer. It is now time to pay. The taco stand's payment policy holds firmly to the honor system. After the plate is relinquished, the patron nods to the man tending the cash box behind the counter and asks, "*¿Cuánto es?*" The moneyman reaches over the counter and takes the bills and coins from the customer, deposits the money in his metal box, and hands back any change due. Sometimes, if he also doubles as a cook, he'll wear a cellophane glove on the hand that handles the money, but only sometimes. The honor system works quite effectively: for the customer's convenience, he is allowed to enjoy his tacos, unencumbered with paying until he is finished eating. For the taco stand's benefit, the tab is left open, increasing the chances for another order of tacos. It is an arrangement at once efficient and symbiotic; it is a relationship built on trust. Lying to the moneyman about how many tacos one consumed is an unthinkable sin tantamount to treason, like stealing from one's own family.

Later in the evening, the taco stand becomes an olfactory magnet for hungry revelers streaming out of the bars and clubs, following their noses and growling stomachs to the source of the seductive aromas drifting through the streets. The activity swarming around the taco stand meets a crescendo at the point in the evening when bars shut down. Drunken partygoers gorge themselves on gluttonous orders of tacos, as bright orange grease soaks through the scraps of corn tortillas resting on their plates. To provide entertainment for the late night crowd and to make a few pesos, a group of street musicians, or perhaps a lone guitarist wearing crusty old leather sandals, shows up and begins belting out the standard compositions of the taco stand soundtrack. As the last remaining appetites are sated and the glassy-eyed night owls teeter home through the yellow patches of sodium-vapor streetlight, the taco stand winds to a halt.

As quickly as it was set up, it is cleaned and dismantled. The cooktop is scoured, ice chests are drained and put away, clattering pots and metal bowls are stacked and stored, trash bags are leaned against the utility pole, the money is counted, and the cash box is stowed. The wire supplying complimentary electricity is disconnected and the light bulbs under the awning go black. The Mexican taco stand, resplendent in its austere compactness and minimalist efficiency, rattles off into the darkness, disappearing from the street corner until the next evening. If only the Mexican government and Mexican mail were as dependable.

≈≈ ≈≈ ≈≈

Pickett Porterfield lives in a small town close to San Antonio, Texas. He has lived in and traveled extensively throughout Mexico. When he's not busy planning another trip south of the border, he writes about his experiences and impressions there.

❦ ❦ ❦

A Visit to Dixieland

"In the dark night of the soul it is always
three o'clock in the morning."

—F. SCOTT FITZGERALD, *THE CRACKUP*

I HAD KNOWN THE OLD PLACE IN ITS BEST DAYS AND IN its worst, having first visited it in its heyday, when it served as a popular stopping-off place for weary sojourners in the Southern Mountains. In those days the people of Asheville, North Carolina knew it as "My Old Kentucky Home," which became the Dixieland of author Thomas Wolfe's coming-of-age novel, *Look Homeward, Angel.* I later saw it as little more than a ghostly shrine almost destroyed in 1995 by an arsonist whose forebears, like many of his generation, apparently bore a heavy grudge against the author for his too-explicit description of Asheville and its townspeople.

It was on my last visit, after restoration was all but complete, that I heard the story that has tickled the fancy of natives for well on three-quarters of a century: how F. Scott Fitzgerald, another author of great power, had crossed the Atlantic and taken a hard, jarring trip by train into the heart of the North Carolina hill country to have a look at Wolfe's boyhood home. The two men had known each other intimately during Fitzgerald's days of debauchery in old Europe.

The trip to Asheville turned out badly, for Fitzgerald had barely knocked when a boarding-house madam (Wolfe's own mother) recognized him immediately, even though, to the visitor, she was still a stranger.

"Sorry, we don't take in drunks," she said, sweeping dust onto the shoes of the great man, drunk though he was and had been and would be again, and poking at him with the end of her broom.

"O house of Admetus," Wolfe had called it, after the abode of a mythical Thessalian king doomed to an early death by the goddess Diana. Like Admetus, Wolfe had felt the sharp sting of alienation and doom, often describing himself as "forever a stranger and alone," drawn relentlessly "inward upon that house of death and tumult, as the guests came with their dollar a day and their constant rocking on the porch."

Fitzgerald had come alone to Asheville, having stopped in Baltimore long enough to deposit his schizophrenic wife Zelda into an asylum for the incurably insane. Zelda, a good old Alabama girl who, like her husband, was seeking to recover from a decade of Continental binges. By some accounts she was suffering not only from schizophrenia, alcoholism, and drug addiction, but was also a certified nymphomaniac.

What a life they must have had in France! My experience has been that you have to spend some time learning how to deal with France before going there for any extended period of time. But Fitzgerald had been there for so long he was almost like a native. His 1935 visit to Dixieland was just one more ignominious event in what had been just about the worst year of his life, creative luminary or not. A drunken and sex-crazed wife for whom he apparently still felt affection even though she spent every spare moment looking for other men—enough in itself to drive a fellow to drink.

Worst, the book that was supposed to have been Fitzgerald's masterwork, *Tender Is the Night*, had been a critical flop and brought in little money—though now, ironically, Modern Library ranks it as one of the top one-hundred novels of the Twentieth century while consigning Wolfe's *Look Homeward, Angel* to the scrap heap. Could the remote, haunted glens of Asheville banish the ghouls and demons that had all but destroyed Fitzgerald and his wife during their last years on the Continent?

It was indeed his last great hope. He had come into these hills hoping to find a magical restorative: his wife, transferred from Baltimore to Asheville, would recover her health and youth and beauty and sanity while he—sober again—might at last begin to produce works that would rival *The Great Gatsby* and win him back his lost critical acclaim.

All for nothing. Fitzgerald's visit was a mere interlude in more long days of failure—and somehow symbolic of what his life had become. He sat drunkenly at his writing desk, typing out magazine articles that were mostly rejected, novels that went nowhere. He turned again to hard liquor and then, repentant, went on the wagon, which, for him, meant the consumption of anywhere from thirty to forty bottles of beer a day.

He would commit himself to days and nights of writing and then say that he needed alcohol for inspiration, claiming that his work was sterile and flat if he wrote in a sober frame of mind. But then he would get drunk and wander the streets, unable to get a single line down on paper. After a really serious binge he would sometimes attempt to straighten himself out. Sometimes, though rarely, he would even try to get off beer and onto Coke or black coffee. But beer was still his only real methadone.

The summer of '35 marked the beginning of what was possibly the most debilitating binge of his life, an experience that eventually found expression in *The Crack Up*, a book that was almost as much of a mess as he was. Yet there were some good things in it, including one of the most memorable lines he ever wrote: "In the dark night of the soul it is always three o'clock in the morning." Mostly the writing was stale, but he began a half dozen or so short pieces, that also found a place in *The Crack-Up*, the best of which were "Pasting It Together," "Handle with Care," and the title piece. But mainly the book was little more than the story of his fall to literary mediocrity and nervous prostration.

The real problem was not simply his binge drinking. He had not cared enough about his work apparently to keep up with the times. He was still writing about the Twenties, flappers, speakeasies, the Jazz age, when people wanted to read about the Great Depression, the woes of the working class, the wars in Europe. Drunk or sober, nothing seemed to work for him in those days. Long after he left Asheville he began to recover some of the old fire in *The Last Tycoon*, a novel that remained unfinished when, in his early forties, he died of a heart attack.

Before his demise, however, free at last and yet still proclaiming love for his wife, Fitzgerald had taken a room at Grove Park Inn, lavish haunt of Henry Ford, Thomas Edison, Enrico Caruso, William Jennings Bryan, and many another creative giant of early twentieth-century America. He would spend the summer there, being drunk, pretending to write, and, with Zelda still ill and more than a little crazy, bedding down at least one wealthy young married woman who came his way. Rosemary he called her, a lovely creature, so we are told, who was visiting Asheville with her sister. Rosemary began to talk of marriage, of leaving her husband, a prospect that the author did not relish. Yet he could not bring himself to break off the affair. That was left up to Rosemary's sister, who threatened to carry news of this tawdry business back to her home in Memphis and to the ear of her husband.

He attempted a second affair with a certain Laura Guthrie Hearne, a palm reader and journalist of sorts, who had also come south for her health. She kept a journal, and worked as a secretary for the author during his rare sober moments. But the affair went nowhere, at least as we have it from Mrs. Hearne, who published a part of her journal in the December 1964 issue of *Esquire*. Of course, we do not have Fitzgerald's side of the story.

For all his failings, Grove Park has nevertheless honored him by placing his photo alongside those of Bryan, Ford, Edison, Caruso, Harvey Firestone, and many another heavy hitter, though little enough it was that he accomplished during his stay.

Wolfe's mother was still renting out rooms—though no longer providing three meals a day—on the afternoon that Fitzgerald came knocking. In Paris he had once asked Wolfe "why he felt that he needed to put everything in his work." Wolfe is said to have replied: "Why did Shakespeare?"

Anyway, there he was, with dust all over him, having taken time out from a blazing affair and from his feeble attempts at writing, in the hope of getting a good look at the inside of the house that Wolfe had described so eloquently in *Look Homeward, Angel*. All he got for his trouble was an ignominious scolding from Wolfe's mother, the formidable Eliza Gant of his first work and its sequel *Of Time and the River*.

"You just go on now. We don't cater to your kind around here."

Built in 1883, The Old Kentucky Home in its best days drew as many as 18,000 visitors a year. The house was old enough to claim a certain renown of its own, but it would have been lost to the bulldozer long ago if there had been no Thomas Wolfe to transform it into an enduring part of America's literary heritage. The youngest of seven children, Wolfe was the only one to know the place as home. His brothers and sisters came each day to help with the chores, but at night they would escape to their father's Woodfin Street stonecutters shop and home, the "warm center" of the author's own early life.

Wolfe had lived at The Old Kentucky Home from the time he was eight until he went away to Chapel Hill and later to graduate school at Harvard. It is the last of its kind on a street once crowded with other high, brooding mansions much like Wolfe's Dixieland.

I had often heard of its numerous hauntings, of the "alien presences" that had bedeviled the author's childhood. I began to wonder how much of what I had heard was true. I had barely stepped into the gloom of the front hall when—already—I began to feel that same dark feeling of "death and tumult," and something even more palpable: a quick fleeing sound of footsteps upstairs, perhaps even a low hum of voices.

"Hardly," said site manager Steve Hill. For I was his only visitor. He at once dragged me to the upper story, perhaps thinking to put me at ease. I'm not sure that is what happened. In the upstairs bedrooms an even more oppressive spell of premonitory gloom fell over me with an insistence that could not be easily explained away— maybe because I had been told that that was where all the ghosts were. The ones that kept staring at you out of all the old news photographs.

If not Wolfe himself, surely his father would have been the happiest fellow in town to see The Old Kentucky Home go up in flames. If the arsonist had got there in time, the old stone-carver no doubt would have hewn him out a special "angel" for his mantelpiece. The elder Wolfe refused to join his wife in her infamous abode for a good fourteen years before falling ill and being forced to come there to die. As the author has his fictional father say:

> "Woman, you have deserted my bed and board, you
> have made a laughing stock of me before the world....
> Fiend that you are, there is nothing you would not do
> to torture, humiliate and degrade me.... Ah, Lord!
> It was a bitter day for us all when your gloating eyes
> first fell upon this damnable, this awful, this murder-
> ous and bloody barn..."

Many of the townspeople of the day shared his contempt for the "murderous and bloody barn," which apparently did not always enjoy the best of reputations. The whole family came off much the worse for it. "You will still find strongholds of people who detested the entire family," said Hill on the afternoon of my visit. "Many people considered the family kind of rowdy. They were into things that they didn't want their kids exposed to. They were often told 'Don't play with the Wolfe children!' And there is one old gentleman in Asheville who says he was always told to walk on the other side of the street from the boarding house."

Mrs. Wolfe's forebears, however, had been respected and relatively well-to-do. Some were among the first settlers of this remote mountain country. Nor was she herself altogether the flinty moneygrubber depicted in *Look Homeward, Angel*. But her neighbors—and in time all of Asheville, to say nothing of Scott Fitzgerald—knew her only as the hard-eyed proprietress of the faintly disreputable boarding house at 48 Spruce Street, known for many years before the arsonist got to it not as The Old Kentucky Home or Dixieland but simply as the Thomas Wolfe Memorial.

The darkly varnished floors, the stark eerie whiteness of the plastered walls, the high, dim ceilings, the dining room set as though to receive guests, the chairs and tables and settees that seemed almost too heavy for their delicately carved cabriole legs—all remained as Wolfe knew them in the first days of the last century.

It was one of those houses that never seemed quite light enough even at the brightest part of the day. Hew down all the great oaks that crowded in upon it, throw open all the doors and windows and it would have still

been the same: some lingering hint of primordial darkness that could never be quite banished.

Indeed, to Wolfe the very idea of light and warmth
were alien to the house. The most autobiographical of
novelists, he once wrote of how young Eugene Gant, his
alternate persona, had fled in panic and dismay from
all those alien presences: "He went into the hall where
a dim light burned and the high walls gave back their
grave damp chill. This, he thought, is the house."

The feeling presses itself on you even more profoundly
as you wander the upper halls, something invisible yet
ever-present, ominous, at once seductive and repugnant,
some of the old anguish and pain and unspoken yearning, as you hear again the forgotten voices, the mur-
murous echoes of those long ago summer evenings, the
guests rocking and talking on the veranda, the clink of
silverware and hearty laughter as the dining room filled
for an early dinner—yet the feeling of death always
there, in summer, yes, and even more so in winter, with
the "remote, demented howlings of the burly wind" raging about the house. And always those haunting refrains
that, once heard, can never be quite forgotten:

> "Which of us has known his brother? Which of us
> has looked into his father's heart? Which of us has
> not remained forever prison-pent? Which of us is not
> forever a stranger and alone?"

After all that how easy to forget that Dixieland was
occasionally the scene of good times as well as bad.
Wolfe fanciers will remember no doubt that he—or
young Gant—returned from college one spring to enjoy
a love affair, his first, with a girl he called Laura James.

The affair ended badly. But it inspired one of the most memorable flights of lyricism in all of American literature, a quality found everywhere in Wolfe and too-seldom matched even by our finest poets:

> "Come up into the hills, O my young love. Return!
> O lost, and by the wind grieved, ghost, come back
> again, as first I knew you in the timeless valley, where
> we shall feel ourselves anew, bedded on magic in the
> month of June."

Laura James, or Clara Paul in real life, died soon after leaving Dixieland, from what we are never told, only that her passing was for Wolfe a reminder of how quickly all life flies:

> "Quick are the mouths of earth, and quick the teeth
> that fed upon this loveliness. You who were made for
> music, will hear music no more; in your dark house
> the winds are silent. Ghost, ghost, come back from
> that marriage...we did not foresee, return not into
> life, but into magic, where we have never died, into
> the enchanted wood, where we still lie, strewn on the
> grass..."

Wolfe's verbal excesses—his tendency to over explain, his sprawling, adjective-laden sentences—were often as great as his virtues. Yet few contemporary writers have been more frequently quoted. And when he chose to set flight into pure lyricism he had few, if any peers, among American novelists—or poets. No, he did not have to bow even to Whitman, another undisciplined literary giant whose few excellent poems have made the world forget the many that are beyond redemption.

Wolfe died too soon, a mere thirty-eight, of a rare type of tuberculosis, just as he was beginning to gain control over his stylistic eccentricities. The Thomas Wolfe Society keeps his name alive after a fashion, and, of course, the house is always there, to remind one of the tumult it created in the young man's life, as well as in the life of his father.

Lamentable though it may be, it appears that we are about to lose him again. Once a giant among American writers, more than a match for the Fitzgeralds and Hemingways and Steinbecks despite his excessive wordiness, he now ranks pitifully low among twentieth century American writers. Not only has Modern Library ignored *Look Homeward, Angel*, it likewise has chosen none of his other books for its list of the one-hundred best novels of the twentieth century. Neither did a Modern Library poll of readers put him there. *Angel*, however, has never been out of print. Still, like the Italian composer Salieri, in his competition with Mozart, his voice grows fainter and fainter until "almost no one reads him anymore." His books remain as little more than literary curiosities, despite the best efforts of his editors to pare down the bloat; so that no longer do his words, as he said in another context, "make new magic in a dusty world."

Much of his best work deals, naturally enough, with the themes of escape. As a young man he thought of himself as "speeding world-ward, life-ward, Northward out of the enchanted, time-far hills, out of the dark heart and mournful mystery of the South forever." For all that he never really escaped the spell of "the house." With the undoubted exception of Ernest Hemingway, he would become the most traveled of authors, leaving his footprint on all the great cities of America and the Continent. But always his thoughts, willingly or not, turned toward home, toward the indomitable hills, toward the house that had infused him with a "grave-damp chill" and premonitions of early doom.

One would always wonder, while wandering those massive halls and hearing the echoes of that far-off time, the muted voices, whether Wolfe could ever have been quite the author he was—if he could ever have been any sort of author at all—had it not been for the house he called Dixieland. Yet, like Wolfe himself, a visitor is never disposed to linger overlong. The house, dark even at midday, casts its inexorable spell, and as one meanders from floor to floor the twilight seems to come ever more quickly. Like the young Thomas Wolfe, one began to think of escape, of fleeing "worldward" and "lifeward," putting the "dark and mournful mystery" of the house forever behind him.

So it was and so it is again, on another summer's day as you walk the halls of a now restored Old Kentucky Home, the gloom once more settling over you as though the alien presences remain ever-present despite the best work of the arsonist. Your footsteps quicken and your breath comes hard as you turn toward the door, toward sunlight, the voice of your tour-guide mingling dimly with the not-quite-heard voices that still abide—yes, you are sure of it now—amid the ruinous clutter of the "murderous and bloody barn." Outside, you pause to look back, at the high gabled roof half hidden in the trees and untouched by the fire, at the young man bus-ily painting a new set of balusters, at the wrap-around porch where Eliza's summer guests—men and women not always of the best character—sat rocking away those long ago August evenings.

It was good to have seen it again, to have known, however briefly, something of the moods that helped shape the life and work of a man destined to become one of the nation's most enigmatic novelists. To have been there, yes, and felt much of what the author had felt; but there would always be more than just an ordinary sense of relief that you had now put it all behind you—that you, too, had escaped into a world where light and warmth were no longer mere "alien presences" and where the traffic and clamor of a busy Asheville afternoon seems a most welcome reprieve.

❧ ❧ ❧

Hunter James has published eight books, spent more than thirty-five years as an editorialist for the Baltimore Sun, Atlanta Constitution, *and other newspapers, and spent a season as a fellow for the National Endowment for the Humanities. He has won numerous awards, including a share of the 1970 Pulitzer Prize for Public Service, and published many articles in nationally-circulated magazines.*

ROBERT L. STRAUSS

❧ ❧ ❧

Next Year in Germany

Reluctantly and without a plan, an American
uncovers his family's poignant past.

FOR MANY YEARS I THOUGHT ABOUT TRAVELING TO
Germany. My father, who died when I was three,
and my mother's second husband, the man who brought
me up, were both German Jews. Although curious about
their roots, I had an ingrained hesitation, an aversion to
Germany and things German that kept me from traveling to their ancestral homes. It was only when my wife
Nina became pregnant that we decided it was time to
learn about the past before starting a new future. When
we crossed into Germany, the border was nothing more
than a small creek on a small country road: no guards,
no passport inspection, nothing but a welcoming sign.
The skinheads we imagined lurking behind every corner
were nowhere in sight.

My grandmother, Hannah Eichenbronner Strauss, came to America from Germany as a teenager in the 1890s. Her only child—my father, Fred Strauss—predeceased her in 1959. Three years later, my mother married Henry Levinstein, my father's best friend. It was Henry whom I came to know as Dad and came to think of as my father. Unlike Fred Strauss, who had been born and raised in New York City, Dad had been born in Germany, in a little town called Themar that wound up in East Germany. Dad died in 1986, never having spoken a word about his first fourteen years in Germany. Neither did his mother, Nanette, who lived more than half her 101 years in Germany and left there only in 1941.

I don't know that my mother or two brothers ever asked much about their experiences. I knew that Dad's father, Moritz, had died in Germany in the late 1930s. I remembered conflicting stories, that he had died in a concentration camp—or perhaps not, but that he had been in a concentration camp. After Dad died I found a few postcards in an old desk. Some were from Moritz, from Buchenwald, making it clear that he had at least passed through a camp.

My wife and I left for Germany equipped with very few pieces of information to guide us. One was the name of the village where my grandmother Hannah had grown up. Weisenbronn is much too small to appear in most atlases. I found it on a tourist map given to me by an old friend of my father who knew a little of the family history.

The other piece of information we had was a photograph of Dad as an infant. There was almost nothing to give away the location of the picture except that the uppermost part of a building could be seen in the background. In the photo, Dad couldn't have been more than two years old, so we imagined it came from 1922 at the latest. The picture could have been taken in Themar or in some other town; we had no idea. By the time we decided to visit Germany, there was no one left who could tell us.

As we drove deeper into rural Germany, Nina and I were surprised how much it looked like the Germany of fairy tales. The dark dense forests. The villages, perfectly nestled in the folds of soft hills, each with its narrow church steeple. The ancient houses, spotlessly maintained, no window without flowers. We found ourselves making fewer comments about skinheads lurking behind each bend and more about the natural beauty of Deutschland Mitte, as our map called the country's midsection.

"Do you have a plan?" Nina asked me for the dozenth time as we approached Weisenbronn. I didn't. I supposed only to go to the cemetery and see what we might find. It wasn't actually until we passed Rödelsse, a neighboring village, that the name Weisenbronn finally appeared on one of the directional signs that were set at every crossroads, pointing to all the tiny villages in the area.

Weisenbronn was one of those tiny villages. It sat in the melded laps of a few low hills and seemed almost to be smug, solidly content in its beauty and long history. There were no large signs welcoming us to town. No drive-through restaurants. Very little that proclaimed itself loudly or garishly to be modern or hip or new or improved.

Fields of corn, hay, sunflowers, and grapes extended in all directions until interrupted by the red roofs of neighboring villages. From the summit of a large hill above Weisenbronn we could see half a dozen such small farming towns, each with its church steeple and gingerbread Rathaus (town hall). It was easy to imagine winter smoke rising from hundreds of chimneys, fueled by the endless cords of stacked firewood that crisscrossed the area like hedgerows. But we arrived in summer, on a warm, sunny Saturday afternoon. A cluster of crosses on the village directory marked the Friedhof, the cemetery. It took just a few minutes to walk there.

Four women were working in the cemetery tidying up. Not a blade of grass was out of place, no stone unpolished. Every grave was blanketed with plants and fresh flowers. We said our *"Guten tag"* to the ladies and began looking around.

"You know, there aren't going to be any Jews in this cemetery," Nina said, pointing out what perhaps should have been obvious to us right away. There was no Hebrew, no Stars of David, on any of the stones.

"Bitte," I said to one of the ladies. *"Meine Obermutter, Eichenbronner, aus Weisenbronn,"* I explained, using up all the broken, incorrect German I had absorbed. The ladies shook their heads. They didn't know Eichenbronner. They didn't know Strauss either.

Sometimes Nina and I travel well equipped, with guidebooks and dictionaries and phrasebooks. This time we had decided to go without. In Germany we wanted to force ourselves to interact with Germans, to question them and depend on them. We arrived in Weisenbronn speaking no German, with no guidebooks and no English-German dictionary.

"Why don't you ask her?" Nina suggested, gesturing to an older woman who stood a few feet away.

"*Namen?*" she asked. Strauss and Eichenbronner, I told her. Hearing Eichenbronner, the older woman said to her younger friends, "*Hebräisch*" and "*Jüdischer.*"

Immediately I became apprehensive. I had no idea how people would react to interloping Jews poking around their towns, their cemeteries, their history. I as much expected to be told to go away as to be helped. But the ladies did not seem the least bit uneasy. I went ahead.

"*Ja,*" I said while pointing to Nina and me, "*Jüdischer.*" I can remember as a kid thinking it better not to identify myself as a Jew, and even telling people that, yes, Strauss was German but that my family was Lutheran. Once I told my mother that I didn't feel Jewish at all. "Tell that to Hitler when he comes back," she said with uncharacteristic bluntness. And here we were, in Germany, telling complete strangers, the fathers of whom did who knows what in the war, that we were Jewish.

The older woman said "*Jüdischer Friedhof in Rödelsse, nicht in Weisenbronn.*"

Before heading back to Rödelsse, we took a quick walk around the town. Weisenbronn itself was as tidy as the cemetery, immaculate homes and perfectly clean, smooth streets that hardly seemed in need of the repaving that was going on. In the center of the village were two inns, a convenience store and a bank with an ATM that would give us money from our account in San Francisco. And not fifty feet away were half a dozen homes that had barns right behind them filled with pigs, and front and back yards piled high with *misthaufen*, neatly kept heaps of manure. Everything in Weisenbronn was the stereotype of German precision—except the air, which reeked, almost burned, with the smell of fermenting pig waste.

"Do you have a plan?" Nina asked again as Rödelsse came into view.

"We'll go to the cemetery," I told her.

"I can't believe we came to Germany without a German dictionary," she said.

We didn't have to enter the Rödelsse cemetery to know we were in the wrong place. Beyond the gates were only crosses. Three women sat outside, keeping company. We greeted them and asked, *"Bitte, Jüdischer Friedhof?"*

This inaugurated a prolonged discussion in which the women clearly disagreed about the least complicated way to find the Jewish cemetery. One of the women finally decided to show us. In the car she chatted continuously, in German, while directing us through town. (A characteristic of all the Germans we met was that even after it was completely apparent that we did not speak German, they would just keep prattling along.) *"Schlüssel,"* the woman kept saying. We arrived at the tidy home of a pig farmer. "Moment," she said before going into the house.

She came back a few minutes later. In her hand she carried a small canvas bag the form of which clearly outlined a book. "Juden Freidhof" was written on the canvas. She turned it over and out slid a key. *"Schlüssel,"* she said.

At the edge of town she told us to stop. She was going to her garden and would not accompany us any farther. Over and over she repeated the directions to the cemetery—in German. Left, then right, then right again. We nodded our understanding, but in front of us there was nothing but farmland and open country. The road wound into the fields and disappeared from sight.

At the first left we curved around a field of blossoming sunflowers. The first right took us among vineyards and stacks of firewood. The next right and we were off the pavement, heading into what seemed to be nothing but open fields. "Oh my," Nina said softly.

Ahead of us a Star of David, silvery in the shimmering heat of the summer afternoon, rose above a small building that formed one corner of a large, walled compound. Inside we could see countless gravestones, most of them hip- or even shoulder-deep in vegetation.

With only the name of a town, we had flown across nine time zones and driven a day and a half. A twist of the key and the lock on the gate popped open. Each link of the heavy chain rattled as I pulled it free. We went in.

The weeds in the cemetery were not forgiving ones. Wild roses with stout shoots and thick thorns grew entangled among flowering purple thistles. Each step was like breaking trail in the brambles of a fairy-tale thicket. Flowers bloomed everywhere. Butterflies and bees swarmed, busily at work, unused to intruders.

Many of the stones had sunken so that only the tops, carved as crowns, were visible. Those still high above the ground were mainly obscured by weeds. Only by stamping could we see the engravings. Within minutes Nina had to stop; the bristles of the overgrowth had already made dozens of small cuts on her bare legs.

The weeds weren't the only obstacles. Termite mounds hidden in the thick grass gave way like rotten floorboards. My ankles caught on the rusting andirons and chains that outlined decaying plots. The jagged edges of broken slabs raked my shins. It was very slow going. Before I had made my way through the first row, Nina called out, "Did you see over there?"

The cemetery was large, perhaps three acres or more. Nina pointed to a far corner I had not yet seen where there were hundreds of graves. It seemed pointless. Many of the stones were corroding, with large fragments flaking away as if from pieces of stale pastry. Only the marble markers were legible. Yet many of those were in Hebrew. It would have taken us forever to decipher them. Nina, pregnant, impatient with the improbability of it all, waited uncomfortably. My "plan" was not working. I finished the first row having found nothing. There were Rossmans, Sterns, lots of Sondheims and one Einstein. But no Eichenbronners and no Strausses.

From beyond the cemetery walls, fields rolled down to red-roofed Rödelsse. The cascade of a church carillon spilled over the cemetery. It was a gorgeous afternoon. My jeans were damp with sweat. Pollen caked my hands and neck. My every pore itched with the heat. I began the second row of thirty graves.

It took me forty-five minutes to work through the first two rows. I thought I would plod through the next four and then take a cursory look at the hundreds of other stones. A few graves into the third row I stepped on the overgrowth and saw "Samson Eichenbronner" clearly marked in black marble. The year of death: 1923. Next to Samson was Louise Eichenbronner, died 1926. I had never heard either of those names. Were these my great-grandparents? The grimy sweat that had soaked my jeans turned chill with the discovery. I continued looking.

We spent two more hours in the cemetery, finding no more Eichenbronners. As I looked, Nina read through the visitors' book that we had been given with the key. There were excerpts from German books on

Jewish cemeteries and hundreds of signatures, mainly in German but many in Hebrew and a few in English. As we left the cemetery an ultralight plane flew overhead. A hot-air balloon rose not far away, perhaps on a late afternoon tour of the vineyards. I leafed through the visitors' book and although I could understand almost nothing of what was written, I was overcome with a sense of connection and deep sadness. Here were dozens of people who had come to this out-of-the-way cemetery, trying to make sense of a senseless past. It felt as though history was washing through us even as it had ignored and abandoned these hundreds of graves.

At the house where we had picked up the key it took a minute or two for the old man to answer his door. Thirty steps away, fifty pigs clustered at the barn gate. The smell was overwhelming. I handed him the book and the key. "*Danke*," I said. His face and hands were rough, hard-worked. He took the things from me and said nothing. I had no idea who he was or why he was in charge of the key. I had no way to ask.

We sat in the car as I jotted down some notes. The old man came out of the house and slowly, stiffly, walked over. He leaned down and put his head in the window. Somehow we signaled that our visit had been worthwhile. He hung around for a few minutes as though he expected that we would learn German just from his presence. But we didn't. He nodded, and went back to his house.

We had dinner that night at the only place that was open in Weisenbronn. Our waiter suggested what type of wurst we should have and what type of local beer I might try. We told him that we were looking for family roots.

"You forgot one small detail," Nina said as the waiter went to the kitchen. I hadn't told him we were Jewish, still nervous about how that "small detail" might be received. The waiter came back and told us that no one in the place knew any Eichenbronners. That's when I told him we were Jewish and that there hadn't been anyone in the town for a long time. "Obviously," he said, quietly. In a word that might have been cynical, he somehow combined his limited English with melancholy and compassion. I explained that as far as I knew the Eichenbronners had left before Hitler. "Anyway..." he said, as though that fact should give very little consolation.

A while later he returned with a name and number. We should contact the Burghermeister, Herr Müller, who knew all the local history and spoke English fluently. He would be able to help us.

The next morning I tried to call Burghermeister Müller. But the pay phone wouldn't take coins and, on a Sunday morning in a small town in Germany, there was no place where I could buy a phone card. Plus Nina was anxious to move on. We had found the cemetery. We had found names. Perhaps that was enough.

"Let's at least drive around town before we leave," I said. In the car it wouldn't take long to cover Weisenbronn's few streets.

We could have missed it just as easily as we saw it. In the first block one of the homes had a signboard with the name Müller carved on it. As we passed, a man came out the front door.

"*Herr Müller?*" I asked.

"*Ja,*" he said.

"*Burghermeister Müller?*" I asked to make certain.

"*Ja*," he said.

"*Sprechen Sie Englisch?*" I asked.

"*Nein*," he answered.

With my crippled, elemental German, I explained about "*Meine Jüdischer Grossmutter aus Weisenbronn.*"

"Moment," he said gesturing for us to wait as he left the house.

Ten minutes later he reappeared with an elegant, sixtyish woman. She had short gray hair and a chiffon scarf draped over her red jacket, which seemed very fashionable in a town whose every corner smelled of animal waste.

I again explained about Meine Grossmutter Eichenbronner and Frau Hoffman answered, in very good English, that she knew "a great deal" about "your great-grandfather," Samson Eichenbronner. "What would you like to know?" she said.

It was 10:30 in the morning. We spent the next five and a half hours with Frau Hoffman.

On the patio behind the Burghermeister's home, Frau Hoffman told us of Samson Eichenbronner's service in the Prussian-French war of 1870-71 and how he had started the local veterans' club after the German victory. She explained his cattle-trading business: buying them in Rhön, an impoverished area far away; shipping them by train to the railhead a few miles north of town; and then hiring local boys to drive them south to Weisenbronn.

Frau Hoffman then took us down Kobaldstrasse and showed us the Eichenbronner home. She told us how the Jewish community leader, Herr Herbert, had resisted on Kristallnacht, the night of breaking glass, when the Nazis ransacked his house, and how he never returned after being taken away.

I still wasn't entirely certain that Samson Eichenbronner was indeed my great-grandfather. From the pay phone on the corner, I called AT&T Direct and was talking to my mother in New York in seconds. "How many brothers and sisters did Grandma Strauss have?" I asked her. It was early in the morning in New York, and it took Mom a while to wake up and gather her thoughts.

"Oh I don't know. There were a lot," she said. "Maybe ten or twelve. I think only three or four came to this country." Frau Hoffman had said there had been eight children.

"What did Grandma Strauss' father do?" I asked. Mom said she thought he was a Pferdehändler, which is literally horse trader. But the German word is very close to Fleischhändler, or cattle or meat dealer. The numbers, the dates, the occupations were all close enough. Samson Eichenbronner was certainly one of the ancestors I had come to Germany never imagining to find.

We wondered why this elegant schoolteacher had become so interested in local Jewish history. She explained that in 1982 one of her sons had begun a history of the Jewish population of Weisenbronn as a school assignment. Many people did not want to talk at that time, but one man, who had once worked for Samson Eichenbronner, spoke so voluminously that the son grew tired and called in his mother for help. Soon she became more interested than he. Now retired after forty years as an art teacher, she continued to research local Jewish history. Nina asked her why.

As a teacher (and a German), Frau Hoffman was very precise with her words. She told us that "bad things, evil things" had happened in Weisenbronn.

She thought people, particularly the younger generations, should know—even if some did not want to know.
Frau Hoffman was also a religious person. She had been
to church that morning, and to the cemetery and to her
garden as well.

She told us that there were things in her past, more
precisely in her parents' past, that made her feel guilty. It
wasn't so much guilt, she explained, but a sense of sadness
and remorse. While she grew up knowing that bad things
had happened to Jews, she first believed as she had been
told: that they had only happened in Berlin and the other
big cities. But there was also the memory of smelling fire
as a six-year-old in her home town of Nördlingen and
then seeing the charred remains of the synagogue the next
day. And the memory of the first time she saw an adult
cry, when a Christian neighbor and family friend came to
her childhood home after his Jewish wife had been taken
away. He sat there among his neighbors and sobbed.

Over lunch at the Gasthaus, we talked about how
thrilled she was when Germany was reunified and how
she had never believed it would happen, how she was
certain it could never happen and how her relatives from
East Germany showed up at her door the very day the
border opened. I sensed that because of the separation
she had experienced in her own family, she understood
why Jews sometimes come back to Weisenbronn.

She explained that the Rödelsse cemetery dated from
1432. "Can you imagine? That's sixty years before
Columbus," I said to Nina, trying to grasp the notion
of Jews, my ancestors, having lived in one place for
500 years. I have moved nearly twenty times in the last
twenty years. Here families once lived—and some still
do—in one place for half a millennium.

Nina asked Frau Hoffman why the cemetery was even still there. She figured that the Nazis would have attempted to erase every trace of Jewish existence, even that of the dead. Frau Hoffman explained that the local people have always been deeply religious and even those who were the most ardent Nazis would not disturb the dead. Somehow that transcended their idea of who should live.

From her file, Frau Hoffman pulled out the Weisenbronn census. The Germans had been very precise about record-keeping. In 1910 there had been 836 people in town and 44 Jews. In 1925, the population had risen to 882 but the number of Jews was down to 27. In 1939 it had fallen to nine. In 1942 the census became more precise, enumerated monthly. In February of 1942 there were three Jews left in Weisenbronn. In March, there were none.

Eventually there were no more questions to ask. It was time to go. We thanked Frau Hoffman and told her as best we could that what she was doing was a very good thing. As we left Weisenbronn, Nina said, "You know what she does is so wonderful. And she's doing it just because it's the right thing to do." It seemed to us that we had been guided to her. There had been too many coincidences along the way for it to simply have been chance.

Had the gravestone been illegible, as so many were, perhaps we would have driven on. Had we not seen Burghermeister Müller's sign, had he not been at home, had Frau Hoffman not been at her home when Herr Müller bicycled over, we would have left Weisenbronn with only memories of graves. There would have been no other pictures, because our camera battery had given out just after we arrived. In a little town in Germany, on a Sunday, there was no place to buy a replacement.

※ ※ ※

Robert L. Strauss served as country director for the Peace Corps in Cameroon from 2002 to 2007.

❧ ❧ ❧

The Purple Umbrella

It quickly became the symbol of an entire culture.

I HAVE A SNEAKING SUSPICION THAT AN UMBRELLA IS A BIT of a security blanket for many Japanese—rather like the soft and fuzzy *ngouk-ngouk* I used to carry around with me when I was five and one day accidentally incinerated on a floor heater. If there is a hint of rain—just one errant cloud in the sky—umbrellas start popping up like mushrooms on rotten wood. Shops have extra ones that they give out to customers who might otherwise suffer some terrible, soggy fate. It's just possible that Japanese are water-soluble and don't want the world to know.

I don't carry an umbrella. My backpack weighs eighty-eight pounds, and that's only after I threw out my flashlight, trashy novel, the bottom half of my toothbrush, and my toilet paper. I am not water soluble, so if it rains I just get wet.

One day as I am leaving a small pension in Tottori, on the back side of Japan, it starts to drizzle. The old lady who owns the place calls after me to wait. She ducks back into her kitchen and re-emerges with a monstrous purple umbrella. It's made of wood and oiled paper and is sadly scuffed and splintered. She hands it to me. I thank her and hand it back. The thing weighs at least four pounds and has a little yellow knob on the top that makes it look like a cross between a giant pimple and a bruise. We stand there and pass it back and forth until I give in, bow profusely, and shuffle off down the road, clutching the center column of my new semi-portable wood-and-paper ceiling.

Two days and several hundred miles later I can't stand it anymore. The umbrella doesn't fit in my pack, won't hook over my arm—and since it hasn't rained for a while, is about as useful as a stick of firewood. I decide to "lose" it. Unfortunately Japan has only two kinds of public garbage receptacles—one for recycled soda cans and the other for newspapers. I feel funny trying to stuff the umbrella through the little round hole meant for cans and am terrified that someone will catch me frivolously disposing of what is clearly a Valuable Tangible Cultural Asset. So I decide to send it to umbrella heaven—the Lost and Found department of the Japan Railway System—where it can party forever with the hundreds of thousands of other umbrellas that get left on trains every year.

I pick a day when I have to make five connections—two of them on the famous bullet train, which stops at each station for less than a minute.

It takes me one connection to get up my nerve. I'm not used to publicly littering. Just the thought makes me hunker down and start looking out of the corners of my eyes like a criminal.

Second connection. The train is standing-room-only. I get up and edge my way to the door. Someone calls out to me. I ignore it. Someone else stops me and gestures over my shoulder. The purple umbrella is making its way towards me, hand over hand. I accept it with profuse apologies, deep appreciation, and even deeper bows, then stand outside the train, waving at a smiling carriage full of good citizens. They wave back.

Third connection. This one is a bullet train, with plush seats and only a scattering of people. I sit down next to an *obasan*—a granny—who compliments me on my umbrella. This is a bad sign. I pray that she either gets off or dozes off. Not a chance—she is alert, awake, and solidly seated. When it comes time for me to go I see her eyeing my stuff and I know it's useless. I reach for my umbrella. She smiles and nods and tells me to take care and good luck.

My next connection is local. I get on. I don't talk to anyone. I don't make eye contact. I quickly stuff the purple umbrella into a rack above me, push it way back, and put something on top of it. When we reach my stop I wait until the last minute, sling on my gear and scurry out the door. I sprint up the steps and down to the next platform. My train is due in less than three minutes. Things are looking good. I half expect the umbrella to magically appear behind me, flying through the air all by itself like Mary Poppins. A minute ticks by. Nothing happens.

I'm free! I feel like doing a little jig. With four less pounds to carry, I may even indulge myself with the luxury of a newspaper at the next stop.

I hear a shout, in English. I'm the only Caucasian in the station. I turn. I can't help it. A young man in a schoolboy's uniform is standing on the platform outside my old train, waving my umbrella. I wave back a lot less enthusiastically. Even if I wanted to, I can't go back and get the umbrella or I'll miss my connection. I feel awkward pretending ignorance while this poor fellow is frantically trying to communicate across two crowded platforms, but the problem will resolve itself as soon as my train arrives. Suddenly, the young man stops signaling and dashes up the stairs. I pray for my train. No good. He's young. He's fast. He's at the top of my platform, taking the steps three at a time. He comes to a panting stop in front of me. He bows. I bow. He offers me my umbrella. I express vast surprise and gushing gratitude. I've already decided to own up to ownership. Someone has clearly seen me with the umbrella and can identify me and that's how the police in this country solve 95 percent of their crimes.

My train pulls up. He gives me my umbrella. I try to give it back to him as a thank-you gift. He won't accept it. I bow. He bows. I bow. He bows. I miss my train.

Then, as he disappears in desperate bounds up the stairs to his platform, his train pulls away.

When I'm about to get off my last train, I notice that it's raining. I grab my umbrella and tuck it under one arm. What's a couple of pounds, anyway? I'm even starting to like the color purple.

≈ ≈ ≈

Karin Muller was a Peace Corps volunteer in the Philippines after graduating from Williams College. She is the author of Hitch-Hiking Vietnam *and her work has appeared in Travelers' Tales* Women in the Wild. *This story was excerpted from* Japanland, *a memoir of a year in Japan, which was one of the New York Public Library's top 25 books of the year for 2005. Her work has been reviewed by* The New York Times, Los Angeles Times, Chicago Tribune, Washington Post, Atlantic Monthly, Outside, Traveler Magazine, *and Peace Corps Writers on-line. A companion documentary to* Japanland *was made into a four-hour series and premiered nationwide on PBS in November, 2005.*

❧ ❧ ❧

The Adventure of La Refrita

They rolled into an extra ordinary town.

Eastern South Dakota is as flat as Holland but without the excitement of even a few windmills. Staying sane with lots of CD's and thoughts of the Sierras, I punched the greasy throttle of La Refrita, our bus that ran on recycled vegetable oil. We had traveled thousands of miles, through riveting landscapes and rock-climbing adventures. This was before Biodiesel became a household name, and we had done our part to spread the good news of a free, environmentally friendly fuel alternative all around the States. Now we were racing home, connecting the dots of nothing towns like Murdo, Kadoka, and Okaton until the prairie was a frying pan and the sun was melting butter.

All of a sudden, I snapped out of my daydream into the flat, boring night. I gave the reigns to Em, my girlfriend and traveling partner. Then I stumbled to the back of the bus to rest up for my next shift. "Canada here we come; at this pace we'll be there tomorrow," I said, dozing off.

"Woohoo!" Em yelled.

I flopped down and let the night slide by at seventy miles per hour. I fell to sleep but dreamed fitfully that the bus had broken down. Around nine thirty, Em woke me up in a panic, ironically living out my dream. "Steve! The engine died!" she yelled. But I was too sleepy and confused to be impressed.

"Did it stall?" I asked groggily.

"The power steering is gone. The brakes are gone. We're going down a huge hill. Oh no!" she yelled.

I realized we were sailing at seventy-five down a long slope. Em wrestled with the steering wheel and cursed. After a few very long minutes we veered off the road and bumped to a violent stop. La Refrita hunkered to the grassy shoulder on the edge of an endless field of wheat and darkness.

We tried to start her immediately. Nothing. The battery was strong, so it couldn't be the alternator. Em insisted that it hadn't slowly bogged down, which would indicate a clogged filter. It had been running at its usual temp and the fluids were O.K., so the engine hadn't overheated. What could it be?

When you break down and you're running your engine on vegetable oil, which in 9,000 miles had never happened to us, you have a grace period of four hours before the grease congeals and clogs up the whole system. We picked our brains until our grace period waned to an ungraceful close, and then decided to sleep on it. It would be better to fix it in the morning, when we could see what we were doing and call up friends for their mechanical consultation. So we spent the night on the side of Interstate 90, not exactly sure where we were.

Given the steep pitch of the hill the steady stream of eighteen-wheelers used their engine brakes as they blasted by every few minutes, screeching like colossal dentists' drills. We heard them approaching from miles away, announcing themselves in the far corners of our dreams. As they drew closer, we began to awaken with quickening heartbeats, calling up all the anxiety that lay dormant since our wisdom teeth had been removed. Then they passed, rocking the bus in their wake. Their headlights lit up the bednest like a stage, giving our thick felt curtains the transparency of wax paper. We were shocked fully awake as if the anesthesia had worn off in the middle of a root canal surgery. Our sleep was had in thirty-second intervals, combat style, in a constant ricochet between the cacophony of the entire trans-continental trucking industry and disturbed dreams where we were chained to those dentists' chairs with our jaws clamped open as heavy machinery bore down on us.

In the morning, we tore the engine apart. We checked the filters. We checked the fuel pump. We checked the fuel lines. We cracked the injectors. We made coffee. We poured boiling water on the injectors, then tried cracking them again. We squirted WD-40 into the air intake, wishing we had some ether. We checked the solenoid to see if it might be clogged or stuck or busted. We cooked some sausages. We rubbed engine grease on our faces, cussed, and prayed to whatever gods might have been listening. We considered calling NPR's Car Talk, then called our friends instead.

Besides telling us to do everything that we had already done, they were clueless.

Diagnostic work is the hardest thing about mechanics, at least for me. It feels like you have to combine the skills of a psychiatrist, a surgeon, and a psychic, only your patient is a deaf blind and dumb mute hunk of stubborn metal. Not knowing what else to do, I heroically collapsed on the bed while Em called AAA. Just then, a state trooper knocked on the door. We hadn't even seen him pull over behind us.

Seconds later, I was sitting in his cruiser, trying to help him overcome a strong belief that the bus smelled overpoweringly like marijuana. Seeing as there was nothing remotely weed-like in our possession, I was at a loss. All I could come up with was, "...ummm, I don't know what to say, officer, I had some sausage for breakfast, that could be what you're smelling..."

He gave me a look that he must have stolen from a cadaver. "No," he began, with the perversely difficult manner of the challenged male, "I've been in this line of work a while now, boy, I know what marijuana smells like. This is the raw smell I'm getting, not the burnt smell. I think you have *a lot* of high-grade marijuana in that..." his mind searched for the word, "vehicle." Again, the cadaverous stare. I looked him over, decided that he most likely hadn't ever done anything except hay fields, play football, and write a few traffic tickets. I would bet money that he had been a quarterback.

I wanted to laugh, but instead I looked him straight in the eye, without blinking, and told him, "You know what, I haven't slept. We've been sitting here on the side of the road all night. I would smoke some weed right now if I had it, but we don't have anything. Why don't you just go search the bus, because I don't have the energy to sit here and argue."

"So you smoke 'weed' then," concluded the Quarterback, scoring a touchdown in his mind.

"No, I don't. Just go look in the bus." This conversation was causing me discomfort.

"So you've never smoked weed?" He gave me an incredulous look as if he had seen my picture in his handbook of what a weed smoker should look like, with a photo of La Refrita next to it to show what a weed smoker should drive.

"Not any time recently," I said honestly, although I was a bit surprised myself when I realized that this was the truth.

"So why do you smell like it?" he pressed.

"I don't. Look, why don't you just go look in the bus?" I said mildly, entering a bit of a funk. This was a plot development I had not expected.

Suddenly his stare came back to life and he changed the subject. "Where are you headed?" he asked, now sounding genuinely interested, even a trifle concerned.

"Canada," I answered diligently.

"For what?" his mouth said while his mind imagined an extravagant drug ring.

"My girlfriend has family there. She goes there every summer," I said, letting him down.

"Where are you coming from?" I think he really wanted me to say Mexico or Columbia or Afghanistan.

"The Black Hills. We were climbing there."

"Rock climbing?"

"Yes, sir."

"Up around Mt. Rushmore?"

"Yes, sir."

"Nice country up there," he went on conversationally, in the way that a lawyer does while cross-examining a witness, just before they tear him to pieces on the stand.

"Yes, sir," I agreed, although I doubted he had ever been much farther than a few miles from this stretch of highway.

He called for backup, in code of course. I wondered if he had a code for "Big Broken Down Hippie Bus that Runs on Recycled Vegetable Oil, Bring Rolling Papers."

"So why do you smell like marijuana?" He lowered his voice a fraction and his piercing eyes found mine once more, indicating it was business time again.

Although innocent, I was as nervous as a long-tailed cat in a room full of rocking chairs. Could fear smell like pot? "Look," I pleaded, "I realize we are driving a big hippie bus, and so maybe we deserve this type of treatment from every cop who sees us. But we aren't smuggling any drugs. We're athletes. We were going to paint it flat black with chrome accents but chrome paint costs an arm and a leg. Do you think we'd be driving that thing around with weed on us? Why don't you just go look?" by now I was whining.

He looked at me for a good long while, too long, and said, "With a Kerry sticker on it, too. You know you're in the most conservative state in the union?"

"Exactly my point." I agreed, forcing a light-hearted smirk at his joke.

"Tell ya what, why don't I go have a peak in the bus, talk to your..."

"Girlfriend. Emilie."

"I'll talk to Emilie and see if your stories line up. Sit tight." He got out of the cruiser.

"Good idea. Come up with that one yourself?" I muttered.

By now another cruiser had pulled up behind us. The Quarterback called his buddy into a little time-out huddle, called out the play and then they split up. A big goofy corn husker who looked like Elmer Fudd lumbered over to me while the Quarterback went to have a little talk with Em and nose around the bus. I was too tired and innocent to care.

"That's quite the vehicle," Officer Fudd said through a chuckle, "What's this vegetable oil shit? That's just weird." If he was attempting to hide the fact that he was enjoying himself, he was doing a poor job of it.

"It runs on recycled vegetable oil," I said with a robotic autonomic response. I was relaxing a bit now, suddenly in the familiar role of tour guide instead of convicted felon. I saw the Quarterback poking his head in the bus door. I hoped that he was too lazy to invest two days of his life searching it here on the side of I-90 in the middle of the summer heat.

I had Elmer's full attention. He continued with the good cop, bad cop routine. "Hyuck Hyuck hyuck, doesn't look like it runs on anything at all, now!" he most astutely pointed out.

"No, sir, it doesn't seem to be."

"Where was you guys headin' in that thing, anyway?" he asked with a version of condescension that was all his own. It was obvious that what he was really asking was "Don't you stupid hippies even realize how stupid you hippies are?" I could imagine him as a child, getting picked on by the other kids, then going alone out to the pond and poking sticks through the eyes of frogs. He pursued the persecution mercilessly, while

the Quarterback did the same with Em. From my un-
nerving position in the cruiser, I could see him lifting a
corner of the quilt in a sad impression of a search.

They had another huddle and then miraculously
decided that we'd all be pals. The Quarterback shook
my hand as if I had made a solid interception and then
flooded me with apologies. Elmer jumped up in the bus
and started spewing questions excitedly. His look of dis-
belief was monumental. I could see his mind attempting
to bend in new directions and failing. I was worried that
we were causing him pain.

The Quarterback turned from property owner shoot-
ing grapeshot at trespassers to apologetic host. He wondered aloud which of his buddies in town could give
us the cheapest tow. He asked how long we had been
there. When we told him thirteen hours he gasped and
immediately offered to take us into town for breakfast
and coffee. We didn't have the foggiest idea where or
what "town" was. But we would soon. There were
no dots anywhere around on the map, so I had grown
comfortable accepting the possible fact that there was no
town, and that we would spend the rest of our lives in
this humble prairie. That ended up being frustratingly
close to the truth.

We finally selected a tow service. They told us our
Triple A was useless around here, and it would be a two-
hour wait. We were out of water, so the Quarterback
and I cruised in to town while Elmer Fudd pestered Em
with his dimwitted questions.

Now that we were friends, Q.B. showed me how
his cruiser could go from zero to one hundred in four
seconds. I joked that I would have to make a citizens
arrest if he didn't slow down and pass me his weapon,

which gave him a healthy laugh. We hit up the gas station, where he bought me a cup of coffee and I jokingly bought him a donut, saying, "Yeah, I know what you like." He looked at me like I had cut the wrong way going out for a pass, causing me to wonder if I had overstepped the bounds of our friendship. But when he laughed so hard that he spit out a mouthful of half-chewed donut, I knew I was definitely in.

Back at the bus, the four of us sat shootin' the shit for three hours. They were fascinated with our stories, our lifestyle, our bus, and our politics.

"So why do you use vegetable oil instead of gas? I'm just curious," Q.B. said with a voice that was weary from many years of brainwashing.

Em didn't mince her words. "Because we don't support this errand-boy Bush, and all his oil wars. Because it's free; and because it doesn't pollute," she said in a tone that couldn't be mistaken for anything except extremely bitter. She had been reading a very liberal book lately. Elmer Fudd chuckled.

"Soy is our number one export," I added, "while oil is one of our biggest imports. If a way exists to run our cars on soy rather than oil, isn't it better to support the industries we have here by using our own resources instead of importing oil from regions like the Middle East?" I tried to sound practical and enterprising, because these seemed like characteristics that these guys would respect. I thought I was leaving them no choice but to join our side. Chances are their parents are farmers of some sort, I thought, what else would one do for a living around here?

"Well, I also own a gas station, that's why I'm curious," Q.B. retorted, proving me wrong.

I floundered, "Well, we're not expecting to completely wipe out the oil industry, we just think it's important to try out some alternatives. I don't think we're gonna put your station out of business or anything."

He obviously wasn't worried. "Well, oil is *never* gonna run out anyway, at least not for another hundred years or so," he said, as if a hundred years was far enough away to absolve us of all our over consumptive guilt today. He continued educating us, and filled us in on the fact that gas station owners don't actually profit from the gas they sell. According to his facts, which checked out to be spot on later, the tax on a gallon of gas was forty-three cents. Oil tycoons were charging nearly a dollar for a gallon. So by the time he paid for it, and paid the tax on it, he could only mark it up a few cents. He was really making his money from the items he sold inside the store itself. So he didn't care what kind of fuel he was peddling, as long as people had a soda while they pumped.

We talked about other products that were made from oil, like all the synthetic clothes I was wearing; made from petroleum-based plastics, like the tires on the bus; each made with more than seven gallons of oil, like beef; which takes oil to make the fertilizer for the fields and run the machinery on the farm. Luckily, I had just read the newest *National Geographic* and knew that a pound of beef took three-quarters of a gallon of oil to produce. So a steer weighing 1,250 pounds had taken almost a thousand gallons of oil to grow. I was getting hungry.

Elmer changed the subject, "So what's this sticker about...this 'Climbing Mountains for Kerry'?" he said with a slow drawl, cutting right to the chase.

I fielded this question before Em could get to it. "Well, I reckon we'll vote for Kerry because for one, he's not George Bush, and two, he has promised to work to preserve more lands that we like to climb on, which is generally our main concern." We told them the story of how we had conquered the Pumpfest and they were duly impressed. We told them all about how climbing works and showed them some gear.

Just seconds before I convinced both of them to become liberals and start climbing, the tow truck turned up, winched La Refrita onto a flatbed, and took us for a two hundred dollar ride. There was no champagne, but we got a good tour of the town of Chamberlain as we tried to find a mechanic who would take on our case.

There were five in town to choose from. The first four said, "Hell no, no way," and so by the time we got to the fifth, they had no choice. It was a cruel scene, shelling out that kind of dough while our immobile home was plunked down and abandoned. We were helpless. Suddenly we lived in the parking lot of Don's Ford, Chamberlain, South Dakota. We were completely at the mercy of a mechanic who had no reason to like us right off the bat.

Now, you most certainly recall that we had promised to solve our endless process of selecting a town to live in by simply calling wherever the bus broke down home. When we said this, I had imagined a cute little Serendip, with a lot of young people doing cool progressive things with their time. Chamberlain is about as far from the place I had idealized as we could have gotten. Our imagined breakdown place was a place with rivers, mountains, maybe some undiscovered climbing that we could develop and become famous for. I had not imagined spending the rest of my life turning a wrench to pay off my debt to Don. I had imagined that we would

fortuitously coast to a peaceful quiet stop in front of a
babbling brook, plant an apple tree in front of the bus
and call it good. But this obviously wasn't that spot, so
the will of the divine promised that all we would need
was a new fuel filter, or in the worst case a new alternator, and then we would drive on to our real fate, right? I
was about to be let down very hard.

"So, this thing runs on vegetable oil?" Steve the mechanic quipped, with a puzzled look that made me very
nervous. Were those dollar signs flashing in his pupils?
If he had said, "Doesn't look like it runs on anything
now," I would have strangled him. He didn't say anything, just stared into the engine.

"Have you ever heard of that before?" I asked, plead-
ingly.

"No, but it seems cool."

Not knowing what else to say, I simply furrowed my
brow like he was doing and joined him in staring at the
offending engine. I could have hugged him.

Steve was good enough not to charge us labor hours
for the three hours it took Em and me to map out the
system we had created and explain to him how the bus
worked. Together, we painstakingly purged the thick,
impossibly congealed grease from the system.

Q.B. stopped by after work to check on us. He was
very sympathetic and extended his apology for suspect-
ing us again. He blamed the pot smell on the vegetable
oil, and suggested with polite optimism that it might be
just a weak battery. It was very charming.

Steve had a lot of other projects going on, but stayed
at work late for us, trying to isolate the problem. He tore
the engine apart. He checked the filters. He checked
the fuel pump. He checked the lines. He cracked the

injectors. He made some coffee. He poured boiling water on the injectors, then tried cracking them again. He squirted WD-40 into the air intake, wishing he had some ether. He checked the solenoid to see if it was clogged or stuck or busted. He rubbed grease on his face, cursed, and prayed to whatever gods might have been listening. He considered calling NPR's "Car Talk," then called his friends instead. He reluctantly came to accept the fact that a big blue hippie bus was going to be parked in front of the office of his garage for a few days. He gave us a car to borrow and told me where I could find some beer.

Em had been catching up on the last eight months of *Time* magazine inside the office. When I broke the news to her that we would not be in Canada for some time, she took it really well. Anybody else would probably have had a serious mental crisis, but she just attempted a smile and said, "At least we have each other."

"At least this isn't a dry county," I responded, for which we both thanked the Powers That Be, and decided that some serious twelve-ounce curls were in order. Cruising back down the creatively named Main Street, we took note that the town hadn't changed character, or acquired any, since we had rolled through in the tow truck a few hours earlier. There was the same barbershop with a barber's poll out front that could have been any barbershop in any town, the same antique shop that sold the same horseshoes and lampshades as any other antique shop anywhere. There was the same drug store that provided the town with all the same needful things as any other town's needful things. There was the prerequisite McDonalds which has to be the staple of an American town. There was the same old Movie

Theater that was showing the same movies that every other Movie Theater in the country had shown a year ago. There was the same Town Hall that could have had any town's name on it. There was the same tiny shoebox of a library that had the same lousy books and hand-me-down computers from before the age of computers that became obsolete in half the time it took for them to turn on…and then there was one place we saw that might be different. We realized instantly, this place had the chance to distinguish Chamberlain from every other town in the country that was cultivating the unmistakable features of terminal decline.

This phoenix from the flames was the Anchor Restaurant. We were rooting for it as we walked in, but it took us all of a second to realize that it is called the "Anchor" because it belongs at the bottom of a dark, murky sea. Upon our entrance, the entire room fell quiet and stared at us as if we had purple skin. They probably hadn't seen anyone from out of town since the last bright blue hippie bus that ran on vegetable oil broke down there. Their faces seemed to say, "Don't blame us for our bad taste; there's no where else to eat in town," "Don't order the fish and chips," and "I married my sister."

My strategy was to pound as many beers as possible before the "food" came; so that I might be drunk enough to trick myself into thinking that it was edible. It worked, but was not, even by the most charitable stretch of my drunken imagination, a good experience.

More beer was required in order to gather the strength to return to the bus, in the parking lot of Don's Ford. We got there, laughing at our predicament until we noticed that Don's Ford was located conveniently close to a manure pile that would have been the tallest mountain in

Connecticut. Conveniently located, that is, for a population of flies that must have been the epicenter of the fly universe. We had left the windows open and now a suburb had sprung up in our bus. I took up a newspaper and commenced swatting them with all of my compiled frustrations until I fell down exhausted and slept.

The next morning found Steve and me staring at the bus again, side by side, each of us with one hand on the hood, the other on our respective hips.

"Hmmmm…" Steve said.

"Hmmmm…." the other Steve said.

"Hmmmmmmmmmm…" the two Steves said together.

It was Steve who decided we should take off the injection pump and look inside; it was probably rusty, time for a new one.

It was Steve who asked how long that would take, and how much it would cost.

It was Steve who said about six hours once we had the part, and a thousand bucks.

It was Emilie who handled it well, and didn't break anything, like Steve did.

When Lewis and Clark came to this area, they remarked upon the abundance of honeybees on the banks of the Missouri River, where Chamberlain is today. Since first arriving with the settlers of Virginia in the 1620s, bees had since spread to not only what would become Chamberlain, South Dakota, but all regions of the continent. Bees were the first Euro-American species that western tribes of indigenous people met, and so they were the first tangible proof these tribes had to support the spreading stories of an encroaching population of white humans. And so the bee came to represent the

white man, just as the buffalo later came to represent the
Indian. In proportion as the bee advanced, the Indian
and the buffalo retired. Indians saw the bee as a har-
binger of the white man and impending doom. Indeed,
long before the economic complex of European animals
arrived, bees were pollinating European crops and
weeds, carving out the niche that would soon be filled
with imported pleasures such as smallpox, agriculture,
cattle, and white people. This is how Old World mi-
crobes, plants, animals, and people accomplished their
conquests in concert. These are the things you think
about when you have five days to spare and you are in
Chamberlain, South Dakota. That's how long we had to
wait for a new injection pump to be shipped.

If you are ever stuck in Chamberlain, South Dakota,
you will know exactly what your options are right away.
That's the good news, there is no grueling decision making about what to do. The bad news is that the reason for
this is that there is nothing to do. We went first to the
river, which they call the lake because it's really wide,
but is actually the Missouri River. We swam around in
the concrete-colored water, and talked to some locals.
They professed that they loved Chamberlain, even a
young girl who in every other town would have learned
to hate her hometown by now. They sent us to the Akta-
Lakota Museum.

We looked at stuffed buffalos, arrowheads, and di-
oramas of Plains Indian's camps. Asking around, I was
surprised to hear that the people here also claimed to
love this town. "Did you see the bridge?" they asked. We
had. "Isn't it spectacular?" they wanted to know. I hadn't
seen what was so spectacular about it, so we went again
to the water and looked. There was a big steel bridge

spanning the river. It looked like any bridge in any town that had sprung up during an industrial boom and then flopped. The only thing I found spectacular about it was that it hadn't fallen down. Sure enough, as we stood there, a man with a beaver on his head waddled up to us, gestured grandly toward the bridge and exclaimed, "Isn't it spectacular!?"

We went to the drug store and bought more beer. To me, Chamberlain seemed like a hard place to love. How were people doing such a good job of it? Or was something fishy going on? The clerk at the package store spotted us for out of towners and asked if we had broken down. Apparently there is a breakdown vortex around Chamberlain, which is how it sustains itself. She was genuinely sympathetic, but remarked, "Chamberlain isn't such a bad place to break down. I love it here. Have you seen the bridge?"

There was a pamphlet from the Chamberlain Chamber of Commerce in the corner. Were these the people who were training everyone to lie and say they loved it here, as a conspiracy to bolster tourism? I picked it up. Sure enough, right there on the cover was the bridge, basking in a flood of glorious evening light. "The bridge is a landmark for both highway-goers and boating enthusiasts," the caption read. Inside the pamphlet, there was a page about the lake and one about the museum, an ad for the Anchor Restaurant, and that was it.

We went to the library and did some research. Here we saw some pictures that proved Chamberlain really was a fun spot...in 1910, when riverboats floating the Missouri unloaded thousands of vacationers into the streets. All the riverboats had stopped running long ago. But the library was still fun!

We set up shop. Em made some illustrations. I typed. We sent some postcards to family and loved ones. Em drew some more. I typed some more. We sent postcards to everyone we had ever known. Em drew some more. I typed some more. We sent postcards to complete strangers. Em drew. I typed. Then we went outside and climbed the walls of the building, which were stone and actually made for decent climbing. This drew quite a crowd in Chamberlain. Well, as much of a crowd as is possible in Chamberlain. Three people and one Labrador, to be exact. Climbing and talking to the developing party kept our minds off our bleak situation. But something else was bothering me now.

I interviewed a few more locals to see exactly how they felt about living in a town that based its economy on the occasional person that happened to break down there. To my increased astonishment, they loved it here. "Have you seen the bridge?" they asked. The Labrador even stared in the direction of the beloved bridge and drooled away his longing.

I began to get seriously introspective. What was wrong with me, that I couldn't be happy with such a place? Why couldn't I live here with these people and be happy like them? Why couldn't I drive around in my big American made car, get a job waiting tables at the Anchor, and be happy with an occasional visit to the bridge? What kind of spoiled, high-standard, highbrow, shallow person was I?

By the time the injector pump had arrived (five days), I felt really guilty for my original pessimism and closed-mindedness. Who was I to judge, and impress my own ideals onto other people? As it turned out, Chamberlain wasn't such a bad place to break down. Just think of it as the Bermuda Triangle of the Midwest. It has all the mystery and the lore but none of the sweltering heat or scantily clad women. Instead, it has bad haircuts and worse food. But something good comes from everything. Em got to do some amazing illustrations. I had some amazing illuminations of self-contentment. In fact, I highly recommend breaking down there. Go and see the folks at Don's Ford. There are plenty of flies to swat, cornfields to mope around in, and prairie dogs to chase. There is even a gay dude dressed up like Meriwether Lewis. The people of Chamberlain, once you convince them you are not smuggling hundreds of pounds of pot through their town, are friendliness itself. They are so friendly it's as if it never went out of style. I promise you, little tips about your own spiritual evolution (and little tips of rat's tails) are hiding beneath every buffalo burger bun at the Anchor. Don't miss the bridge. It's spectacular!

❧ ❧ ❧

Steve King is a writer, photographer, artist, and avid crazyman based out of Boulder, Colorado. He is currently working on a documentary film about the Rupert River and the Cree Indians of Northern Quebec. The Adventure of La Refrita is an excerpt from his book by the same title.

✒ ✒ ✒

Fishing with Larry

They got together for one last adventure.

Don Juan says the Río Grande de Quetena holds
trout. To make the point, he extends a muscled
arm as if signaling a left turn: long as this and thick, too.
He'll meet us four days from now at his hotel, Mallku
Cueva. "*Voy a llevarlos.*" I'll take you there.

I'm skeptical about the trout, but that's not important. I only hope the guy shows up. We've just booked a
five-day trip across a remote region in southern Bolivia
where there are barely any roads, much less gas stations.
Don Juan will be carrying our extra gas.

A nagging voice whispers caution. The Bolivian tour
operator talks and smiles big. Like just that, an operator.

"What do you think, Larry?" I ask, and immediately
the answer shoots across my synapses. Go for it.

What the hey, we're here for the adventure. So we

pack our gear into Larry's '84 Toyota Land Cruiser and set off for the Salar de Uyuni, the world's largest salt lake. With my sister-in-law Babette and her friend Christophe, my wife Jeanne and me, plus our Bolivian guide Dieter, the car is stuffed to the max.

My brother Larry makes six, but he doesn't take up much room. He's in a Ziploc inside my fishing fanny pack. Larry died a year ago. I'm carrying his ashes.

Larry was a man of grand schemes that had an uncanny way of coming to fruition. His last was the grandest. Driving the Land Cruiser from New Mexico to Tierra del Fuego was only half the plan. The other half had Babette's Peugeot maneuvering from Corsica to parts east. He'd ship the Toyota from Chile to New Zealand, then north eventually to Southeast Asia. They'd crash the vehicles head-on in China. Larry would collect the insurance.

Traveling six weeks at a crack, over the course of several years the Land Cruiser had gotten as far as Bolivia, weathering a Colombian earthquake that created pandemonium in that already chaos-riddled country and a Peruvian mudslide that left Larry with a concussion and he and Babette trapped in the car neck deep in a raging river. My brother always kept his head above water. But he didn't survive pancreatic cancer.

One of his last requests was that his ashes be divvied amongst his loved ones to do with as we chose. Jeanne and I brought our cupful on our hundred-day South American sojourn organized around learning Spanish, visiting our Peace Corps volunteer daughter in Paraguay, and meeting Babette in Bolivia. We began our trip at the tip of the continent in Punta Arenas. On the ferry ride across the Strait of Magellan, halfway between the mainland and Tierra del Fuego, I flung a scoop over the railing. It felt right. Larry was a nautical guy—a boater, diver, fisherman. On the return ride, in the afterglow of a blazing midnight sunset, a Patagonian dolphin surfaced at the same spot and paralleled the boat for a forever moment, eyeing me and nodding his head as if agreeing: good decision.

I'd only scattered half my Larry, though. I guess I still needed to keep him near.

Now, a month later with Babette and Christophe in Sucre, we've resuscitated the car, dormant four years. Three days of a whole family of mechanics' time cost fifty bucks, but we also had to pay an $800 ransom to liberate it from their brawny and resolute mother, who owned the garage and swore the deal was five Bolivianos a day.

We made our way through the massively wrinkled 14,000-foot desert landscape that is the Bolivian Altiplano, south to Potosí, where, booking a tour of Cerro Rico, once the world's richest silver mine, we met this thickly built, charismatic fortyish guy Juan Quesada, whose employees call him Don Juan. A chef by training, he's a born entrepreneur.

We leave his office about a thousand dollars lighter with an itinerary to some of the most isolated reaches of Bolivia.

After rendezvousing with Dieter—his only explanation for his German name is, "my father was crazy"—he directs us onto the somewhat slushy Salar de Uyuni. "*No hay problema*," he says, the salt is ten meters thick. We dodge piles of drying salt destined for shakers as we drive to the Salt Palace Hotel, built entirely of blocks of the white crystals. The rooms are little igloos, complete with salt stalactites and comfy, if a bit dazzling salt furniture. It was Don Juan who built this curiosity that actually works. I gain a little confidence.

Traversing the open Salar at our pedal-to-the-floor sixty miles per hour, the white is so intense, the lack of reference so complete that we have no feeling of movement. Babette says she feels as if she's in a boat on a perfectly calm day. Larry would have loved this. She scatters half her Larry out the window.

At the foot of Volcán Thunupa, its flanks streaked with the red of iron, the yellow of sulfur and the green of copper, sits a small village, tiny yellow and red flowers pushing through the salt soil of its church courtyard. Larry, an artist, would have loved this, too.

Dieter guides us unerringly off the Salar and through a landscape soaked in salt, borax, and a periodic table's worth of other minerals that is at once stark and intensely vivid. We summit barren mountain passes and ford unmarked streams up to our floorboards. Sometimes there's a road, sometimes just wheel tracks that flare off in random directions.

Our stops—other than the ones to blow rust particles out of a frequently clogged fuel filter—are as compelling as the environs. We stroll through an Inca necropolis in a field of coral boulders, the tombs containing the misshapen skulls—from being bound—that gave Inca noble kids that fashionable oblong look. We're voyeurs to male llamas draped lazily over lounging females: llaid-back llama llove. We view through a haze of heat all three species of Bolivian flamingoes, the black-winged Andean, the all-pink Chilean and the James with its brilliant red-orange wings. An equal number of the magnificent birds stand upside down in the reflection of the unnamed salt lake. My overstimulated eyes find elephants, vultures, a

throne and two lovers in the bizarrely sculpted lava for-
mations of the Rock Valley. Maybe the coca leaves I'm
chewing are working better than I thought.

Exhausted and encrusted in salt, dust and sweat,
two days later we reach Mallku Cueva, another of Don
Juan's hotels. This one is built into the side of a cliff;
its rock face forms the rear wall of our bedroom. The
shower even has hot water. Better yet, as we follow our
noses to fresh baked bread from the hotel's wood oven,
Don Juan shows up with our blessed petrol and a bottle
of Sangini, Bolivian cognac. He's brought his fishing
rod, too, a decrepit looking spinning outfit.

So we're a bit furry-mouthed and anvil-headed when
our trout expedition sets out the next morning. I ride
with Don Juan down a dirt track that keeps getting
worse, finally narrowing to a footpath that plunges
down a steep hillside, barely squeezing between two
boulders. The blue Toyota bravely follows, Jeanne at the
wheel. Don Juan's impressed.

After maybe an hour, we reach the Río Grande de
Quetena. Grand it's not, so choked with weeds that you
can hardly see water. Here and there are open spots
through which a gentle current trickles. No way is this
a trout stream. We climb a rocky hill to an overlook and
peer down. Trout. Huge ones! A few spook and swim
beneath the blanket of weeds, but several, including one
monster matching the size and bulk of Don Juan's arm,
just lie there. "*Ahora, ¿Me crees?*" Don Juan asks.

Yeah, I believe. Lordy.

That's when the pressure hits me. With so little water
to work a fly through, how am I going to hook a fish,
much less land it? And Babette has built me up as some
kind of fishing maestro, whereas the truth is I'm not

much of a trout fisherman. We have streams in northern
Wisconsin, but a lot more lakes. I grew up with a spinning rod in my hand and a minnow bucket at my feet.

So I try to conduct myself in the manner of every
trout fanatic I've ever met. I prepare fanatically slowly.
I return to the car. Ease into my waders. Rub each
section of my five-piece *caña de mosca* on the oily
spot on the side of my nose before putting it together.
Check each guide as I string it. Unwind, stretch, and
restretch my fifteen-pound leader. Snug the loop-to-
loop connection.

I open the large compartment of my fanny pack to
pull out my fly box, and instead encounter the baggie of
Larry. Whoa. Could this be the place?

"What do you think, bro?" I whisper it aloud.

One thing about my brother. Type-A though he was,
he believed in letting people make their own decisions.
That's why he left a dozen of us with ashes and no instructions.

Oh, the magical fishing days we shared. Northern
Manitoba on the solstice, hammering the pike and walleyes as the sun dipped down and came up an hour later.
Loreto, in Baja, Mexico on my fortieth birthday, one of
those cosmic jokes with me as the butt when I couldn't
catch a fish to save my life, but it didn't matter, not
even when the skies opened up and cancelled our last
two days, because the sight of the orange, swollen river
dumping into the aqua of the Sea of Cortez was unforgettable. Or another time camping in Baja when his
outboard conked out and our next landfall, by Larry's
reckoning, would be Australia. Or that final time in
Captiva, Florida, a week before he died, when, under a
double rainbow, Larry outfished us all.

But most treasured of all were evenings on the lakes of Northern Wisconsin, in the cold or the rain, that ended with grins on our faces and a stringer of walleyes, basket of slab crappies, or memory of wide-shouldered bass caught and released.

We worked together twenty years. He was eight years my elder, ever my sounding board, but eventually our talk about relationships or kids or our current passions, his painting and my writing, had been as peers. We shared blood, genes, a somewhat obsessive commitment to family and a lot of wine. Yet of all the bonds between us, fishing was as important as any. When we fished together, the world was always right.

How Larry would have loved the utter improbability of this trout stream in southern Bolivia. I make up my mind: this is the place. Whether the fish are catchable is immaterial.

When I ask Don Juan permission to put Larry's ashes in the river, he says he'd be honored. We return to the rock overlook. Babette decides to scatter hers as well. The wind carries them to the edge of the weeds, where the double dose of Larry gently settles and sinks.

Don Juan takes out his spinning rod, gives it a quizzical look. He admits he's never fished with anything other than a seine net. I show him how to hold it, flip the bail, make a cast. He flips his one spoon from the overlook and whoops when one of the monsters turns to it, but the fish flashes off. I try to get him to come down to the river with me, but Don Juan is gaga over being able to see the trout below. I scramble down alone.

With the help of a wood pole, I slog through the weedy gook to where I can cast. I have no idea what to throw. I've seen a few dragonflies, so I try one. The wind behind me, I make a perfect cast. Phew, at least I didn't embarrass myself right off the bat. The fly floats back toward me. Nothing doing. I try several more times, then switch to a green tongue depressor, a Wisconsin smallmouth fly similar to a wooly bugger that Jeanne ties. *Whammo*. Don Juan sees the hit and is screaming like a kid. Fish on.

I'm glad for the heavy leader. The fish is strong, but, pulling horizontally, my six-weight affords good leverage, and I'm able to keep the trout from the weeds. Dieter has followed me with a landing net, large enough though the frame is way flimsy. I tire the fish out and instruct Dieter: hands on the frame, not handle. *La cabeza primero*. Head first. Fish in. Twenty-one inches, four and a half pounds, a fat, beautiful rainbow. In Bolivia. Thank you, Larry.

"*¿Quieres comerlo?*" I shout up the outcropping. Don Juan gives me the thumbs up. Hell yes, he wants to eat it.

I climb up with the fish. Time to help my host, who's still after the big one. Time after time the fish refuses the spoon, though it never spooks. So I thread the spinning line through on a bobber I fashioned last night by boring a hole in a wine cork, then pinch on a split shot and attach a wooly bugger. A trout snaps at it immediately, but Don Juan misses the hit. He's chattering nonstop, having the time of his life.

I still can't get him to come down to the river. So I return. Wham. Twenty-three incher, another shimmering rainbow of a rainbow.

So the day goes. We eat lunch. Jeanne, Babette, and Christophe tire and leave. Don Juan, Dieter, and I, to say the least, don't tire. The boss is determined to tease

that monster trout from on high. I don't have the heart
to tell him that even if he hooks the fish, there's not a
trout's shadow of a chance he'll raise it up a twenty-five-
foot cliff.

Moving upstream to another hole in the weeds with
a large boulder in the middle, in no more than six casts
I land a twenty-three and two twenty-fours, all six to
eight pounds. We have plenty for dinner for us and
the staff; I'm ready to catch and release. But Don Juan
wants me to keep every fish. He's having a party for his
brother, who's turning fifty in a few days. The brother
has cancer. This will be a birthday to remember. I feel
Larry smiling.

By now, it's mid-afternoon and hot. I finally convince
Don Juan to move to the stream. I want to take him to
my boulder, but he insists on fishing downstream. Oh
well, it's his river. I try to place him where he can get
some action with his spoon, but he's not much of a lis-
tener. We see no fish for a good half mile.

So we return to the overlook rock. Yep, the behemoth
is still there. Don Juan stands above to direct me. The
wind has shifted and is now blowing down the river; it's
tough casting. Staying in the shelter of the rock overhang, I can just manage to put a fly into position. A fish
hits. Twenty-four inches. Beautiful. But Don Juan wants
me to fell the giant. I keep casting and break lines on
two fish I never see. So I tie on a piece of twenty-pound
shock tippet and return one more time. My fly sinks,
drifts, stops. Yeah. Fish on. "*Un caballo,*" I yell.

I can't stop it from swimming under the weeds. I'm
patient, though, applying constant pressure, and finally
out comes the trout, running downstream. Not good.
But it stays on and begins tiring. The landing net has

long since broken, so I keep working, tiring the fish, which always seems to have strength for one more run. Finally, the oversized trout lies quiet on the surface, allowing me to cradle it. Twenty-nine inches, eleven pounds. A horse, for sure.

Don Juan is all grins as we pose for a photo, holding the fish between us, as long as our outstretched arms. He thinks there's still a bigger one down there. "*Bastante*," I say. Enough. I try to impress upon him the importance of leaving some fish in the river. We return to the car and share a *trago*. Another universality, that post-fishing drink.

I pour a bit of Sangini on the ground both as offering to the earth goddess Pachamama and farewell to my brother. It's not easy to get into Don Juan's jeep and close the door. But it's necessary. Thanks for one more great day, bro.

The next day we walk through a field of geothermal pools with roaring steam vents and burbling pots of brown, pink, and gray goo. Then we cross an expanse of soft blond sand dotted with large dark brown boulders, bleak yet ordered, and appropriately named Salvador Dalí Desert.

Larry would have loved this.

≫ ≫ ≫

Tom Joseph's fiction, essays, and travel writing have appeared in regional and national publications, including Travelers' Tales Central America. *He lives in northern Wisconsin, but often escapes to warmer climes. Currently, he's working on a historical novel set in southwest Florida. This story won the Grand Prize for Best Travel Story of the Year in the first annual Solas Awards.*

❧ ❧ ❧

The *Mukhtar* and I

An exile's very last summer in the old city.

T HE MORNING MY GRANDFATHER AND I TOOK A WALK
together—after feasting on a breakfast of *ka'ak*
(over-sized sesame bagels) and *bayd hammeem* (oven-
baked eggs) that my grandmother bought from a street
vendor by yelling and dropping a basket-on-a-rope from
the dining room bay window overlooking the market
in the Christian Quarter—he turned to me and said,
"Today you get to spend the day with Sido (grandfather); you are now old enough to come help me at the
qahwe (café)."

The year was 1966 and I was barely eleven years old. We
were living in Beirut. Often during the summertime my
mother would take me, together with my younger brother
and my sister, to visit Tata (grandmother) and Sido in the
Old City of Jerusalem. It was a summer holiday I often

resisted and fought against, for I preferred to spend my time on the beach in Beirut with my best friends Mounir and Imad instead of visiting my grandfather—a stern-looking, *tarboosh*-wearing (fez-wearing), *za'oot*-sniffing (snuff), nargileh-puffing, mustachioed man who to me looked more like an Ottoman Pasha than a grandfather, a man almost feared by everyone around him (at least that was my perception), someone who had never shown the slightest interest in me or any affection towards me.

I not only feared my grandfather, I was petrified by the sight of all the ugly, bearded monks who occupied the Greek Orthodox Convent where my grandparents lived after their forced exile from their home in the Katamon Quarter. The intoxicating smell of incense and burning candles, the spooky, narrow, cobble-stoned alleyways of the convent grounds, the robed priests roaming around in the dark (they gave me the creeps every time they looked me in the eye and whispered *kalimera* and *kalispera*, which I didn't know at the time meant good morning and good evening in Greek)—all contributed to a feeling of anxiety and discomfort I could do without.

My grandfather Issa Toubbeh, known to everyone as Abu Michel (father of Michael), was the *Mukhtar* (literally, the chosen), the head of the Eastern Orthodox Christian Arab community in Jerusalem, whom he dutifully served for over 50 years, as his father had done before him and his eldest son after him. As *Mukhtar*, he was given a residence inside the Convent, which consisted of several large, high-ceilinged rooms abutting the walls of Mar Ya'coub (St. Jacob's Orthodox Church) and the Holy Sepulcher, located on the Convent grounds. Two rows of sweet-smelling potted plants and flowers, including gardenias and jasmine, lovingly tended to by my grandmother Tata Maria, graced the front entrance of the house and provided a welcome antidote to the unpleasant and overpowering (at least to a child) holy scents one encountered along the way. From the rooftop—the makeshift playground my cousins and I frequented—the view of the Mount of Olives, the Dome of the Rock, the al-Aqsa Mosque, and the Church of the Holy Sepulcher overwhelmed my eleven-year-old eyes every time I gazed in the distance.

Everyone spoke highly of my grandfather, the *Mukhtar*, and his important role in Palestinian society. Abu Michel was quite erudite and always commanded people's attention and respect. He spoke fluent Arabic, Turkish, Greek, Armenian, and Russian. And he could even swear in English—with a posh British accent, nonetheless—something he picked up during his numerous dealings with the "cursed" British before their departure from Palestine in 1948. He survived the rule of the Ottomans, the English, Hashemite Transjordan, and the Jewish state, and was considered a shrewd and highly experienced problem-solver—a necessary prerequisite for the job of *Mukhtar*. His reputation as a successful mediator spread beyond his flock in the Eastern Orthodox Christian Arab community and his services were highly sought after by people in the Muslim as well as Jewish communities in Jerusalem. "Abused women rushed to our house for protection while their abusers waited patiently outside for the arrival of my father, the mediator," my uncle Jamil once told me. It was also rumored that whenever my grandfather accompanied an entourage of men assembled for the purpose of asking for a girl's hand in marriage, it was guaranteed that their request would be granted.

Such was the importance of *my* grandfather, the *Mukhtar*. But no matter what people said about him, no matter how much praise was bestowed on his position in the society, it never really impressed me much. My older cousin Basima once came up to me and proudly told me that she saw Sido's picture in the newspaper walking next to the Greek Orthodox Patriarch of Jerusalem at the head of the procession on Easter Sunday. Big deal, I thought. My aunt Widad, the sweetest of my six aunts, bragged that no marriage in the community could take place without the official stamp of the *Mukhtar* on the marriage certificate; no birth could be legalized without his seal; no divorce approved without his counsel; no death authenticated without his presence. The more stories I heard about him the less affection I felt towards him. There is someone, I said to myself, who is doing good deeds all over town but has never said a kind word to me, let alone given me a grandfatherly hug. I was puzzled. How could a person have so much power over a community? Many more questions crossed my eleven-year-old mind: Do I really have to get his approval before I get married? Will he stand in my way if I choose to marry the belly dancer I saw in the Beirut restaurant a month ago? Must I steal the round, brass seal with Arabic calligraphy he keeps chained to his vest in order to do so?

The side I saw of Sido was in stark contrast to his reputation on the street. The verbal abuse he often unleashed on my aunts (mind you, never on my uncles) was shocking. The time he yelled at my mother for her disrespectful act of lighting a cigarette in his presence, and his refusal to speak to her for several days afterwards, was quite upsetting to me. The way he treated my Tata (the world's kindest grandmother) was also painful to watch—especially the evening ritual of her taking off his shoes and socks and massaging his feet in a bowl of hot water for hours on end after his return from work. As if her days were easy when compared to his, I used to complain to my mother. I remember my mother scolding me one day for asking why he never massaged her feet as payback or reward for taking her away from her family at age thirteen and impregnating her ten times (not counting the several miscarriages she had to go through) without a break in between.

Spending time at home with my grandmother and watching her slave away in the house all day made me very resentful of my grandfather's behavior. Maybe I felt this way because I grew up in cosmopolitan Beirut. Or maybe it was because I never saw my father treat my mother in this manner. I was too young to understand the role customs played on his behavior and attitudes, too naïve to fathom how deep-rooted in tradition some people can be.

But despite all this, I was not too young to understand that being "the grandson of the *Mukhtar*" had its benefits too. And I shamefully admit that I exploited them to the maximum. I wasn't about to let these brief, unpleasant family episodes stand in the way of having fun on my summer vacation in Jerusalem. Everybody in the community knew the *Mukhtar* and, in very short time after my arrival, people everywhere would say: "Ah, you must be the *Mukhtar*'s grandson." The local grocer would give me free sugar-covered chickpeas, the juice vendor, free lemonade. I got free ice cream, free falafel sandwiches, free bicycle rentals, free olive wood crosses (which I later sold to tourists a few blocks away), and—most important of

all—free donkey rides. The *Mukhtar* connection opened
so many doors for me that the Old City was soon transformed into one big amusement park. I would spend my
days roaming the streets, going from quarter to quarter,
hanging out with Hassan and Ahmad in the courtyard of
the al-Aqsa Mosque while they waited for their father to
come out of Friday prayer services, playing in and around
the Church of the Holy Sepulcher with Charlie and
George, sons of a souvenir store owner, and watching the
mini-skirt clad *ajnabiyyat* (foreign women)—some pretty,
I thought, but no match to the love of my life, the dark-
haired belly dancer in the Beirut restaurant.

I had the freedom to go anywhere I wanted in the
Old City—no worries there, since I was the *Mukhtar*'s
grandson and the *entire* community would look after
me (be responsible for my safety is more like it). My
only condition was that I return to the convent before
the 8:00 P.M. closing time of the small, studded, metal
door carved in the center-bottom of the monstrous iron
door that sealed off and protected the fortress known as
the Greek Orthodox Convent. I was constantly warned
about the closing time by my mother and always allowed
ample time for the walk back home—except once.

It was Sunday evening and I was having so much fun
flying Salim's kite that I lost track of time. When I got to
the convent, the dreaded metal door was shut. And that
was a lesson to remember. The street was almost deserted
and the amplified sound of occasional hurried footsteps
on the cobble-stoned sidewalk did little to ease my fears.
Alone, I stood outside the convent door sobbing for what
seemed like eternity (it couldn't have been more than ten
minutes) until a nice, elegantly-dressed lady came up
to me and uttered the magic words: "You must be the

Mukhtar's grandson." She gently held my hand and let me rest my head on her chest (later I thought of marrying her too) until someone sent a message to the monk inside who unhappily came and opened the door. After I thanked and bade my savior goodbye, the monk with the foot-long keys hanging from his belt slammed shut the squeaky metal door behind us, and I quickly ran to the house—totally ignoring the angry Greek words he spewed in my direction.

The "walk" with my grandfather took place the morning after this incident. And I dreaded it. My time of scolding has come, I said to myself, especially after his total silence on the matter the evening before. But to my surprise, there was no mention of it. Instead, he extended his hand to me and gave me a warm and loving look—something I was not accustomed to seeing. As we passed the frowning monk at the convent entrance, the one whose prayer I disrupted the night before, Sido looked at me and gave me a wink and a smile. That was the start of a day I will remember and cherish for the rest of my life.

The first order of the day was a visit to the *Batrak*, the grand old Patriarch of the Greek Orthodox Church in Jerusalem—a real treat and a privilege very few people get, Sido told me. I was not only special but also the oldest son of his youngest daughter, he went on to say (a reason only a real smoothie would think about). Our audience with the *Batrak* was very brief. I remember feeling dazzled by the opulence of his quarters, but had little time to absorb any details except for the long baton with the round, golden head the *Batrak* held in his right hand. I was not thrilled at having to kiss the wrinkled old man's hand, and I had to do it twice—once at the beginning and another time after he placed around my neck a gold chain with a black and gold cross. This gift was special and would protect me from future evil, Sido quietly whispered in my ear, since the gold cross had inside it a wood splinter that came directly from the cross of Jesus Christ. (This valuable piece of information came in handy when I later sold the cross to my Lebanese Maronite schoolmate, who paid me the desperately needed Lebanese pounds to shower on the love of my life, the belly dancer, the next time I saw her.)

My memories of that day are as vivid and as bright as a silver coin in the sun. Sido and I, hand in hand, walked through the streets of Jerusalem, stopping every few paces to greet people he knew and those who knew of him. Along the way we passed the market, a bustling collection of colorful fruit and vegetable vendors. I instantly felt the flow of musical energy emanating from the place and its people. Music was simply all around: from the unforgettable melodic chanting of the muezzin's call to prayer—often juxtaposed against the ringing of church bells—to fruit and vegetable vendors in the market singing praises about pickling cucumbers (as small as babies' fingers) or prickly pears (so delicious they melt in your mouth); from the cheerful foot-thumping sounds of children practicing *dabke* dancing to the powerful emotional songs of Oum Koulthoum blasting from transistor radios on window sills. To this day I am still able to close my eyes and transport myself back to the Jerusalem days. I am still able to smell the delicious food sold by street vendors, especially the wonderfully rich and evocative scent of roasted chestnuts and, of course, the sumptuous sweets drenched in *'ater* (sugar syrup) sold at Zalatimo's; I am still able to see the old street photographer with the wooden camera whose head often disappeared underneath a black cloth; still able to touch the olive oil soap stacked in the long cylindrical towers at the corner store.

But the one thing that intrigued me most of all, the one person that had a profound influence on me, was the juice vendor who walked with his body leaning forward and his Bordeaux fez with the black tassels tipped back. Not only did he carry a big tank filled with *sous*, *jellab*, and lemonade on his back as he traveled by foot from neighborhood to neighborhood, but he was a percussionist of the highest degree. I was fascinated by how he announced his arrival, and mesmerized by how he played beautiful, intricate rhythmic patterns, using brass cups and saucers, to entertain customers and alert them to his presence—rhythms very similar to the ones the belly dancer in the Beirut restaurant moved her hips to. From that moment on I was hooked. I would sit on the sidewalk with my eyes fixed on the juice vendor's hands so I could learn his art. Back at the house later on, to my grandmother's horror, I would practice the same rhythms using her china, which produced disastrous results and, it goes without saying, a spanking. This marked the beginning of what was to become a life-long passion for Arabic music and rhythms.

Adjacent to Jaffa Gate was my grandfather's long-established café. Known to family and friends as al-Mahal (The Place) and to others as Qahwet Abu Michel (Father of Michael's Café) or Qahwet *al-Mukhtar*, the café was a renowned Jerusalem institution frequented in its heyday by the Palestinian literati, nicknamed *al-sa'aleek* (the vagabonds). According to my uncle Jamil, it was Palestinian author and educator Khalil Sakakini "who bestowed the title of *sa'aleek* on the group of intellectuals who met at al-Mahal. Members of the *sa'aleek* included Yusef el-Issa, publisher/editor of the daily *Alef Ba*, and Issa el Issa, publisher/editor of the daily *Filistine*, as well as Anistas Hanania, Adel Jaber, Ahmad Zaki Pasha, Khalil Mutran, Yacoub Farraj, and others." Poets, musicians, historians, storytellers, folks who wanted to be seen in their company, young Palestinians who aspired to be like them, or simply those who just wanted to listen to the exchange of ideas taking place, gathered at *al-Mukhtar*'s café.

The café was buzzing with people when my grandfather and I arrived from the market. As we walked in the door, we were greeted by my uncle Mitri, who gave me a kiss on each cheek before going behind the counter to prepare an order of *mezze* for a customer. I was immediately put to work cutting cucumbers, chopping parsley, and preparing plates of olives and pickled turnips for the busy lunch crowd. *Arak* (a Lebanese alcoholic drink made of distilled grape juice flavored with anis) and nargileh were present at almost every table, which accounted for the lively, albeit smoky, atmosphere of the place. For the next hour or so Sido attended to the business of recording births, deaths, and marriages in his oversized leather book, giving advice in between, and stamping official documents that required his seal. When he was done, he signaled to me with his walking stick to follow him to the café backyard, a large paved area with rows of plants on each side, a round tiled fountain in the middle surrounded by tables and chairs, and a massive cage that housed chickens and over a hundred pigeons.

As we sat in the sun and snacked on watermelon and *Nabulsiyyeh* cheese, he told me funny stories and answered the many questions I had stored up over the years.

His answers to silly questions like "Why do you wear a *tarboosh*?" and "What's that stuff you sniff and makes you sneeze all the time?" and more serious ones like "Why did you leave Katamon?" and "Why did you not fight the *Yahood* (the Jews) when they took your home?" kept me enthralled the whole afternoon. He told me about the bombing that demolished the Samiramis hotel down the road from their house in Katamon and how the blast that Menachem Begin masterminded at the King David Hotel, close to my uncle Michel's office, instilled fear in the community and was the catalyst that drove many Katamonians to flee their homes. I laughed when he described how one morning, on orders of Haj Amin Al-Husseini, the *mufti* of Palestine, he received a delivery of antiquated guns and ammunition loaded on five donkeys to be distributed to the men in the community at a time when the *Yahood* were parading the streets with tanks and cannons. I cried when he told me the story of the massacre that took place at the village of Deir Yassin. A quick change of subject to the art of pigeon flying restored my smile. And before we headed back home, he gave me an impressive demonstration by releasing all the pigeons and showing me how to fly them in a circle and then guide them back to their cage—all with only the help of a black piece of cloth tied to the end of a long stick. What he failed to tell me was that this exercise is done to attract other flying pigeons to the flock and ultimately back to the cage so that uncle Mitri could later serve them to the customers.

Back at the house that evening, while my grandfather rested his feet on a chair in the living room, Tata asked me to run over to the neighbor's place to borrow a bowl of rice. Along the way, I met another neighbor who asked,

"Where are you headed, son?" I told him about my mission to which he inquired, "Why? What's going down at *beit al-Mukhtar* (the *Mukhtar*'s house)?" I shrugged and kept on going. My guess was that he told another in the neighborhood, and another told another, and in no time more than twenty or so family and friends descended on my grandparents' house, which sent my grandmother—and a dozen or so female helpers—scrambling to the kitchen to prepare food for the guests. The feast and the festive atmosphere that ensued were like nothing I'd encountered before. Suddenly musical instruments appeared from nowhere, and poetry became the flavor of the day. While the men sang and played music in the living room, the women danced in the kitchen, and the children shuttled back and forth between the two. In between solo improvisations on the *oud* (a fretless lute), the *qanoun* (a zither-like plucked instrument), and the *nay* (a reed flute), that brought sighs of appreciation, the singer sang soulful *mawwals* (vocal improvisations in dialect) and made up new lyrics to familiar tunes. I recognized many of the rhythms the juice vendor played and I was encouraged to join the musicians on the tambourine. The fun was interrupted when Tata ordered everyone to the dining room table. And what a table that was! There were *keftas* and *kababs*, *hashwet jaaj* (chicken with rice and pine nuts) and *koosa mahshi* (stuffed zucchini), and meze plates as far as the eye could see: hummus (chickpea dip), *babghannouj* (eggplant dip), stuffed vine leaves, glistening black olives, braided white cheese, glossy vegetables, plump nuts, and lush juicy fruits. It was like magic: Where did it all come from? I wondered.

After stuffing ourselves to the chin (an Arabic expression often used by my mother), we all retired to the living room and the music resumed. This time the men and women danced together to the soothing and hypnotic compositions of Zakaria Ahmad and Sayyid Darweesh, Mohammad Abd el-Wahab and Fareed el-Atrash. And I, naturally exhausted by the events of day, fell asleep on my grandfather's lap.

Early the next morning, a crowd of family and friends lined up at the convent entrance to bid us farewell. We got into the *service* (taxi) that drove us to Amman and from there back home to Beirut. From the car window I waved goodbye to my teary-eyed Tata and Sido and yelled *kalimera* to the bearded monk with foot-long keys.

That was the last time I saw my grandparents; the last time I saw Jerusalem.

~ ~ ~

Michel Moushabeck is an essayist, editor, publisher, and musician. He is the founder of Interlink Publishing, a Massachusetts-based independent publishing house. His books include Beyond the Storm: A Gulf Crisis Reader *(with Phyllis Bennis) and* Altered States: A Reader in the New World Order. *He is a founding member of Layaali Arabic Music Ensemble. He plays* riqq, tabla, *and* daff *on the music soundtrack of an award-winning BBC/ WGBH documentary on Islam, which aired as part of the series "The People's Century." His recording credits include two albums:* Lost Songs of Palestine *and* Folk Songs and Dance Music from Turkey and the Arab World.

Acknowledgments

Introduction by Tony Wheeler published with permission from the author. Copyright © 2007 by Tony Wheeler.

"Bread" by Nicholas Seeley published with permission from the author. Copyright © 2007 by Nicholas Seeley.

"The Barber" by Dustin W. Leavitt published with permission from the author. Copyright © 2006 by Dustin W. Leavitt.

"Sunday Dinner" by Patrick Pfister published with permission from the author. Copyright © 2007 by Patrick Pfister.

"Blood Ties" by Michael Engelhard published with permission from the author. Copyright © 2007 by Michael Engelhard.

"My Military-Industrial Complex" by Gary Buslik published with permission from the author. Copyright © 2007 by Gary Buslik.

"Confessions of a Water Pipe Smoker" by Carolyn A. Thériault published with permission from the author. Copyright © 2007 by Carolyn A. Thériault.

"Kick Boxing for Pride and Peanuts" by Antonio Graceffo published with permission from the author. Copyright © 2007 by Antonio Graceffo.

"Rilke Was Miserable Here" by Kathleen Spivack originally appeared in *The Harvard Review*. Copyright © 1999 by Kathleen Spivack. Reprinted by permission of the author.

"Bad Country" by J. Spencer Klein published with permission from the author. Copyright © 2007 by J. Spencer Klein.

"Argentina on Two Steaks a Day" by Maciej Ceglowski originally appeared at www.idlewords.com. Copyright © 2006 by Maciej Ceglowski. Reprinted by permission of the author.

"The Girl Who Drank Petrol" by Tanya Shaffer excerpted from *Somebody's Heart Is Burning* by Tanya Shaffer. Copyright © 2003 by Tanya Shaffer. Reprinted by permission of Vintage Departures, a division of Random House, Inc.

"Mr. Hat's Neighborhood" by Richard Sterling published with permission from the author. Copyright © 2007 by Richard Sterling.

"Dervishes" by Rory Stewart reprinted from the Summer 2002 issue of *Granta*. Copyright © 2002 by Rory Stewart. Reprinted by permission from Gillon Aitken Associates.

"At the Foot of Mount Yasur" by Usha Alexander published with permission from the author. Copyright © 2007 by Usha Alexander.

"Only Fish" by Bonnie Smetts published with permission from the author. Copyright © 2006 by Bonnie Smetts.

"Grandpére" by Ken Matusow published with permission from the author. Copyright © 2007 by Ken Matusow.

"Smackdown in Tijuana" by Jim Benning published with permission from the author. Copyright © 2006 by Jim Benning.

"The Howrah-Puri Express" by Gregory Kennedy published with permission from the author. Copyright © 2007 by Gregory Kennedy.

"Immortality and the Art of Losing It" by Thaddeus Laird originally appeared in the Summer 2000 issue of *Mountainfreak*. Copyright © 2000 by Thaddeus Laird. Reprinted by permission of the author.

"Over There" by Paul Theroux originally appeared in the Winter 2003 issue (Issue 84) of *Granta*. Copyright © 2003 by Paul Theroux. Reprinted by permission of The Wylie Agency.

"The Mexican Taco Stand" by Pickett Porterfield published with permission from the author. Copyright © 2007 by Pickett Porterfield.

"A Visit to Dixieland" by Hunter James published with permission from the author. Copyright © 2007 by Hunter James.

"Next Year in Germany" by Robert L. Strauss originally appeared in the 9/8/99 issue of *Salon*. Copyright © 1999 by Robert L. Strauss. Reprinted by permission of the author.

"The Purple Umbrella" by Karin Muller excerpted from *Japanland: A Year in Search of Wa* by Karin Muller. Copyright © 2005 by Karin Muller. Reprinted by permission of Rodale Press.

About the Editors

James O'Reilly, president and publisher of Travelers' Tales, was born in England and raised in San Francisco. He graduated from Dartmouth College in 1975 and wrote mystery serials before becoming a travel writer in the early 1980s. He's visited more than forty countries, along the way meditating with monks in Tibet, participating in West African voodoo rituals, living in the French Alps, and hanging out the laundry with nuns in Florence. He travels extensively with his wife, Wenda, and their three daughters. They live in Palo Alto, California, where they also publish art games and books for children at Birdcage Press (www.birdcagepress.com).

Larry Habegger, executive editor of Travelers' Tales, has been writing about travel since 1980. He has visited almost fifty countries and six of the seven continents, traveling from the Arctic to equatorial rainforests, the Himalayas to the Dead Sea. In the early 1980s he co-authored mystery serials for the *San Francisco Examiner* with James O'Reilly, and since 1985 their syndicated column, "World Travel Watch," has appeared in newspapers in five countries and on WorldTravelWatch.com. As series editors of Travelers' Tales, they have worked on more than eighty books, winning many awards for excellence. Habegger regularly teaches the craft of travel writing at workshops and writers' conferences, and he lives with his family on Telegraph Hill in San Francisco.

Sean O'Reilly is director of special sales and editor-at-large for Travelers' Tales. He is a former seminarian, stockbroker, and prison instructor who lives in Virginia with his wife Brenda and their six children. He's had a lifelong interest in philosophy, theology, and travel, and recently published the groundbreaking book on men's behavior, *How to Manage Your DICK: Redirect Sexual Energy and Discover Your More Spiritually Enlightened, Evolved Self* (www.dick-management.com). His most recent travels took him through China, Thailand, Indonesia, and the South Pacific.